"I HAVE BEEN FISHING"

JOHN RENNIE

LONDON

Seeley Service & Co, Ltd

196 Shaftesbury Avenue

1949

Printed in Gt. Britain
By W. S. Cowell Ltd, Butter Market, Ipswich

LIST OF CONTENTS

LIST OF PLATES

ix

TEXT DIAGRAMS

EARLY DAYS

IT is usual to say where you were born—what started you
fishing—how you had the patience to fish, etc.

I have never been very patient with anything, except fishing. I never considered that fishing required patience. It is so ab-
sorbing that you do not think of time, and as it is time which
makes people impatient, it does not require patience to be a
fisherman. That's the way I look upon it.

My first impression of fishing is this. I must have been about
five or six years old. I spent a great deal of my time fishing a small
pond at home, which was full of carp, roach and gudgeon. One
day I was alone, and holding my cane rod, when an enormous
animal settled on my rod just above my hand. I flung down the
rod and ran, yelling. I said that a dragon had settled on my rod.
It was the first time I had met a dragon-fly. It was some days
before I could go back to my pond, and even to this day I shudder
when a dragon-fly comes very near me.

I caught my first trout at Tunstal Hall, Market Drayton, Shrop-
shire, where we used to go and stay as children. There was a
little stream which ran through the park, and John, the Irish
coachman, taught me to fish with a worm for trout. I caught quite
a nice number, and it made me keen to catch them with a fly,
but as I had no fly tackle I had to wait a bit.

We boys had permission to fish at Gatton Park for pike, perch,
carp and tench two or three times a year. What a preparation it
was to get ready for the day! My job was to go and catch gudgeon
for live bait for my eldest brother. I was never allowed to use

them myself, which was rather hard lines. As I got older, I thought the time had come when I should catch a pike. I bought a large float—I remember it, green and white, and it cost four-pence—and with a triangle and a gudgeon I threw out my bait. Soon after, my brother came walking down the bank. 'What are you doing?' he said. 'Fishing for pike', said I. 'With my live bait!' said he. 'Well, I caught them', said I. Then my backside was kicked and I was told I was a cheeky little brat, so that was the end of my first day's pike fishing. Forty years afterwards I proposed a similar fishing trip to Gatton Park with my two brothers—by that time one was a Diplomat, the other a General. Sir Jeremiah Colman kindly gave us leave, and the only difference was that I insisted that my eldest brother should get the live bait. We had a grand day, and everything was just the same as it had been forty years before. We took up our same places as in previous years: we caught ten pike, and finished up the evening with a merry dinner and, as I was going out of the front door, I got my backside kicked! Everything just as it should have been.

When I was about sixteen years old I went to Scotland with my father and we stayed at Hunter's Quay. We found that the River Eck was not very far away, so we hired a pony and cart and drove there. My father made me go up to the house, which, if I remember rightly, belonged to Sir George Younger. I was terribly nervous walking up to the house to ask leave, and there, standing in the porch, was Sir George himself. I must say he wasn't very encouraging to the nervous youth, and told me that I could not fish the river, but if I liked to go up to the burn in the hills I could fish there. By this time I had a rod and reel of sorts and a few flies I had collected. We had a happy day and I caught a few very small trout, but—they were caught on a fly!

On another day we went to Loch Eck, and my brother gave me a lesson in casting a salmon fly. I don't think he was very good himself, but he said I was rotten. Never mind, that was the first time I ever handled a salmon rod, and I was quite deter-mined that I would have a salmon rod of my own and learn to use it properly, and I have every reason to think that I kept to the resolution I made that day.

In after years I won the Open Salmon Fly Casting Competition, and in 1929 Mr R. B. Marston, of *The Fishing Gazette*, wrote to me as follows: 'Dear Mr Rennie, I cannot find any records for amateurs to beat your forty-three yards cast. I shall put in a note saying we believe your cast is the amateur record and would be glad to have particulars if anyone questions it'.

·It was in the year 1894 that I went off to stay with my brother George, at Inveroran Hotel, Loch Tulla. The hotel had about three miles of fishing rights on the River Orchy. This was my first salmon-fishing trip; my equipment was very poor and I had great difficulty in casting against a wind, indeed, in casting at all. It was towards the end of September; it was very cold, and the hotel was very primitive and not too clean, and there was no bathroom. It was owned by Duncan Forbes, and although his hotel was none too good he did give me some useful tips about casting, and even lent me his rod, which was a mighty thing of eighteen feet.

And talking of casting, there was a certain Colonel Wilson staying there—he was a mighty caster, with a huge rod, and was credited with the immense feat of having cast a fly to the other side of the Fank Pool. I looked upon him in awe and wonder. Thirty years afterwards I happened to have a day's fishing on this water, and found that I could do the same feat of casting with a twelve-foot rod! Rods and tackle have improved a lot since those days, and what a difference there is in the pleasure of fishing. My impression is that people did not tell me very much when I was young—they were not very helpful to the inexperienced youth. I think the older folk are now far more inclined to help the youngsters—that is to say, if they want helping, but some of them think they know all about the game, and these I let alone.

Well, to go back to the Orchy. There were a lot of fish jumping about, but they all looked very black to me, whereas the salmon I had always seen on fishmongers' slabs were bars of silver. Nobody seemed able to tell me why this was, but simply said 'late fish'. That conveyed nothing to me, but it was all the answer I got.

One of the rods, Mr Metzler, used to come in most days with a fish. He had his own gillie. The other rods were mighty jealous, and he never would say on what fly he caught his fish. I made friends with him, and the day he left he told me that he had got all his fish on the 'Canary' fly. Now, this is a fly which, as you all know, is entirely yellow, and is made up of dyed yellow hackles, yellow body and wing with a topping. He gave me a pattern and sent his gillie down with me next morning to the Canal Pool, where he told me that he had seen a big fish rise at the head of the pool. Unfortunately the gillie did not think much of my casting and took the rod from me, and, when he got to the right spot, up came the fish. He handed me the rod. I was terrified at the enormous weight at the other end. Well, the fish was kind for a few minutes, and then took a sudden run down the pool. I do not suppose he really ran for more than thirty yards, but I thought that he was taking all my line away, and I pictured everything disappearing; something had to be done to stop this. I put my hand on the reel! I got a very sharp knock on my knuckles: there was a bang and a slack line. The fish had gone off with my beautiful 'Canary' fly and left me with two feet of cast.

What the gillie said to me I won't repeat. He called me a silly little b—— and left me on the river bank. I never saw him again. But, believe me, it was a very valuable experience. I have never since then tried to stop a salmon running.

I have seen the same thing happen to several beginners. On the last occasion to a lady on the River Dee, when I was fishing at Cairnton, in 1941. I was coaching her in casting, and she made a very good cast. I said 'That ought to catch a fish', and sure enough, up came a big fish. I told her 'Whatever you do, don't put your hand on the reel if the fish wants to run'—this fish did want to run, and away it went to the other side of the pool. This was too much for the lady and she put her hand on the reel, with the same result as happened to me forty years before. I think she wept a little, and then went sadly back to fish again. I was kinder to her than my gillie was to me—I hope it has had equally good results.

In 1895 my father sold his property in Surrey and took a house in Scotland, Killicrankie House, on the River Garry which runs into the Tummel at Pitlochry. This was the first time that we had had a piece of fishing of our own. It was most exciting. By now

I could cast a salmon line quite well, as I had had lessons from an old cousin of my father's, Rennie Cockerell. Although he was an old-fashioned salmon fisher he knew the right way to instruct. Instead of holding the rod with the lower hand in a firm grip, he showed me how to use this hand as a 'ball and socket' joint, that is to say, keep the rubber ball end of the rod in the palm of the hand, with only the thumb uppermost. Never grip it, but control it near to your side and never allow it to get very far away from the body. It was wonderful the difference this made to my casting, and the ease with which I could throw a line. He used to put down a halfcrown fifteen to seventeen yards away on the lawn, and when I hit it, it was mine. I got quite a number of halfcrowns, and they were scarce in those days. So, after a time, this part of the instruction stopped!

But I know now that those lessons he gave me in 1895 were the making of my casting. I have coached a number of people on the same lines, and they have all turned out well. I don't mean the halfcrown part of the teaching, but the 'ball and socket' principle.

Other people, other methods. If I had found anything better I should have adopted it.

The Garry is quite a good river in the spring, but in the late summer and autumn it is pretty hopeless with fly. Possibly a bait or prawn might have caught fish, but I knew nothing about such things.

Nowadays, I am sorry to say, many salmon fishermen on such rivers as the Wye, Usk, Avon, etc. know nothing about fly fishing, and seldom take a fly rod down to the river. In fact, they have never learned to fly fish. What a pity this is, because I am quite sure that the more a water is fished with bait, the less chance there is for a fly, although I have known occasions when someone has been through a pool with a bait on the opposite bank, and a fly coming down afterwards has secured a fish, but this is exceptional.

There is a time and season for everything. On many rivers it is pretty useless to use a fly before the end of March, but after that the fly is best every time. Then again, take such rivers as the Tay, Tweed and Dee. Forty or fifty years ago a bait was almost unheard of, and all the catches were made with fly. I was talking to John Stewart, head keeper of Grantully Castle water on the Tay, only a short time ago, and he told me a bait was unheard of in his young days, even in January and February. But they caught more fish then than they do now.

But to continue; on our way back from the Garry, my brother George and I took coach to Rannoch and stayed the night in the hotel there. We passed beautiful Loch Tulla where I had previously stayed a night. Loch Tulla had some fine trout and I got one beauty of three pounds, the largest trout I had ever caught up to that time. But to return to Loch Rannoch; I remember taking a walk in the evening down the river where it runs out of the Loch. There was a wonderful show of trout, and big ones, too, rising and jumping all over the place. We had no trout rod, so could do nothing about it, but I promised myself that I would someday return there. This visit did not take place until many years afterwards, in 1918. There were still plenty of small trout, but I never caught anything large. Perhaps they were not so large as I thought they were in 1895.

Next day we went on to Inveroran by coach over Rannoch Moor. This was before the West Highland Railway was completed. Time was of little consequence in those days. The Inn at Inveroran was much the same as it was on my previous visit, very crowded, and as there had been a spate that day, the prospects of fishing were not very good. It was decided that the only chance was a worm. How I hate them, and always will. But I did get a fish and some nice trout. We were only there two days, as I had to get back to Cambridge for my second year at Trinity Hall.

I was up at the Hall for two years; my career was a short and happy one. I did no work, and was generally mixed up with a noisy and happy crowd. It was at the Hall that year that I met my friend David Campbell Muir. We have fished together in many places ever since that time, and we still continue to do so.

I have often wondered if I have spent too much time and money on fishing, and my answer is—I would do it all over again; but I wish I had had a little more money in my early days, so that I could have had better fishing. Good fishing is an expensive game and always has been, and that is why in later years

Plate 1

I HOLD MY ROD IN THIS WAY, THE LEFT HAND MAKING A 'CUP AND BALL' JOINT, THE THUMB UPPERMOST. THE LEFT HAND SHOULD BE KEPT NEAR THE BODY, AND PREVENTS THE ROD GOING TOO FAR BACK. THERE IS NO GRIP WITH THE LEFT HAND.

I took to going to Norway, Canada, Iceland, Sweden and other places, where fishing was not so expensive. Think what one would have missed if one had not been a fisherman. Fishing has taken me to some of the most lovely spots in the world to which I would never otherwise have gone, as I am not particularly fond of travelling and sight-seeing. Fishing has given me all my best friends.

In 1896 I went up to stay with my friend David Muir at his home on Loch Awe. What excitement and what fun we had. We were a noisy party, but his parents were very good and kind to us, and we did exactly what we liked. Walter Steton, McLaren, Esdale Muir, David and myself. They owned the Brander Pass beat on the Awe, and a launch took us down to the fishing every morning. It was difficult fishing for a beginner on the left bank, as a huge mountain runs down almost to the edge of the river. You have to keep your line very high, otherwise a touch on the rocks behind, and your barbe is gone. I don't think I owned a dozen salmon flies in those days, and most of them were de-barbed before I had finished my stay. David Muir was a grand caster, and had a big eighteen-feet Castleconnell rod with which he was able to get his fly right over to the other side. There is a bank over there, where the big fish lay. One morning he got into a really big one, probably forty pounds or perhaps more. It sulked, so he got into the boat with the old gillie, Nicol, to see if he could move him. I did not know that any rod could stand the strain that he put on it. But the boat got too near the fish and the rod doubled up and something broke. Soon after, he got into another, which we got out. It was thirty pounds. These things I remember as if they had occurred yesterday. They made a deep impression on my youth. One thing I found out in after life, the more you pull a big fish when he is first hooked, the deeper he goes, and the more likely you are to get broken in a rock. I found this out on the Shannon many years after, when I had been broken by a number of big fish. The Shannon boatmen always used to shout at you 'Hold him, your Honour, hold him, or you will never get him'. So I did hold, and the result was usually a smash of some kind or another. If a big fish wants to run, let him run, without too much strain, and he will seldom rock you. Anyway, that is my experience, and I have caught quite a number of big fish since then and would have caught many more if I had not been so rough with them.

Later on in this book, when I come to the Shannon, I shall have more to say about this.

We got into sad trouble on Loch Awe. One night we thought we would go and raid the two Hotels up at Port Sonnachan, and when it was quite dark we set off in the launch. We found both hotels closed, so broke into them through a window and collected anything we could lay hands on. God knows what beset us to do such a thing. A canary in a cage was one of the things we took. Having broken into both hotels without being discovered, we steamed home.

Of course everything was returned next day, but what a row there was about it, and we were lucky to get off with a good wigging. Mr and Mrs Muir were really upset about this, and I am not surprised.

David had a wonderful old gillie, Nicol Macintyre. He thought of nothing but fishing and whisky, both of which he was very fond of. Whisky was only three shillings a bottle in those days. Two stories I will tell about him. When sawing a branch off a tree about ten feet from the ground he sat on the branch he was sawing, with the result that when the branch came down, so did Nicol, and he broke his leg. After the last war, in 1919, David was complaining of the quality of the whisky. 'This is damned bad whisky', said David. Nicol said, 'Mr David, Mr David, there is no bad whisky. There is good whisky and better whisky, but there is no bad whisky'! He was a great old man and lived to be over eighty.

Here I find some epigrams in my diary which are very true and which amuse me more perhaps now, than they did then. I do not know their origin.

1. Acquaintance—a person whom we know well enough to borrow from, but not well enough to lend to. A degree of friendship called slight when its object is poor or obscure, but intimate when he is rich and famous.

2. Advice—the smallest current coin.

3. Barometer—an ingenious instrument which indicates what kind of weather we are having.

4. Bore—a person who talks when you wish him to listen.

5. Consult—to seek another's approval of a course already decided on.

6. Egotist—a person of low taste, more interested in himself than in me.

7. Hospitality—the virtue which induces us to feed and lodge certain persons who are not in need of food or lodging.

8. Patience—a minor form of despair, disguised as a virtue.

9. Politeness—the most acceptable hypocrisy.

I remember quoting the following words when I was occupying the Chair at the Fly Fishers' Club Dinner—'Man's knowledge and ingenuity has grown out of all proportion to his moral development'.

This sounds rather true in the light of present-day development, and can also be applied to the many contraptions used in catching salmon!

The Eyed Hook. I think I am right in saying that it was sometime in the 'nineties that the late Mr H. S. Hall invented the eyed hook.

This lead to a great deal of controversy in the sporting press as to its merits or demerits. The chief opponent to the eyed hook was George M. Kelson, well known as a fisherman and as the author of *The Salmon Fly*, published in 1895. One has only to look at the frontispiece of this book and see the portrait of Mr Kelson to understand what a terrible opponent he might be in any controversial matter. There he stands in long waders and a bowler hat, a rod in his hand. His beard and moustaches would frighten any timid man. But Mr Hall also had a beard and moustaches, not quite so fierce, perhaps, but very strong and intellectual. Apart from inventing the eyed hook, Mr Hall had also invented Hall and Knight's algebra, so you can understand the sort of man he was.

A battle royal raged between these two great men and, if I remember rightly, the correspondence in the press had to be shut down. On page 35 of Mr Kelson's book he says 'I hope that I seldom find fault without just cause, but when the mania for eyed hooks broke out afresh I pointed out the faults and persistently maintained that they never could and never would become popular. . . . I need not make quotations, for the student who has followed the foregoing arguments will clearly perceive the awkward results of attaching a cast to a hook of this sort . . . etc'.

Some time after the battle Mr Hall sent me the following verses relating to Mr Kelson. They amused me much at the time, so here they are:—

THE CASE IN A NUTSHELL

Piscator magnus sum

Let others all be dumb!
For when I write
I wield the might
Of all things right.
By Jove! By GUM!
I make things hum.
Without dispute
I am so cute
That not a man dare flout me,
Of this there can no doubt be.

Piscator magnus sum

To state my creed I come:
A man who ties
His choicest flies
On hooks with eyes
All sense defies.
Be such taboo!
While anglers who
Use not gut loops
Are nincompoops.
Piscator magnus said it,
And 'F.G.' readers read it.

H.S.H.

I will leave my readers to judge.

THE TURN OF THE CENTURY

IN 1896 my father took a place called Burn Foot, on the banks of the border Esk, Dumfriesshire. Such a jolly house with a bit of shooting of all kinds and about two miles of the Esk. There was always a lot to do and quite a number of sea trout, and an occasional salmon. There I learned how to get sea trout with a worm, fishing up stream. The Esk fishermen were adepts at this form of fishing, and it was really rather fun. I have seldom fished with a worm since those days.

Sometimes I went further down the river to Canonby. Lots of salmon were showing down there, but there were also many fishermen, and I would find four or five fishermen on some of the best pools, one behind the other. I remember the road makers were blasting rock on one of the pools, and after every explosion the fish started jumping all over the place.

I was in sad disgrace at home at that time; I thought of nothing but shooting and fishing and a bit of hunting in the winter, but eventually I did settle down, so there is hope for everybody.

In 1897 my father took a delightful place called Denford Park, Hungerford, with about 1,000 acres of shooting and two miles of the Kennet and side streams. Since that time I have fished the Kennet every year, with the exception of one, 1898, when I went to Central Africa. It was here on the Kennet that I learned most of what I know about dry fly fishing. What a sight it was in those days when the May fly was on. It always started on our water the first week in June, and continued for about three weeks. Why was it that the fishing was so much better in those days? I have my ideas on this subject, which will be given in a subsequent chapter.

I find that in August, 1897, I went over to stay with my

Cambridge friend, Harry Low, in Ireland, at Kilshane, Tipperary.
We shot grouse and fished a nice little river which had sea trout
and salmon, of which we got quite a number. One of the party
was Tom Gubbins, whose brother Jack Gubbins had just won
the Derby with 'Galtee More'. I was much impressed at being
so near a Derby winner!

From there I took boat and went to the west coast of Scotland
to stay with another Cambridge friend—Charles Henry. His
father, Col. Henry—God bless him—had a place called
Strontian. It was quite a good deer forest—a nice lot of grouse
and two small rivers with sea trout and an odd salmon. I killed
my first stag there, and what a day it was for me. In after years
I killed a great many beasts in Central Africa, but the excitement of that first stag was better than anything afterwards.

When you are young, it seems to me that you are naturally
bloodthirsty, but when you get on in years this craze to kill
dies off, and I am glad to say it died out with me. In catching
trout and salmon, I have no such feeling and the pull of a salmon
has all the thrills to me now as the first pull I got over forty
years ago.

In my time I have caught over 1,000 salmon, and as old age
comes on I never tire of the sport, and I fish much better now
than I did in my youth. More steady, more mellow than I used
to be, and in consequence more capable of enjoyment. I cannot
understand those folk who will rush up and down the river
when they see a trout rise or a salmon jump. Their behaviour
shows absence of peace of mind, and they would catch far more
fish if they did not run about so much.

In 1898 I went to Central Africa, to Lake Nyasa. In those
days there were no roads or railways; the country was nearly as
wild as in the days of Livingstone. My excuse for going there
was to erect a gunboat on Lake Nyasa. It was a grand excuse
to offer my father, and he was kind enough to let me go. This
boat was about one hundred and forty feet long. It had been built
in England, was named the *Gwendolen* after the sister of the late
Lord Salisbury, and was carried there by barges up the Zambesi
and Shire rivers and then over country and the Highlands to
Fort Johnston, Lake Nyasa. This was all done by natives. There

were hundreds of them, and the extraordinary thing was that only one parcel was missing when the time came to assemble the boat, and that part was replaceable.*

It was a grand experience for a boy of my age. My fishing companion, David Muir, went with me. We saw a lot of life, shot a great deal of big game, and learned much about human nature.

The only fishing we got on this trip was occasional sea fishing on the east coast of Africa, and some fish in the river which runs out of Lake Nyasa. We had little tackle, and before long this was all lost in some very large fish—we never discovered what size or kind they were; they might have been crocodiles for all we knew! Anyhow, our tackle was not up to these monsters.

We were ten months away from England, and I think that this is the only year since 1896 that I did not fish the Kennet. I always remember the year 1899 for one particular reason. I happened to go to the Oban Gathering, and stayed on Eddie Hargreaves' yacht. Esdale Campbell Muir was one of the party and he asked me if I would like to go on a motor tour with him for a week. I jumped at the idea, for in those days it was an adventure. The car was a two-cylinder Daimler, with tube ignition and tiller steering. For those who do not know what tube ignition is, I will explain by saying that there was no electric ignition in those days, but only a tube which entered the cylinder and which had to be heated by a lamp before you could start the engine.

Well, we had a wonderful trip, and we actually negotiated the 'Rest and be Thankful' Hill, and it had no surface or easy bends as in these days. We slept that night at the Tarbet Hotel, Loch Lomond. When we drove up, everybody was at dinner. One and all left their dinner and rushed out to see a motor car! The whole trip was rather like a circus in any town we went through. That is why I remember 1899.

* Years afterwards, in 1914, when we went to war with Germany, this same gunboat set out to attack a German gunboat and sank her. Some time after the war I met a man who was there at the time and he told me that it was not the gallant sea battle which I had pictured. In his own words 'It was rather like shooting a sitting pheasant', as the German boat was hauled up on the slipway for repairs.

For the next few years I went from place to place. My sport was not great, but I learned quite a lot. The River Awe always attracted me with its big fish and really good sea trout fishing. In 1903 I went for a trip to the Belgian Ardennes, and stayed at a dear little village called Lignonville.* Here was a stream which ran through water meadows—very like our Hampshire chalk streams. The little river was full of trout, but the most successful man was a Frenchman, who rejoiced in the name of Monsieur le Capitaine Bott. He always came back with a large handkerchief full of fish.

It annoyed me to find that this man was welcomed at the hotel each evening with cheers, and then proceeded to empty his handkerchief of twenty to thirty fish into the porch of the hotel, whereas I could only produce some six or ten small fish. What was the secret? I determined to find out, and find out I did. It was this—he had a long bamboo rod, I should think about sixteen to eighteen feet. He caught a number of grasshoppers—the grass was full of them—then he stood sixteen to eighteen feet from the bank, impaled a grasshopper on the hook and let it drop within a few inches of the bank. Immediately there was a fish, which he heaved out over his head. That was his secret, and that was why he was a 'hero'—in France.

A friend told me to go to the River Laune, Killorglin, in Ireland. It was practically free fishing, and there were sea trout and salmon. I stayed at the Station Hotel, Killorglin. My hat!—it was then the most awful, dirty place I have ever been in. Probably it is now first rate, with three stars attached to it, but in 1905—well, I will leave it at that.

As free fishing goes, it was quite good. There were numbers of salmon and sea trout, but the best time for salmon is June and July. From there I went on to Lough Caragh, and from there to Waterville. Before I leave Killorglin I must tell one story. I had a gillie, Pat Redden. He was a merry soul and kept me amused all day. Before I left he asked me if I would like some chickens sent over to England, price two shillings each. Of course I agreed, and

---

* In December, 1945, this village was the scene of a great battle lasting for two weeks.

the arrangement was that I should send him ten shillings a time and he would forward the chickens. The chickens arrived and they were very good ones, and this went on for some weeks. At last one fine day the chickens stopped coming and he had my ten shillings. As I could not get any answer from him I wrote to the police. They replied that Pat Redden was in prison for chicken stealing! I left it at that and heard no more.

I was at Waterville only for a few days, but I liked the place, and the sea trout fishing was quite good. There was a nice little river, the Linny, I think, with pretty pools and an odd salmon to be got here and there. I was not so particular in those days, and one salmon in a day was an event—now I want more.

I had a relation who had cultivated a taste for cheap cigars; he could not afford expensive ones and he liked his cheap ones. He would never take an expensive one if offered to him, as he said 'It would spoil my taste for the cheap ones'. Fishing is something on the same lines—if you have never had first-class fishing you don't miss it. Dear old Coggeshall, beloved by all members of the Fly Fishers' Club, used to say to me, 'John, you never miss what you haven't had'. 'Well', said I, 'I don't quite follow you, Coggy'. 'Well', said he, 'do you miss not living in Buckingham Palace?' 'No, certainly not', I would say. 'So there you are', said he, and there was nothing more to be said. I was quite happy in my young days with bad fishing. I must own now that I am not contented with the kind of fishing I used to get. I think that the reason is, as one gets older, one has the horrid feeling that there are only a certain number of years left, and if one can afford good fishing it is a waste of time to go to bad fishing. That's how it appears to me, and has done so for the past twenty-five years.

I have been lucky—a word that I hate to use; so let us say fortunate—in having had some of the best fishing that can be got. When I think of the wonderful rivers I have fished in all parts of the world, the beautiful scenery and places I have visited, I can only say 'Thank God for His blessings'.

I once had an old employee who spent all his money on gin, then two shillings and sixpence a bottle. I said to him one day, 'Jimmie, what would you do with all the money you have spent on gin?' 'Spend it again on gin' was his immediate retort.

So would I in the case of fishing, and much more too, if I could have had it.

In 1906 I went to Garrynahine, Isle of Lewis. I had intended to take a rod on the Grimersta River, but I discovered that no ladies were allowed in the Lodge, so I gave up my rod and went to Garrynahine instead, which is about two to three miles away. Both rivers run into the same Bay, but for every one fish that runs up the Garrynahine River, there are probably a hundred run up the Grimersta.

I shall never forget the long drive across the island from Stornaway to Garrynahine in an old open one-horse wagonette. We had had a bad passage to Stornaway; moreover, something on the way had badly disagreed with my tummy. It took about four to five hours to make that journey. It was pitch dark, and the rain pelted down all the way. We were much relieved to get to the hotel at twelve o'clock that night.

My recollections of the place are very pleasant. The country is without a tree, but with wonderful colouring over the bogs and heather, seaweed and very blue seas. The hotel was comfortable—it was a tin affair, and the only fault was that you could hear every word and sound going on! The other fishermen were two old stagers; one had been there for twenty-five years, the other for twenty. I don't think they fancied a youngster coming there very much and one had to be very careful not to sit in their chairs, otherwise one was 'for it'. One of them was the most conceited man I ever met fishing. He pounced upon one when one arrived, and let one know everything he had done in the last twenty years. There was a large photograph of him hung up in the hotel with ten or twelve fish—this was not forgotten. All went well until one day I returned with a large basket of sea trout and a salmon—a really good basket. He had returned home with nothing. Later in the evening I heard someone walking up and down the dining room talking to himself, and this is what I heard—'No, I shall never fish again. I must give up fishing. To think that a young man should go out and bring back a basket like that, whereas I caught nothing. No, I shall give up fishing.' There was more of the same kind of thing, and it went on for some time. However, next day he had recovered and went out fishing, but can you understand the mentality? I can't.

At Garrynahine there is a chain of lakes, connected by a small river, and finishing up with about a mile of river running into the bay.

I had very good sport and got a number of sea trout and salmon; if I had known more about fishing I should have done much better, as there were loads of fish about. There are two things I remember—one, I rose a salmon twice on a dry fly; second—the other old boy fishing used nothing but a March Brown in various sizes. He was just as successful as anybody else, so adding evidence to Mr Wood's theory, some twenty-five years afterwards, that there is nothing in a fly—size only counts. But oh, how dull! Half the fun is in changing the pattern of your fly, and I shall never quite believe this theory, partly because I don't want to, and partly because I have a great deal of evidence that this is not so.

I think if I had tried the dry fly for sea trout in these waters I might have done well. I say this from my experiences later in Harris. But I was only learning then—I am still learning, but I have learned much since those days.

On the way back home, I stayed the night at Stornaway, as Walter Parrot had given me a day's fishing on the Castle water. It was reputed to be very good. There is a large lake and small river which runs into the sea at Stornaway. I was unfortunate, as there was heavy thunder and rain most of the day. At one moment, when the thunder was at its worst, every salmon in the lake started rolling about on the surface. I never saw such a sight. They were moving all round the boat and as far as one could see; but they were not takers!

At Stornaway I had my first sight of the herring industry. Women, up to their knees in fish offal, gutting and throwing the fish into tubs. It took me some time after that to face a herring for breakfast.

I look back with pleasure to my trip to Lewis—it has great charm.

From Stornaway I went on to stay with my brother-in-law, General Oxley as he now is, at a place called 'Dalnagla' in

Perthshire. We had some jolly grouse driving and on off days I went fishing in a little river close by. One day I hit it lucky and came back with a bag full of small trout, about three to the pound. I tried them fishing up stream with what I suppose we should now term a 'nymph'—the result was wonderful.

1907—my first motor car—shall I ever forget it? I chose an 'Adams Hewett'. The gear was epicyclic, and when you wanted to change you pressed a pedal. It was rather like playing an organ. It had one huge cylinder under the seat and when you wanted to get at that you raised up the whole body and got at the works. This happened pretty often. There was no windscreen and no side doors, but apart from these little omissions, it was comfortable, and on occasions could go at thirty miles an hour.

We motored all the way up to Ayrshire to a house on Loch Ken and the Kirkcudbrightshire Dee. The Dee is a nice little river, and if it had not been so overnetted, would have been quite good. The Loch has the reputation of harbouring the largest pike in the British Isles. The Castle on the Loch has the skulls of immense pike—I think one of them was labelled fifty-two pounds.

From there I went on to Cassillis House, the third oldest inhabited house in Scotland. The pretty little river, the Doon, ran underneath its walls. There are some fine sea trout in this river, and a certain amount of salmon. Mr John Strain had a lease of it in those days, and he had spent a great deal of money in restoring it and making it fit to live in. The walls were at least six feet thick, and the windows very small. These old places are all right to live in for a short time, but I always want light—the more the better. John Strain was very punctilious about the time of meals, and fishing was a secondary matter. One night I remember getting busy with the sea trout at 7.30 p.m., forgetting all about dinner, when out walked old Mr Strain, all dressed for dinner, saying 'Come along, dress for dinner or you'll be late'. 'Oh, Mr Strain', said I, 'can't I go on fishing? They are just beginning to rise.' But no—he was adamant, and I had to stop when they were coming on well.

I have often suffered in this way from kind hosts who had not that keen sense of fishing that we fishermen have. It is trying at the time, but must be endured.

For several years running I used to stay with a friend on the Tweed. His house was on the banks—or nearly so—of the river. His time for starting was 10.30 a.m. That meant starting fishing at 11 a.m.; at 1 p.m., punctually, we had to be back to lunch. Then there was a cigar and brandy, and at 2.30 p.m. out we went again. At 5 p.m. we stopped fishing. I asked the keeper if we could go on a little longer, but he would not hear of it, although we were getting into salmon every ten minutes. If you live on the river this is all very well, but when you have come all the way from London for three or four days' fishing it is a little trying. The last time I went there was for a short week-end. I got there on Friday night, fished Saturday and got ten salmon on greased line, fished Monday and got six, and returned to London on Monday night. What a week-end, and all done between the hours mentioned above. This was the last time I stayed there, as my friend passed away soon afterwards. Bless him; he gave me many a happy day.

I think the Tweed fish are the free-est risers to the small fly and greased line of any fish I have ever met. Perhaps I was lucky in my visits. Another thing about them—they have a great liking for a dropper, whereas on other rivers I have never done very well on a dropper. I wonder why this is?

Fig. 1   THE DROPPER ATTACHMENT

This is a good dropper I designed—Tail: a topping. Body: first half silver, second half black floss. Hackle: blue, as in blue charm. Wings: a pair of Golden Pheasant tippets tied back to back, size nine. This fly as a dropper was irresistible on the Tweed, and I got quite a number at Cairnton, but at other places, not so good.

1908.—This was a sad season. My father, who had been failing for some time, passed away in November. As my family were all scattered about and my mother could not live there alone, we decided to give up Denford Park, with all its pleasant memories, on the Kennet, which we had enjoyed for twelve years.

In August I went to the River Awe, Argyllshire. There were lots of salmon and sea trout that year and we had quite good sport. I remember my brother-in-law got his first salmon. He had never fished for salmon before, but he picked up casting pretty quickly, and threw quite a nice line. One day I was fishing above him, about one hundred yards or so, and I saw he was in difficulty. I went down to give some help, and found he was in a good fish, but the trouble was, his reel was in the bottom of the river, and the salmon about seventy yards below him, taking off line! The only thing was to wade in below, and try and get a shot with the gaff as he drifted down. This I did most successfully, but wading ashore, I slipped and fell. I had the presence of mind to throw the fish and gaff on to the bank—he was twenty pounds—but I got a ducking!

In spite of all this excitement he never became a salmon fisher, and very soon afterwards sold his rods and tackle.

The hotel at Dalmally was very full but comfortable. There was a Dr Hood staying there, who was very successful with sea trout. His method was a short line, rod held high and flies 'dibbling' on the surface. It was certainly a very killing method on the Awe, and I have tried it at other rivers with success, more especially in the Aurland River, in Norway, with a sedge as a dropper. Big fish used to follow up the flies to one's feet, and sometimes take with a bang. This method is worth remembering, more especially in rough water. From the Awe I motored on to Kirkcudbrightshire to a place called Airds on the Kirkcudbright-shire Dee. A pretty river, and which would have been good but for the overnetting. Salmon were scarce. One day I got two salmon on the fly. This was a most unheard-of event for those parts, and made quite a stir in the neighbourhood. That finished my season for 1908.

ON KENNET TROUT, Etc

UNDOUBTEDLY the fishing on the River Kennet has fallen off a great deal in recent years. My own ideas were set forth in an article I wrote to the *Fly Fishers' Club Journal* in 1942, which ran as follows:—

'I think everyone who has fished the Kennet this year (1942) will agree with me that it has been the worst season ever known. What is the reason? Naturally one's mind goes back a number of years: mine goes back forty-six years, and with the help of my diary and a very good memory as far as fishing goes, I can say with certainty that I have never seen such a season. The weather was not too bad and there was plenty of fly the few days I was on the water, but the utter disregard of the fly by the fish makes one ask "Why is it?"

'I have come to the following conclusions: There are some fish that rise to the fly and some that don't. In the same way there are some people who drink cocktails and others who don't. If you gradually eliminate by catching the fly-rising fish or the cocktail fish, then you have a breed who feed otherwise—on snails, shrimps, minnows, on the one hand—on beer, whisky and soda, wines, on the other hand. Now this may sound only frivolous, but I should like to go back to the days I remember long ago. When the May fly was on, you saw on a good reach of water fish feeding on every spent gnat or green-fly that came over them, taking them one after another for a quarter to half an hour. Do you ever see that happen now? Never. I don't think I have seen it for seven or eight years.

'In the old days everybody stocked their water and there were hatcheries on all the principal waters from Benham to Ramsbury. Those waters which had no hatcheries turned in an appropriate number of fish, from Loch Leven or other parts of England. So instead of relying on the natural breed of Kennet trout, you got new blood into the water and introduced fish who rise to the fly. The majority of Kennet trout are bottom feeders and do not come to the surface for food.

'It was about eight or ten years ago that a great "Voice" went round, "No stew bred fish. Let us have wild fish". From that time on, sport on the Kennet started to go back. There were complaints of the weather and all kinds of things, but the fact remains that all these waters that used to bring new blood into the river ceased to do so, with the result that, year by year, sport in the

May fly season declined until we come to the present year, which has been as bad as it could be up and down the most famous stretches. Perhaps it is not right for me to draw attention to these things, seeing that now I am only a guest on these privileged waters, but I want to find a reason and can find none except that which I have stated.

'The Houghton Club, which I think you will agree with me is one of the best conducted fisheries in the country, continues to breed and let loose great numbers of trout every year, and the sport these fish give is every bit as good as your natural bred fish, and better, because they rise, and your natural bred fish prefer to feed on the bottom. I have no doubt that I shall be condemned for this heresy, but my thoughts over forty-six years have not led me astray.

JOHN R.

'P S.—Since writing the above remarks, I have heard from Mr L. R. Dunne that he had excellent fishing this year at Littlecote during the May fly season. Littlecote, I believe, is the only fishing that keeps up its Hatchery. The fish were magnificent.'

This article brought forward quite a lot of correspondence, some agreeing, others not, but I don't think anybody else was able to put forward any other theory as to why the Kennet trout had ceased to rise as they did in past days.

My article was followed up by a letter written by the Editor of the *Fly Fishers' Club Journal*, Dr Barton, which I quote below. The interesting part to me is what Sir Ray Lankester has to say. This confirms my theory in every respect, and he even goes on to say that 'this unpleasant result can be avoided by the introduction of a fresh strain of fish.' I will leave it at that.

Genetics in Fish, by Dr Barton

'Mr John R. in an article in the last issue of the Journal bewails the absence of rising fish in the Kennet in places where only "wild" fish exist and where there is no re-stocking from other waters. In contrast, he notes that the Littlecote water fished well last season, due, he opines, to the fact that the water is constantly re-stocked. I would point out that the Littlecote water is controlled by a Head Keeper who is fully cognisant of the evils of inbreeding, and replenishes his stews with fish and ova from waters not heavily fished and in which the wet fly is more commonly used.

'Now any naturalist acquainted with the A.B.C. of Genetics—that is, the science of Heredity—would at once point out that the inevitable outcome of systematically destroying the rising fish results in their place being taken by those who do not do so, and which prefer to live on sub-aqueous food. It is purely a matter of survival of the fittest.

'When both parents, birds, fish or humans, have a marked proclivity in one direction, the offspring tend to exhibit this tendency in an exaggerated degree,

Plate 2

AT THE BEGINNING OF THE CAST, RAISE THE LINE OFF THE WATER BEFORE THE BACK CAST IS MADE. THIS TAKES THE WEIGHT OFF THE ROD. SNATCHING A SUNK LINE OFF THE WATER IS FATAL TO A ROD.

and to hand on the same characteristic to their next generation. In like manner cattle breeders, by mating animals both of which possess some desirable factor, and by afterwards eliminating all those offspring who do not display it, retaining only those which do and then inbreeding these, can in a few generations produce at will—and "fix"—any desired peculiarity. By "fix" I mean that all, with rare exceptions, breed true, the throw-backs becoming fewer and fewer with each generation. So it is with trout, the sub-aqueous feeders breeding true, to the detriment of sport.

'The late Sir Ray Lankester, that great biologist—turned his attention to this same problem in one of his delightful articles in *Science from an Easy Chair* (fifth edition, p. 226) from which I venture to quote: "The principle of natural selection and survival of the fittest accounts for the increased caution in trout in well-fished rivers in the simplest way. Assume (as is perfectly reasonable) that some trout are more shy than others 'by nature', that is to say, are *born* so, that some are born with slightly more natural response to the sight of food than others—as one sees often enough with a lot of the young of any animals—then the increased shyness or pretended 'intelligence' of the trout after many years' fishing follows as a necessity. The rash fish are caught and destroyed, the shy fish remain in the river and—here is the important point—propagate their like. Every year the selection goes on till you get a race of the fish in a well-fished river which are so shy that they cease to rise at all." He goes on to state that this unpleasant result of over-fishing a water can be avoided by the introduction of a fresh strain of fish which do not possess this innate shyness of character.

'Thus, where inbreeding of wild fish is allowed and where no outbreeding is permitted, those fish which rise are killed off and their place is taken by those which do not do so. These multiply, and transmit their sub-aqueous feeding factor, which, being exaggerated in every following generation, removes from our rivers the sport-giving factor. Thus slowly and innocently we are destroying the sport in our rivers, unconscious of the evils of inbreeding.

'The cure for all this is too obvious to discuss. If we want sport with dry fly we must cross-breed with fish from wet-fly rivers, which would soon find interest in the floating fly through change of environment to our opulent chalk streams.'   E.A.B.

On Greased Line Fishing

In 1941 I had the privilege of fishing on two of the best beats on the Aberdeenshire Dee, and at Delfur on the Spey. I learned a great deal, because in the past I had at times suffered from short-coming fish. Fish that boil at you and give you a pull and you don't connect. There are times when this never happens, and on the Tweed I hardly ever suffered from this; neither did I in Norway or in Iceland to any great extent. But there is no doubt that in 1941 I lost a great many fish on the Dee and Spey in this way. As you will see in this article, which I wrote to the *Fly Fishers' Club Journal*, I was able to overcome my trouble when I went to Cairnton.

This article brought me into correspondence with a number of people.

My friend Captain Bostock did not agree with me and wrote a letter in the following number of the Journal. He says that to the best of his knowledge Wood hardly ever gave line to his fish. However, I was quite certain that Wood had made that statement about giving slack line, but at the time I could not put my finger on the article. Since then I have found it in an article written in *Fisherman's Pie*, where the writer relates a short talk with Mr Wood. The part to which I refer was as follows:—

'I often hold the rod upright above my head with as much belly in the line as possible between the rod and the water, *and some more slack line* in my left hand. If, when fishing thus in very strong water I see a fish come to my fly, I immediately drop the point of my rod downstream and in towards the bank *and let go all the slack line before I feel the fish*. By doing this I have got rid of the exasperating pulls or breaks that so often occur under these conditions; but try it before you condemn this trick.'

This, I think, proves what I tried to convey in my article to the Journal in 1941.

I here quote from the two letters in question published in the *Fly Fishers' Club Journal*, and must leave it to my readers to judge for themselves. There is no doubt, to my way of thinking, that fish come much quicker to the fly in April than they do in May, so that the slack line may not be so essential in April as it is in May. I have known fish in May and June that will 'mumble' the fly, just as they do a prawn, before taking it, and if the line is at all taut, they will not have it, but if there is plenty of slack, they will take it in the end.

Article from the 'Fly Fishers' Club Journal'.

SLACK LINE IN GREASED LINE FISHING

'Thanks to kind friends, I this spring enjoyed some lovely days with greased line and very small flies, Casts 7/5 to 9/5, flies from No. 7 to 10.

'I learned a great deal on the Spey and the Dee, where I had the privilege of fishing two of the best beats on these rivers. But the chief point I want to dwell upon is the slack line in this form of fishing.

'On the Spey I killed a number of big fish on a single-handed Leonard eleven feet three inches, but I should have got many more if I had fished this water with the two yards of slack in my hand which is so necessary in this form of fishing. Sometimes a fish takes you with a bang. It does not matter then if your line is under the first finger; but many other fish come quietly and give a pull and, if you have a tight line, there is no connection.

'It was not until I got on to the Dee that I thought one night of Wood of Cairnton's doctrine. Wood told us to keep a yard or so of slack line without any resistance. This may sound easy, but it isn't when you have been fishing for forty years with your first finger on the line. I determined to try this out at Cairnton and was astonished at the results.

Fig. 2   THE 'CAIRNTON' OR 'WOOD' KNOT

'A fish would come and touch the fly like a leaf in the water, then the two yards of slack would run out quite gently, and a turn of the rod, not a strike, and the fish would be caught in the proper place—the corner of the mouth.

'Sometimes, after having been fishing for a considerable time without a rise, the finger crept back, not tightly, but still just enough to give resistance; a fish would come and give a pull—no contact.

'In those few days at Cairnton I can think of no occasion when the line was without resistance that I failed to hook my fish, but there were several occasions when my finger was on the line and I got a pull with no result.

'If one cannot manage to keep one or two yards of slack in one's hand, and it is not easy to do this at times without disturbing the fly, then a very free running reel with little resistance will answer the purpose nearly as well.

'As I have said, my rod is eleven feet three inches single-handed, and has a six-inch butt which I put on as soon as I get a fish. I have killed fish up to thirty pounds with this rod, and I was surprised how quickly I got them beaten.

'I am only writing this to remind some anglers of the soundness of Wood's doctrine.'   JOHN R.

I feel for ever thankful to this great angler.

SLACK LINE IN GREASED LINE FISHING
Captain Bostock's reply
To the Editors of the 'Journal of the Fly Fishers' Club.'

'Dear Sirs—I cannot see eye to eye with John R. about giving line to a fish rising at your fly when using the greased line. It seems to me that as soon as the fish has got the fly properly in its mouth there must be a strong resistance to drive the hook home. It is undoubtedly best to have the line as slack on the water as possible, so that at first the fish feels no resistance. The line should then travel on downstream till the pull of the water drives the hook home, and at this moment the line should be firmly held in the fingers.

'To the best of my knowledge there was only one occasion when Arthur Wood gave line to the fish, and that was when he was fishing fast water with a short line. He then held the rod point up very high, so that there was as much belly as possible from the tip of the rod to where the line entered the water. When a fish rose he threw this slack at the fish, plus the loop of slack he was holding in his hand. This line then was carried below the fish and the pull of the water on it hooked the fish, "coupled with the fact that he had a firm grip of the line".

'I think it must be this particular and not too common instance that has caused many fishermen to think that Wood gave slack to the fish when it rose. As a matter of fact, except in this one special case, he swept his rod towards the bank, thus causing a belly for the stream to pull on, and when he felt the fish, raised his rod point to drive the hook well home. By this method the fish was normally well hooked in the side of the mouth. This is exactly what I do myself and find most successful.

'It is interesting to note that some fishermen prefer double hooks to singles in the smaller sizes. Wood never did, and personally I agree with him. Can the reason be, and I expect it is, that different fishermen have different styles of fishing, and that is what makes it so difficult to dogmatize?

Yours faithfully,

NEVILLE F. BOSTOCK.'

Since this correspondence, I have developed a new way of treating this slack line method. But what suits one kind of temperament does not suit another, and my last wish is to be dogmatic on these things.

For those who are worried about the number of fish that pull them and the number they lose, I give this information for what it is worth. It is as follows: I often found that letting go that 'yard of slack' was not quite so easy as it might seem to be. The fish caught you 'unawares', with the result that, instead of letting it go, one's thumb and finger involuntarily held the line. Well, there was not much good in having a yard of slack if one was going to do that!

In 1943 I tried having a very free running reel, so that when the fish came and pulled you, he took off a yard or so of line. Without touching the line I swept the rod—not upwards, but sideways—towards my bank. This gave off another couple of yards. But the fish was hooked, and in nine cases out of ten in the proper place, far back in the side of the mouth.

In eleven days fishing, I killed fifty-four fish and only lost three.

I taught this method to someone else, and down went the percentage of fish hooked and lost.

That is all I want to say. You can try it if you like. It may not suit your particular temperament—it suits mine.

I have recently seen letters about the fish that are lost when they take the fly straight downstream below the angler. I can only say that I caught a great many this year when my fly was straight below me: I was fishing the above-mentioned way.

The difficulty of the 'yard of slack' on one's hand is to let it go at the right moment, when you have not seen your fish rise, and only feel the tug. I find it very hard to let go the line under these circumstances, but that, as I have said before, is a matter of temperament.

I am sure the successful greased-line fisherman is the one who changes his fly very often. There may not be much in a pattern, but I always hope that there is. There is a great deal in size.

I will quote one instance on 'Pattern' theory. I was fishing with a party in Iceland. The river was low and clear, and we could catch them only on a silver blue, very small—Nos. 9 and 10 and lightly dressed. Other patterns of the same size were tried, but with no success. We had only three or four patterns of silver blue and they soon went, as they always do if you have only one or two patterns.

I had my fly-tying materials with me and managed to keep the party fully supplied for the remainder of the trip.

There are three flies I use on the Dee in April and May: (1) Blue Charm, (2) Jeannie, (3) Logie.

I have a supply of these in all sizes from No. 1 to No. 11. Eighty per cent of the fish I get on the Dee are on Blue Charm, but other fishermen I find are getting their fish on a Logie, Jeannie, or some other pattern. On comparing notes at the end of the day one usually finds that although the pattern was different, the size was the same.

There is one fly I would mention which I always put on just as it is getting dark. It is a pattern of my own and is as follows:— Tail: a topping. Body: lower half, light yellow floss. Top half to the head: black floss. Ribs: oval tinsel spaced widely apart. Hackle: a long black heron, the full length of the hook. Wings: two narrow strips of Cinnamon Turkey laid flat. Hook No. 1. I have killed a great many fish with this fly from 8 - 10 p.m. in the latter part of April and May.

IV

'A FEW TIPS'

HERE are a few tips I have picked up from various friends and all kinds of people.

My friend, Edward Corbett, who kindly asked me to the Evanger River in Norway on several occasions before the 1939 - 45 war, had more 'tips' and ingenious ideas than anyone else I have known, and several of the 'tips' I mention here are his line of thought.

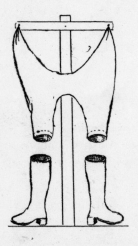

Fig. 3

1. Drying gum boots. Corbett rigged up a wind sail, something like this: a canvas supported by a cross arm to spread out and

catch the wind, which was taken down the two legs of the boots. In a few minutes the boots were dry. Another way, not so good, is to stand a piece of flat board in the boot and point to the wind.

2. After your line has dried and when you wind it on again next morning, run it through a piece of paraffin wax. It keeps a fine surface on your line, and is splendid for undressed spinning lines.

3. When a number of people get into a car with their rods and lines up, there is generally a fine tangle at the end of the journey, and sometimes a broken rod top. To avoid all this, hitch a wooden match to the point of your line and reel up to the top ring. You will never have any more trouble.

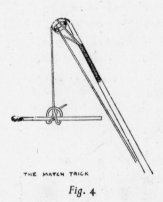

THE MATCH TRICK

Fig. 4

Personally I always do this whether I am walking down to the fishing, or motoring. Your cast is in the damper, where it should be, and at the end of the journey you have only to catch hold of the match and tie on your cast, which is now properly soaked.

4. In these days of lack of gillies it is convenient to have some means of carrying your fish, besides the heavy and clumsy bag which usually smells and attracts flies. Get a light netting, such as is used to catch rabbits, make a handle of round wood, tie on some strong string to the handle and net and you get something like this:

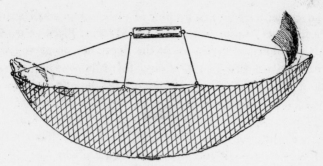

Fig. 5 A HOME-MADE FISH BAG

You can put half a dozen of these bags in your pocket or fishing bag and you hardly know you have them. If you are alone and get four of five fish and have to walk half a mile, you will appreciate these bags. Another form of carrier is made by cutting a piece of broom handle. Bore a hole through it and pass a double piece of fine cord through the hole. One end has a loop, the other a piece of strong wire in the form of a hook. You put the hook through the gills of the fish and into his mouth and the loop pulled tight over his tail. Either the carriers or nets, particulars of which I have already given, are very handy.

6. Removing varnish from rods. Apply a coating of Bergers' 'Solroid' from a coachbuilder. Then scrape away the old varnish, clean and re-varnish two or three coats.

7. Your cork handle on your rod will in time get black and greasy. I dislike this, and if you want it clean, rub it down with a cloth and ammonia, and it will come up quite clean again.

8. I have tried all kinds of brogues and boots, but for the past ten years I have used nothing else but a pair of brogues made by Eadie, Bootmaker, Builth Wells. These are very soft leather with thick felt soles, leather heels and spikes or nails. Before I used this type of brogue I was always 'taking a bath', but since then I have only had one bath! They give you great confidence. I have had mine re-soled four times.

9. Golden Sprats. I now always dye and preserve my own. They are generally brighter than most shop sprats and do not smell so strongly of formalin. This is how I prepare them: Get nice fresh sprats, wash them well and be careful not to remove scales. I use a pair of forceps to handle them. After washing, place them

in a jar containing, say, half a pint of water and a small quantity of 'Acriflavine', either in solid or liquid form. Place your sprats in this solution until they are of the depth of colour you wish. After this, place them in a solution of formalin (one part formalin to about forty parts of water)—about a teaspoonful to half a pint of water, and leave them there for twenty-four hours. I generally do this process before dyeing. At the end of twenty-four hours take them out and wash them well. Then place them in your jar of very strong salt and water—as much salt as will dissolve. Bottle them tight and they will keep for a long time. The advantage of the salt solution is that it takes out all the formalin smell and the baits are tough.

10. This is how I preserve prawns and shrimps. Get some nice fresh prawns of the size you want. Wash them, place in a small saucepan and put some bright red dye in the water before you put in the prawns. Bring your water almost up to the boil and keep moving your prawns with forceps. When they are a nice red colour take them out, wash them, and place in the same solution of formalin as you did for the sprats, for about four hours, Then bottle them in salt and water as in the case of sprats. They keep well and still smell of prawn. Glycerine I find is messy, and not easy to obtain. I straighten out the prawns and put a needle through them before treating them. I always like prawns with eggs—I catch more fish with them.

11. Some people are clever about knots, others forget them, so I put these illustrations in again, in case anyone has forgotten them. One must always remember that making a knot in a gut cast reduces its strength from twenty-five to forty per cent. It does not matter what knot you tie—some are better than others. I am only illustrating a few which I think are the best.

Mr Nuttall, who knows more about knots than anyone, wrote to me on this subject and I quote his letter in my chapter on 'Tackle and Equipment'. Mr Nuttall has tested, with a ballistic tester, every type of knot known to the angler, and you can be sure that what he says is correct.

12. 'Terrors.' I mention this as they have been the means of my catching a large number of salmon. Many years ago I was fishing the upper reaches of the Tummel, late in the year. My com-

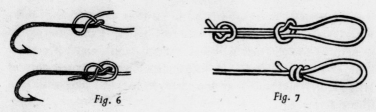

Fig. 6

THE FIGURE OF EIGHT. EQUALLY SUITABLE FOR
EITHER GUT-EYED OR METAL-EYED HOOKS

Fig. 7

THE LOOP KNOT

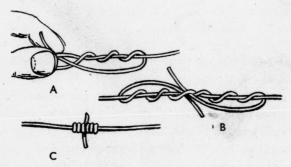

Fig. 8   THE BLOOD KNOT

A. THE FIRST HALF OF THE KNOT   B. THE WHOLE KNOT, LOOSE

C. THE KNOT PULLED TIGHT

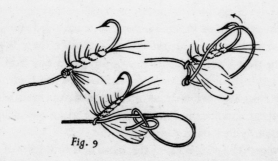

Fig. 9

THE 'TURLE' KNOT. THIS WAS STRONGLY RECOMMENDED BY THE LATE
F. M. HALFORD IN 'DRY FLY FISHING', A RECOMMENDATION REPEATED
BY MANY SUBSEQUENT AUTHORITIES. THE ILLUSTRATION SHOWS HOW
THE KNOT IS MADE

panion, Charles Burtt, and I had been using every kind of lure, with little success. One day I said to Charles, 'I am going to try something tonight that will make them jump', and I produced a large 'Terror', three and a half inches long, composed only of a flight of hooks and four long badger hackles, like this (see illustration):

"TERROR"

Fig. 10

The body was made of twisted gut, and the hooks wound with silver tinsel.

The next day I had immediate success, and during my stay on the Tummel I got many fish. I have tried this fly on the Shannon, in Norway, Iceland, Scotland and Ireland with great success.

On the English rivers I never had much success. On the west coast of Scotland little success, on the east coast of Scotland very successful. In Norway and Iceland, great success in most places. Of course, it represents a sand-eel, and if the fish have been feeding on this in the sea, then they take it; if they have not been feeding on this you get little success—anyhow, that is my theory. You fish with it in the ordinary way, down and across. The hooks should be small doubles. It casts quite well.

13. On keeping lines in order. Now you have got me! I don't suppose there are many people who look after their lines with more care than I do. I strip them, polish them down to get the dirt off. I rub them down most days. I used to put them in a hat box with talcum powder; I have hung them up in an airy loft, in my sitting room, and in all manner of places—yet, in spite of all this, my lines have gone 'tacky'.

Mr Coggeshall, who dressed the most beautiful lines of anyone I know, told me that it was the inferior quality of boiled oil that was then on the market—that a litharge was put into the oil to make it dry quickly, and that did the damage. I have a salmon line which I have had over twenty years; it is as good today as ever it was; also one of Coggeshall's trout lines which I had for fifteen years, and which never went sticky.

On the other hand, lines made in the last ten or fifteen years, I find, go sticky quite suddenly. Last year I sent two lines to be re-dressed; the other day I found two salmon and two trout lines which I had fished with all one season (1943) and which suddenly went sticky in November.

I was given a tip the other day as follows: If a line is only slightly 'tacky', uncoil it in fairly large coils and place it in a solution of a tablespoonful of lime in a quart of water. Give it a thoroughly good soaking and then stretch it up to dry. Do not rub it down, but when it has been drying for some days, rub it down and give it a final polish with Mucilin or Cerolene. I have not yet had an opportunity of trying this, but the tip was given me by an old professional who knows what he is talking about.

(Later). Since writing these lines I have tried this tip on a very sticky line. When the line was dry I rubbed it down with a bit of 'Loofah' and then a silk handkerchief. Then I took some boiled oil in my fingers and worked this well into the line. It is now dry and hard after four weeks and with no sign of stickiness at all.

Apart from this I know no cure, except re-dressing. You can remove the sticky oil from the line, but when you have done this you have a line without dressing.

Lines, I consider, are one of the most important items in your fishing. They can make you fish well or badly. I seldom find a rod I can't fish with, providing I have the right weight and taper on the line. I have seen many a rod condemned on account of the wrong weight of line being used. Of course all this is well known to the experienced fisherman, but you would be surprised what a number of fishermen there are who won't take the trouble to try different lines on their rods.

When one goes to the expense of taking good fishings, it is surely worth while spending a few pounds on your casting lines, and the pleasure you get out of a good line that suits the rod is beyond all price.

14. *On tying Flies.* I won't say much about this, as there have been so many books on Fly Tying of recent years, more especially

two books, one by Major Sir Gerald Burrard, the other by Mr
Eric Taverner on Salmon Fly Tying.

At one time I used to tie all my trout and salmon flies; but
recently my dry fly fishing has been restricted to a comparatively
few days in the year and my eyesight is not so good as it was, so
that I now tie very few trout flies. Another thing is, I have
become such a lunatic about greased-line fishing for salmon in
May and June that it seems hardly worth while taking any dry
fly water, where May and June are the best months. So beyond
the privilege of fishing as a guest, with the few remaining old
friends I now have, my dry fly days are few in a season.

In the winter I have tied up to eighty or one hundred salmon
flies. It has the same soothing effect on me as knitting has to a
woman. I tie by artificial daylight lamps, when I can get them!
After a long day's work I know nothing more soothing than
tying flies.

There are few tips I can tell you that have not been given in
those two most excellent books I have already mentioned.
During the past two years I have had a most delightful correspondence with Mr William Barry who, by general consent, is
one of the finest, if not *the* finest, salmon fisher in the world.
What Mr Barry does not know about salmon fishing is hardly
worth knowing. Mr Barry, in this correspondence, has touched
on all kinds of subjects, but I will refer now only to the question
of flies. His idea—and he is probably right—is that it is a question
of size and not pattern. I have put several questions up to him
to try and refute this argument, but he always has some ingenious
answer to account for this or that. Nevertheless, I do find little
weaknesses in his armour which tend to show that he does like
to try some new pattern, although he has his favourite patterns.

The fact is, none of us like to wear a suit of clothes of the
same pattern the whole year round, or the same tie. We all like
a change, no matter whether in clothes, food or salmon flies.
It would be a dull business if one used the same pattern of fly
all day and every day, simply varying the size. Take, for example,
my first experience in salmon fishing, recorded earlier in this
book, where the fisherman caught all his fish on a 'canary' fly,
and nobody else got any. Next year, everybody used 'canary'

flies, and they were no better than any other. How can you account for that? What I was going to say about salmon flies was that I am convinced that one can modify one's dressing to a very great extent; that is to say, leave out a large amount of the dressing in the wings and keep the body as 'lean' as you can.

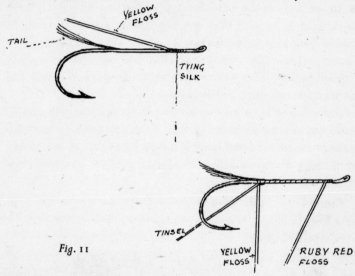

Fig. 11

In order to do this I now dress my flies as follows: Supposing that you want a Logie. Tail: a topping. Ribs: silver oval tinsel. Body: pale primrose one-third, and ruby-red the other two-thirds. I proceed as follows: I tie a few turns of tying silk down the hook from the eye; I then tie in a strip of pale primrose Floss and I wind this down the hook towards the bend. About half-way down the shank I tie in my Golden Pheasant Topping for the tail, with my yellow floss. Then I work down the yellow floss over the topping until I reach the point I require. Then I tie in my silver ribbing and work back my yellow floss to the point where I tie in my hackle. Next I take a fine strand of ruby-red floss silk. Tie this in and work it down the body over the yellow floss, smoothing each turn with a stiletto, until I get to the point where I want to stop, then I work this back to the hackle point. I then take up the silver tinsel ribbing which is securely tied in by the floss silk and wind up the body in open turns to form the ribs, and tie in. You will see by this that I have not used the tying silk at all in making the body, but only for tying in at the head. This method makes a much slimmer body than the old method and is quite as strong. If you want a flat silver body, take a length of thin tinsel and tie in at the head. Work this down towards the tail and tie the tail in with the tinsel. Then work the tinsel back to the head and tie in. For working in this way, the tinsel must be very thin, but the double layer of tinsel up the body is just as strong as the single and thicker layer, and you can make a surprisingly strong and slim body if you want it for summer fishing. This method is also much quicker. The hackle and wings are tied in, in the usual way.

I have lately been experimenting with summer salmon flies with enamel bodies instead of silk. Silk goes quite dull and lifeless in water. An enamel body shines and gives off flashes of light. I don't suppose this is a new idea, but I give the information for what it is worth.

1. Enamel the body with white enamel, or aluminium paint, for a foundation. When dry, paint on your colour enamel. This gives a brilliant finish.

2. Choose what colour you want for the body, say half yellow and half ruby red. Paint half a dozen hooks like this and let them dry.

3. Tie in your fine silver tinsel at the head of the fly, this to form the ribs. Wind the tinsel in open turns down the body, then take it back in open turns to the head and tie in.

4. Then tie in your blue hackle and wing your fly in the usual way, with mallard, dyed swan and jungle cock cheeks and you have a very pleasing, fine water 'Logie'. You will notice that there is no tail, but I do not think this matters in these low water flies.

I always give it a small touch of celluloid varnish after every two or three turns of the tying silk.

In case there are readers who do not know how to make clear celluloid varnish, the following is the recipe I always use: Get some old films and thoroughly clean off the filament, cut it up into small strips and place in a small wide-necked bottle. Then pour in amyl acetate and shake the bottle every few hours, when

Plate 3

THIS IS THE END OF THE BACK CAST. THE ROD SHOULD SELDOM GO BEYOND THIS POINT. THE LEFT
HAND CONTROLS THIS.

the films will dissolve. Keep this mixture about the same thickness as treacle and pour a little into another bottle and add more amyl acetate so as to make it of the required consistency.

Amyl acetate is a fine cleanser for the fingers when they get wax on them. When tying flies your fingers must be kept clean, so must your tinsel.

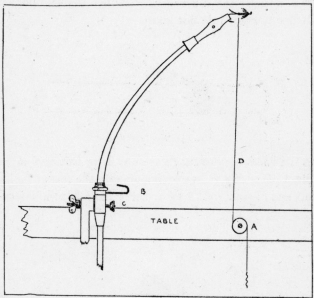

Fig. 12   VICE

This is an illustration of the vice I have used for thirty-five years. It is adjustable to any angle and the arm is well bent over. On the table I screw a circular piece of rubber. The tying silk can be hitched round this and it does away with pliers and weights to hold the silk taut.

The jaws are held by a screw and hold both big and small hooks tightly. If the jaws of your vice do not grip, slip in between the jaws and the hook a piece of very fine glass-paper. Hooks will never slip if you do this.

A is the rubber disc.

B Revolving hook to wax your silk, etc.

C Set screw to hold the arm in any position.

D Tying silk.

One more thing about tying flies. It is customary, after having tied the body, to tie in the hackle. It occurred to me one day to tie on the wings next and finish up with the hackle. You can certainly keep your wings nice and flat that way and make a head much smaller. The result was very pleasing. I showed these flies to a number of salmon fishers, and was surprised to find how few noticed the difference. Whether the salmon will be equally unobservant I do not know.

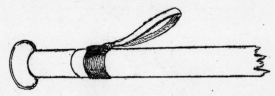

Fig. 13   BUTT OF ROD

This is a handy way of attaching your fly or bait to your rod.

Whip a piece of soft leather bootlace in the form of a loop at the butt end of your rod. A fly or bait seldom becomes detached.

V

MORE DIARY

HAVING written on all kinds of subjects in the previous chapters, I am now going back to my diary, but shall leave out a great deal for fear of becoming tedious.

One incident which is well worth relating was in 1909 when I went to Fortingall on the River Lyon, a tributary of the Tay. It was in March, and the weather was cold and bright. This is a very pretty little river and fishes well in the spring. When I was driving to the hotel, I stopped on the bridge and there I saw an old gentleman spinning with a tray strapped round his middle. I had never seen this before and was fascinated. The fisher, I was told, was Mr Philip Geen, well known to all salmon anglers. The line, as he gathered it in by hand, was coiled into the tray, and in throwing his bait he was able to drop it within a few inches of the spot he wanted. I have never seen this before nor since, but I always wanted to know what happened supposing he hooked a fish when most of the line was in the basket! I suppose he managed all right, as he was a most successful angler.

Spinning with a 'Killin' wire trace, was a new thing to me. I don't think it had been in fashion for very long. My gillie insisted on my using it and as I was always ready to try a new thing, I consented. I had a lot to learn in the spinning line, as I found out later on. There may have been 'Silex' reels in those days—I don't know. But there were no Illingworth or Pflueger or Elarex reels in those days. Mine was a good old-fashioned Nottingham, the best thing for anyone to learn on. If you can manage that, you can manage anything. Lots of over-runs and birds' nests! Here is a tip my gillie told me—keep a button-hook in your pocket—it will save you hours when you get a really nice over-run.

But these sort of gadgets are not necessary nowadays. The reels are so perfect that you can go a whole day without an over-run. The only time I ever get one now is when the line has got kinked, and that is only due to carelessness. Put on a spinner that turns the opposite way, and it soon comes out.

When you have caught a heavy fish, it is not a bad tip to run out your line, without any trace on it, in quick running water.

Kinks can be got rid of by trailing the line, say thirty or forty yards, through rough grass, but almost everybody knows this.

To go back to the Lyon; I have often wanted to go there again but have never done so. We got a few fish and spent a happy time.

In August I took a beat on the Awe. The water had been taken over by an enterprising couple, Mr Plevins and, I think, Colonel Macdonald. They took off the nets, or a great deal of them, and thought, quite rightly, that they were going to turn the Awe into one of the finest rivers in Scotland. But it was not a great success, and I am under the impression that the river did not improve very much. The fish ran through.

The 'Stepping Stones' was a great pool for sea trout at night, and many a good basket I got here.

If only one had known about small flies and greased line in those days I feel sure one would have caught far more salmon than one did. Salmon would constantly come and take one's small sea trout flies and so depart, for want of a heavier cast and more line on one's reel. I fished for salmon with an eighteen-feet Castleconnell rod and good big flies!

No spinning was allowed on the Awe in those days, and quite right too.

1910. In the spring of 1910 I went back to the Awe and stayed at Taynuilt. It was wonderful weather, and I always remember it for the first tragedy I had with a really large fish. In a few words it happened thus:

I went down to fish the Oak Tree Pool, which is just below the Bridge of Awe. The month was March. The river was big and I saw a couple of clean fish move on the other side. This is a long cast, fishing from the left bank, but when I had got my fly over the other side I got a very heavy pull and I knew I was into a big fish, a really big fish. Like most big fish he started to move about very slowly at first, cruising round the pool. I was standing on a big rock a little way from the bank: I asked the gillie to give me a hand as I was very unsteady. He did not want to get his feet wet. At that moment the fish came right under my feet. I struggled to the bank, and I suppose this woke him up, for like a streak of lightning he charged the heavy rapids above me and went up about seventy yards. Now I knew what size fish he was, somewhere about the forties. Then he suddenly turned and went to the other side of a big rock in the middle of the river—and all was over. I have never forgiven myself for not being quicker on my feet. If I had been, and got away after him, the story might have been different. But there it is—we live and learn. We had a pleasant time there, and got a few fish and many kelts.

In May, 1910, my brother Ernest arrived in England from Peru or some such place where, as far as I remember, he was Chargé d'Affaire. He said, 'Look here, John, I want to go salmon fishing for three or four days'. I answered, 'Where do you propose to go? Scotland is a bit far for three or four days'. 'Oh', he said, 'somewhere handy'. This was a problem. Then I thought of the Usk at Abergavenny. The Angel Hotel advertised a piece of water about two miles below the town. So there we went. The Hotel was very comfortable and was owned by a man by the name of Stocken. He had a very good cellar, and we were thoroughly comfortable. There was a nice stretch of water, and he charged us ten shillings a day each for fishing. It was on the 14th May. King Edward VII had suddenly died, and there was a great gloom over the whole of London, so we were glad to get away. We had a nice rise of water and during the week-end we each got two fish, twenty-two, twenty, ten and ten pounds, and very evenly divided. Not a bad catch for ten shillings a day each. In 1939 this water was letting for £450 per annum. What a difference! All the beats on the Usk were fetching the most ridiculous prices about this time, which I attribute to the development of the motor car. People could run down there from London in three or four hours, but in 1910 there were practically no motors.

In August I paid another visit to the Awe and stayed at Taynuilt with my friend, Charles Burtt. From that time on, Charles Burtt became one of my chief fishing companions for many years. He was the most unselfish and delightful companion and generous sportsman. Salmon and sea trout were very plentiful this year, and we did pretty well. We had some grand fun with sea trout in the Garavelt pool, just above Awe Bridge, and were constantly getting into salmon on our small trout flies and light rods. We knew nothing of greased line in those days, but if we had, I feel sure we should have caught far more fish, as was proved in after years on the same pools.

From the Awe we went on to stay on the upper part of the River Deveron with friends. They had a place called 'Invermarkie'. The fishing was not up to much, but it is a pretty river. We made up for it by some nice days with grouse driving. I think this was about the end of the fishing season as far as I was concerned. Altogether I had not done so badly considering the limited time I had at my disposal in those days. I might have done better in my profession if I had not spent so much time fishing. But I am glad I fished, and now in my old age I do not grudge one single day I spent on the river bank. So much for 1910.

Now a few notes on 1911. At Easter my brother-in-law and I took a beat on the Upper Wye about two miles below Rhayader. It was really the top beat of the salmon fishing. Although it was the end of March fresh fish used to get up there and, what is more, they rose to the fly. Now I don't suppose they often get there, and hardly ever pull a fly, until May. There was hardly any bait fishing in those waters, and this may account for it. L. J. Graham Clarke, one of the finest salmon fishers and salmon fly tyers that ever was, fished the opposite bank. Dear old boy— with his long white beard and artistic clothing. He used to worry

us a good deal with his kind advice. I must say I liked his good
intentions, but my brother-in-law, being considerably older
than myself, resented it very much. I learned a lot from Graham
Clarke—amongst other things, the art of tying salmon flies.
From that time I determined to do the same, and I cannot say how
grateful I am for his inspiration in introducing me to this delightful and useful occupation. And I am quite convinced it has been
the means of helping me to catch many more hundreds of salmon
than I should have done, if I had not been able to tie my own
flies. It has also been the means of catching many salmon for my
friends when on fishing expeditions in such places as Norway and
Iceland, where there was no possibility of being able to buy some
particular size or pattern which the salmon felt inclined to take
in those waters.

Graham Clarke was a fine amateur artist, having spent his
early days studying art in Paris. Some of his pictures are now
in the Fly Fishers' Club—unless they were 'blitzed' in 1940.

In those days, salmon flies were dressed with very heavy
dressings and huge turkey wings, but the fish liked them. I doubt
if you would get a pull on them in these days. He bred turkeys
simply for their feathers, which were cinnamon.

One day I thought I was into a really good spring fish, and my
gillie said he was quite sure it was. He put up a good fight, and
I got him near a rock. The gillie put his gaff into him before I
could see the fish. Then I heard a voice from the other side of
the river say 'Do you usually gaff kelts?' This was G. C., and
he was a conservator of the Wye Board. He told me afterwards
that my gillie was the worst poacher on the river and would
take that kelt home. I felt very small! On another day he said
he would teach me 'switch' casting on his water. I was delighted
to learn from such an expert, and was getting on quite well—so
I thought. G. C. came up and took my rod and said, 'You have
not got it quite right—let me show you again'. I handed over
the rod, and at about the third cast he was into a fish. I am
afraid I felt at the time, and always have since, that he had seen
that fish move before I got down to it, but I may be doing him
an injustice, and I don't grudge him the fish one bit, as it has
given me many a laugh since.

In July, 1911, I decided to go over to Nova Scotia. A year before I had bought a fruit farm with my friend, Eddie Hibbert. It was a nice little farm in lovely country in the Anapolis Valley—not far from Halifax. We used to ship 3,000 to 4,000 barrels of apples to this country, but beyond being a comfortable living for one person, there was little money in it as far as I could see. We went to Quebec in the *Empress of Ireland*, a lovely boat and very comfortable. Splendid food and '98 Pol Roger at seven shillings a bottle. When I am on board ship I always try and find fishermen and at last I got into conversation with an oldish man by name of Van A——. He was a member of the syndicate who had a lease of those famous rivers, the Restigouche and Cascapedia. I got very little out of him: he was not a very forthcoming person. Later in the day, a very nice fellow came up and said, 'I hear you want to know something about the Restigouche River'. I said 'Yes, I should like to hear something about it and the wonderful reputation it has'. So then he started telling me that it was leased by a syndicate of millionaires; that they did not care much about fishing; that there were fine hunting lodges up and down the river and they used to gamble all night, and no wives were allowed. He himself did most of the fishing, which was really quite wonderful, etc.

Someone came up to me afterwards and said, 'Do you know who you were chatting with?' 'No', I said. 'That was Van A——'s valet!' was the reply. All I could say was 'Much more forthcoming than his master'.

I eventually arrived at Nova Scotia, and before very long I had planned a fishing trip. Nova Scotia has a chain of lakes roughly from North to South, connected by rivers. The lakes are full of trout, but I caught nothing large; the average was about one pound. There was a delightful Club called the Kegimakougie Rod and Gun Club on the big lake of the same name. A great big log-built house, most comfortable, and everything one could want. We had the Club practically to ourselves, as we were a little late in the season; the best time is May and June. In two or three days one caught so many trout that it ceased to interest. The gaudier the fly, the more fish one got. So, after staying at the Club for a bit, I decided to go by canoe through the Lakes and rivers and work down to the coast. At night one stayed at farmhouses, and all the folk were very hospitable and kind. One day we went to a bear trap, but there was no bear, and I was very pleased. I have always hated the idea of trapping. My guide, John Lewis, was an enormous fellow and afraid of nothing, except snakes. One day we found a biggish snake in our pathway. Now snakes never worry me and I have no fear of them, so I took this one by the tail and threw it into the rough grass. My guide had much more respect for me after this little bit of 'bravado' on my part.

On the Liverpool river I had very good fun with small salmon and a trout rod: with greased line and better tackle I feel sure that one would have done very well on this river in June.

We were bothered very little by mosquitoes and flies, and for anyone who is thinking of a change of fishing, I should recommend Nova Scotia. The whole trip was ridiculously cheap in those days. Of course I do not know what it is now, when prices of things have gone 'sky high'—the best split-cane rod of twelve feet costs £25 and Champagne is £3 or £4 a bottle!

In September of this year I had an invitation to go and fish the Sand river in Norway, not far from Stavanger. This is a very late river and does not close until 15th October, as there is a late run after the summer run. This was my first fishing trip to Norway, to be followed by many more after this; but it was not my first trip to Norway as, when I was a boy twelve years old, my father took my brothers and me to Norway on a round cruise. I remember the most wonderful lakes and rivers boiling with trout and I don't think this was my imagination. One day I was much excited; I actually saw a man catch a salmon. I came in for the end of the fight and never shall I forget it. The man who caught it did not think much about it and said it was only a small one. To my young eyes it was huge.

The boat I now crossed in was a very small one, about nine hundred tons, and when we left Newcastle it was blowing one of those awful equinoctial gales. I have never been pitched about so much in my life. We left on a Saturday evening and I never saw a soul from that time until Monday morning when we arrived at Stavanger. It was an awful trip.

We found the Fjord boat had already left for the Sand, so it was a case of staying three days in Stavanger or going round the town to find some sort of boat to take us up the Fjord. After a long search I found a small tug about forty feet long and after much bargaining I persuaded the owner to take us there for a five pound note. We arrived at Sand in the evening and had a long drive of some twenty miles to the head of the river where it runs out of a great lake.

We got to our primitive little inn at midnight. Although it was primitive it was comfortable, and I find in my diary that it cost us 3.50 kroner a day, all in—about three shillings and ninepence as the exchange was then. The food was good, and it was warm, but no bathroom.

The river is magnificent, but so large that all fishing is from a boat. The salmon were turning a bit red, but were good fighters, and there were plenty of sea trout. My largest fish was thirty-three and a half pounds caught on a No. 5 'Jock Scott', and altogether we got thirty-seven fish of an average of sixteen pounds in ten days' fishing. A number were caught spinning, and the favourite bait was a gudgeon. We had no prawns, and golden sprats were unknown in those days, or we might have got many more. Our *kleppers* were paid three shillings and sixpence a day and were pleased with a five-shilling tip at the end of our time.

This trip gave me a taste for Norway which I never forgot.

Thus ended 1911, a year in which I had a great deal of experience and fished in many places.

1912. I find that I went down at Easter to the Carnarvon Arms Hotel, Dulverton. Beyond catching a large number of diminutive trout, about three to the pound and having a very pleasant week, there is little more to say.

In May and June I fished the Kennet, as I had taken a rod on the Hungerford Town water. In those days I think it was the cheapest and best dry-fly water you could find anywhere. When the May fly was on I got my limit of three brace most days, from two pounds up, and a number of fish over four pounds.

In August I went up to the Spey and fished Lady Seafield's water, which is now the water given over to the town of Grantown by Lady Seafield. I caught a few salmon, and fished new water, which is always interesting.

I hear that this water is now managed by an Association in a very efficient way and affords very good sport to those who are unable to spend much money on fishing. A season ticket, so I understand, costs only £10 for salmon and sea trout. In June and July there are plenty to be caught. The fishing extends for about ten miles.

From there I went on to Invermarkie on the Deveron. In October, Douglas Graham asked me to go down to fish his water on the Usk at Clytha. It was a dirty dreary pub in those days, but in later years it was rebuilt and refurnished and for many seasons afterwards I stayed and fished there. In 1940 a flood came and swept away the bank, and the hotel, for the most part, fell into the river. I was there a few days after and it was a very sad sight to see. For the expenditure of a few hundred pounds, all this might have been averted.

The only other time I had been to the Usk was in 1895 when I stayed with a school friend, near Abergavenny. I went off fishing one day and took out a five-shilling licence, paid a man five shillings to show me the water, then promptly fell in. I had no waders, I broke my rod, so thought the best thing to do was to go home as I had a long way to go. Rather an expensive day for a boy without much money in his pocket.

I shall say more about the Usk later on.

My impression of the Usk in those days was that the fish were not nearly so particular as they became in later years, and took the fly well. It was not until later that bait fishing became so popular and every kind of contraption was thrown over a fish as soon as it showed itself. They never got a chance of settling in the pool, and fly fishing before May was of little use.

1913. I was very busy in these days and had little time to spend fishing, and beyond a few days on the Kennet I did not get away until August, when I took a rod at Rodel, South Harris. It was a syndicate water then, and one stayed at the house belonging to Lord Fincastle. It takes a long time to get there, but when you do get there it is worth it. Like most of these Hebridean fishings, there is a chain of lakes and a river to the sea.

There was a semi-tidal Loch—quite a small one, called the Mill Pool.

When I arrived there was an east wind, brilliant sky, and conditions looked hopeless. It was no good going to the Upper Lochs, as there had been no rain for weeks. My gillie was the 'dourest' thing I have ever struck. Although I saw plenty of sea trout jumping in the Mill Pool he said it was quite useless. Then I told him I had come a long way and I intended to try. In a way, he was quite right. We fished with a wet fly for an hour or so, but with no result. After lunch I asked him if he had ever seen a dry fly used. He said 'No' he had never heard of it.

I had with me a few 'variants'—grey, with long hackles. So, much to his disgust I said I would try for the sea trout with a dry fly. The response was immediate, and a two-pounder was landed. This was followed by a four-pounder, and so the fun went on. That afternoon I got twenty-seven sea trout weighing thirty-eight pounds. During the whole of this time he never said a word, and when I asked him at the end of the day what he thought of the 'dry fly' he said, 'I dinna care about it at all!' There was nothing more to be said.

Throughout my stay, which was a short one, I continued to have success with the dry fly, but nothing so good as that first day.

Below the Mill Pool there was a sea loch about a half mile long. The tide came in through a narrow neck in the rocks and I noticed that the salmon came from the other end of the loch and worked up to the bore as the tide rose. I suggested to my boatman that we should go and have a try for them. I had a few small salmon flies with me. He did not think much of the idea, especially as I only had a nine-feet six-inch trout rod. We had not been fishing for five minutes when I got into a fish. He rushed into the kelp—of which there was much about—and broke me. At the end of forty minutes, I had killed two and got broken in three.

This is the first and only time I remember catching a salmon on a fly in salt water.

The sea trout rose very well to a dry fly in salt water, mostly caught on a 'Tup' and grey 'variant'.

There is one story I must tell about this place. Not far away was 'Finsbay', a little fishing village and a good-sized hotel. The story as told to me is as follows:

A certain 'gentleman' insisted on going out to fish on Sunday in the boat. He could get no boatman, so went by himself and came back very pleased at having caught quite a number of sea trout. When he came ashore he offered some to the people standing by. They all turned their backs on him. Nobody would take the fish, and nobody would go out with him in a boat after that. There was nothing for it but to leave the place, which he did by the next boat.

From Rodel I went on to Mull—I think it was the wettest place I have ever struck.

Thus ended my 1913 holiday.

WAR 1914

VI

THE FIRST WORLD WAR

1914 was the year of the Great War—needless to say there was no fishing.

In the spring I took a lease of Denford Mill, a very picturesque old mill spanning the River Kennet below Hungerford. The place was a ruin and most of the inside fallen away. I employed three carpenters and a bricklayer and started to put the place in order. We made a grand job of it and it turned out to be a most satisfactory summer home. There was one very large room which faced up and down the river so that one could sit and watch the fish rise. And there were some fish in those days! I passed several happy years there and was able to entertain a large number of fishing friends who delighted in the place.

In 1915 I wanted a rest, so decided to go to Dalmally for a week and fish the Awe. On the second day I had a curious accident. I was sitting in my bath and did not notice that the hot tap was running slightly. Suddenly the boiling water came in contact with my foot and removed the entire skin. I had to get a doctor and get it bandaged up, and there was nothing for it but to go back home. It laid me up for a fortnight; thus my trip was cut short. It was a lesson I never forgot in after years.

In 1916 my brother-in-law came back from the front and wanted to go away for a quiet holiday for ten days, and as I, too, wanted a holiday from my labours, we decided to go to New-burgh on the River Ythan—Udny Arms Hotel.

62

I think Newburgh is the most healthy and bracing place I have ever been to, and for those who have never been there I will explain briefly what the fishing is like.

There are two ways to catch fish there—one by fishing off the bank and the other what really amounts to harling from a boat. Take the boat fishing; you start at the mouth when the tide is coming in, and row gently backwards and forwards across the river, gradually drifting up river all the time until you come to the bridge, which is about a mile and a half above the mouth. Then later in the day, when the tide has turned, you start up by the bridge and gradually work down to the mouth. One varies one's lure with 'Terrors', sand eels and small herrings. Generally a large Terror at the tail and a smaller one as dropper. The Grey Terror is a good imitation of a sand eel—the small Blue Terror is a herring. The most deadly bait of all is a sand eel, freshly dug up in the morning when the tide is low. They are not easy to get. You might think that the bottled sand eel is just as good, but it isn't. I repeatedly tried putting on a bottled eel and got no tugs, but as soon as I put on a fresh eel, I got a fish right away. You must fish pretty fine and your hooks must be light and small.

From the bank, I found a very light spinning outfit was much the best—practically a thread line on an Illingworth reel. I think most of the big fish were got in this way. They are magnificent fighting fish and up to every kind of dodge. Above the bridge, where the water is brackish, trout take a smaller fly, and you can spend a very pleasant day there with small fish. Always remember when you get home to strip your line into a bath or basin and get out the salt water: also to cover your reel with vaseline before you go out, and wash it and grease it when you get home. If you don't do this, your tackle will soon be all to pieces through the influence of salt air and water.

It was a pretty sight to see hundreds of sea trout jumping all over the river. Occasionally one got three and four pounders, but the bag was mostly made up of fish between one and a half and three pounds. A few really big fish of six and seven pounds were caught. One night I got one so big that he would not go into the net. He got out and the hooks got caught up in the net, so a seven or eight pound fish got away.

At the end of ten days we all returned home very much better and happier. The hotel provided wonderful food, considering the circumstances.

In 1917 I had to go to Aberdeen, in March, in connection with some Admiralty work and my friend, Nathaniel Dunlop, asked me to stay a few days with him on the Dee at Durris. This was the first time I had ever fished the Dee, and my excitement was great. I arrived in a very heavy snowstorm and next day there was two feet of snow and roads were blocked. We went down to the river and found 'grue' coming down in great masses. Fishing was out of the question. It took a couple of days to settle down, and then we got fish. I like Durris; but I very much prefer the higher reaches above Banchory and from there up I don't think there is anything to compare with it in the world—or shall I say British Isles—which is just the same thing. Park was on the opposite bank to Durris. Late one afternoon I saw a round little man in tailcoat and striped trousers and patent leather shoes come down to the pool just opposite the house. On the Park side there is a gravel and concrete path. I was wading and fishing fly from my bank. He started behind me with his little seven-foot rod and to my surprise with the greatest ease and dexterity threw a prawn right over to my bank. He had not been fishing for five minutes before he was into a fish. Now, I wondered, what are you going to do, you have no gaff. But at the right moment he produced a telescope gaff from the leg of his trousers and gaffed his fish as smartly as anything I have seen. Having caught his fish, he went back to the house. The butler, I presumed.

There are some grand pools on this water from Durris Bridge down to Park Bridge. Kirk Pot and Castleton fished best that year. So ended another happy visit with kind and delightful people.

I see that I had a grand day on the Kennet this year—fifteen fish averaging nearly two pounds on 11th June. Fish rose in those days—very different from what they do now.

In 1918 I got to know Holford Dixon through our mutual friend, Agnew Severn, whom I had known since I was a boy at St. David's, Reigate. I was his guest on many occasions after this and I shall always remember his wonderful hospitality and kind-

Plates 4-5

Top. THIS IS THE ORDINARY FINISH OF THE CAST. NOTE THE BODY IS NOT BENT FORWARD.
Bottom. WHEN CASTING INTO A WIND IT WILL BE FOUND THAT BY RAISING THE LEFT HAND
UNDERNEATH THE RIGHT ARMPIT THE LINE WILL BE DRIVEN INTO A WIND WITH EASE. THE BODY
IS TURNED SLIGHTLY SIDEWAYS.

ness in after years. He had a lease of Mottisfont Abbey on the Test, and also shared the salmon water down at Nursling.

Mottisfont Abbey is a wonderful old place, part of it Norman, but spoiled by the additions made from time to time. From my bedroom I could see trout rising.

It was Easter Sunday, so I thought I would go to church, which is partly Norman, and has some fine windows. The service was a nice simple country affair, and when we got to the Commandments the old verger, a man with a huge bushy beard, was very loud in his responses—much above everybody else, and very noticeable. But—when we got to the Seventh Commandment there was absolute silence from him—I suppose he did not agree. The following Commandments he picked up the same as before!

I paid a visit to the church the other day, but the old verger was no more.

When I got back from church, I found a row of fish on the lawn. Holford, Agnew and Jimmy Whishaw had all three been up to some fine game—certainly not dry fly. That night my bed was filled with all kinds of indescribable things, so I had my revenge on Jimmy Whishaw and festooned his pyjamas with Phantoms and all kinds of baits.

We were all very happy, like boys at school. Jimmy Whishaw must have been nearly seventy by then, and was the greatest boy of the lot.

From Mottisfont it is a short run to Nursling, and there you get salmon fishing which is different from almost all other places. Beautiful water meadows, cows, ducks and every sort of bird life, but in the smooth and quiet waters of the Test the salmon are there in great numbers. I went to Nursling many times during the next few years and we caught a great many salmon. On one occasion I got eight salmon in a day, and usually we got two or three each in a day. In the early months most of the fish were caught on some form or other of bait—the prawn was very popular. One would walk down the little river and see two or three fish lying below the small wood croys built out, or under a plank bridge there was a fish or two. When they took under the bridge the trouble was to get your rod under the bridge quick enough, as the fish always ran downstream as hard as he could go. I once did a thing which I should be ashamed of, but it was so tempting and was done on the spur of the moment. I hooked a fish in the bottom pool of the water, a large round pool. He went round and round the pool, and the water being clear I saw that five other fish were following him all round. When the time came for gaffing him I saw to my astonishment that one of the fish that had been following round was still close up to the tail of the fish I had hooked. I said to the man with me 'Gaff the second one'. He did, so we got two fish—very naughty and terrible, but done without a second's premeditated thought. There was a pool, known as the 'drawing-room pool' just outside the keeper's cottage. There were always a lot of fish in this pool. By lying flat, face down, one could see the fisherman's bait coming round. Several times I saw a salmon come up as if to take the bait and then suddenly turn round and give it, or try to give it, an unholy smack with his tail.

I think this often happens in salmon fishing. You feel a bang, and the fish goes off like a scalded cat and the hold then gives way. You say to yourself and your friends 'I can't think why I lost that fish—he came with a tremendous bang, and then the hold came away.' The above explanation may account for some of these fish.

I think the trout on the Nursling water were quite the finest trout I have seen in any part of the world. People were so busy salmon fishing that they did not bother very much about the trout. In the May fly time, the big ones came out, but so often it happened at that time of year that people above would start cutting their weeds. Now there appears to be no rule on the Test to put in weed stops, as there is on the Kennet. Owners cut their weeds and send them to the next man, whereas on the Kennet you are bound to have weed stops at the end of your water, and two or three men pull them out as fast as they come down. This is as it should be, and I can't understand why the same plan cannot be adopted on the Test. Many a good day's salmon and trout fishing has been ruined for me and those I have fished with, for the lack of a little consideration for those below.

As I was saying, the trout on this section of the Test were the

I have ever seen. Great deep shoulders and the smallest
of heads, so different from the fish on the upper reaches.

There were sea trout at Nursling, but for some reason or
another we seldom caught them; perhaps they were only night
risers—I don't know, as I never had the opportunity of fishing
at night. But what I do know is this. On one occasion—and I am
talking of twenty-five years ago—the keeper told me that a few
sea trout were wanted for the table, and would I like to see the
net drawn through the tidal pool.

We had one draw with the net, and as far as I can remember
we took out about forty to fifty sea trout, mostly from two to
four pounds. We only kept enough for the table, and the rest
went back. It was a wonderful sight, and showed what a really
fine lot of sea trout came up the river in August.

As I have already said, there is a great charm about the fishing
at Nursling. You never knew what you were going to get hold of.
There was one fish I remember well—I hooked him on a No. 6
Black Doctor. I knew he was a very big fish as soon as I got him.
He was hooked just above the Rustic Bridge, where the mill race
joins the water. For forty minutes I played that fish with every
prospect of getting him at the end. We saw him several times,
and he was not less than forty pounds. Just at the end, he came
away and I found the gut loop of my fly attached to the cast!

Ah! How many will say 'Fancy fishing with a fly on a gut eye—
it serves you right.' I quite agree—it did, but that was twenty-five
years ago. I don't think I have fished with a gut eye since, except
in the case of really large flies, when I always have a gut eye.
They are so much kinder to one's gut-cast than a metal eye.

I have never forgotten that fish, for it was one of those fish that
remain in one's memory until all fishing is finished.

Since my good friend, Holford Dixon, gave up the water, I have
never fished it again, but on several occasions motoring through
that part of the Test, I have stopped on the way and looked at
the water. It has brought back to me many happy days in the
company of the kindest of friends and the best of sportsmen.*

And so we go on to other rivers and places.

A very jolly holiday, I remember well, was in the autumn of

* Holford Dixon died in 1945.

1918. The war was coming to an end and Charles Burtt and I took a little cottage on the River Tummel. This cottage was about two miles below Loch Rannoch and had fishing rights of the Tummel for about three miles. We were delighted with the place, and the river was but a hundred yards from the cottage. There were plenty of salmon to be seen—of course rather red and not inclined to take any fly or other lure. After fishing for several days without an offer, I said to Charles one night, 'I am going to tie a "Terror", such as we use on the Ythan for sea trout'. That night I tied a Terror, and for those who do not know the dressing, here it is—a gut body about three inches long, with a double hook at the tail, another one half way up, and a single hook at the head: silver tinsel on the hooks. Wings; two pairs of long badger hackles, set flat, and about two turns of badger hackle at the head.

Next morning I started at the pool just below the house. I don't think that I had taken half a dozen casts when up came a big fish of twenty pounds. I waited a bit and he came again. But that was the end of him—I could not move him any more. This was encouraging, so down the river I went to a nice quick-running stream. Very soon I was into a fish and got him. Just at that moment a lady was coming down the bank: the local hotel at Rannoch had the right of fishing this water. Well, the lady was very beautiful—she had a pearl necklace, diamond ear-rings and a very bright red blouse. She congratulated me and said, 'What a lovely fish; I wish I could catch one like it; I have never caught a salmon'. After looking at the fly she said, 'Donald, have we a fly like this?' Donald had never seen anything like it in his life.

The end of it was I promised to tie her one like it, and if the gillie would call for it in the morning, it would be ready.

I forgot the incident, and the lady, but about two days afterwards I saw in the rough water above where I was fishing a lady hurtling down the bank, evidently in contact with a good fish.

Then I recognised my lady—her hat was off, the pearl necklace was flapping, her hair was any way, and there was a fish—quite seventy yards below her and completely out of control.

I got out of the river and said to Donald, 'You have not got any waders—would you like me to wade out and try and get

68

the fish?' He was very agreeable. Meanwhile the lady was shouting out 'I got it on your fly'. So I waded out below the fish, a risky proceeding, and as he came 'waddling' down the water he was quite near to me. I took a chance and gaffed him, waded ashore and laid him at the feet of my lady—twenty pounds. All highly dramatic. I think with a little encouragement she would have embraced me.

I never saw anyone so pleased at getting a fish. We must come and dine at the hotel that night—no excuse. So Charles Burtt and I trudged off to the hotel about two miles away and we had the most sumptuous repast that anyone could wish for—champagne, old brandy—everything. Both the lady and her husband were charming hosts and we went our way home, very late, and the distance seemed longer on the return journey. I never met them again, but I have always felt that I gave the lady one of the best thrills she ever had in her life.

We caught quite a number of fish on this fly, and the experience gained for me many other fish in after years in rivers all over the world, more especially on the Shannon, Norway and Iceland.

So ends the year 1918.

In November the war was over, a sudden collapse.

I find an interesting note in my diary for that year. I rented a small tributary of the Kennet—the Witton Ditch as it was called. It ran into the Kennet below Ramsbury. The rent was £20 all in. The water was as clear as gin, and big fish used to run up it from the Kennet. There were lots of fish from two to four pounds. It must have been the feeding conditions which attracted the fish to leave the main river. It was full of shrimps and a very good hatch of duns and May fly. I kept this going for some years but the rent gradually mounted up to £100 per annum plus rates and taxes and I then decided to give it up, with many regrets. All dry fly fishing rents were going up in those days.

VII

MORE FROM MY DIARY

1919 saw me down at Nursling again and on March 29th I see
that I got a twenty-nine pound fish and a twelve and a half pound
fish the same day. Both these fish were caught on a small No. 5
yellow dressed fly, rather like a 'Canary'. It was early in the year
to get fish on the fly. Temperature of water was the cause, I
expect, but in those days we did not think much of these things.

I had a rod on the Hungerford water this year, and what
remarkable good sport one had. A season ticket was £25. It was
a grand May fly year and I never saw so many fish in the water.
Every day one came back home with two and three brace of
fish from two to three pounds, with occasional four-pounders.
Of course I was ideally situated, as my house, the old Mill below
Hungerford, spanned the river and I had only to look out from
the big bay window at the water below me and see when the
rise was on. Big fish used to rise in the pool below the window.
The same rods used to hurry down in the morning and take up
their favourite places—just like a peg-out competition. One
night Jimmy Whishaw was dining with me and we were laughing
over this and after dinner we cut a lot of sticks and wrote the
names of all the people on cards. Late at night we went down
the bank and planted all these sticks with the names attached.
Next morning from the Mill house we watched the fishers troop
down. Some were furious—others took it in good part. I think
they all guessed who had done it. One man never spoke to me

again afterwards! It rather spoiled a good and harmless joke.

In the autumn, my brother George wanted to go to Scotland for sea trout, so I booked rooms at Overscaig. I went up there in advance of him, but soon saw it was a 'wash-out' so far as I was concerned, so managed to get out of the rooms and wired him to meet me at Newburgh on the Ythan. From 24th July to 5th August we managed to get one hundred and fifteen sea trout. I found my old friend, Sir Archie Ross, there, and we had a very jolly time.

1920 saw me again down at Nursling on the Test. On 13th March I led off with a twenty-three pounder, followed by an eighteen pounder, and in the afternoon a nineteen pound fish. Not too bad to open the season. At Easter I went over to the Pang to fish with Charles Burtt and Hedley Norris. What a lovely little river this is—so clear and bright, and so far away from noise and motor cars. The Pang fish are game little chaps, and a fish of one and a half pounds is a good one. They are very difficult as the water is so clear and shallow, but very interesting fishing, and a good hatch of fly.

I see that on April 23rd I again went down to Nursling with Holford Dixon, Agnew Severn and Daye Barker. I find that on the 23rd I rose and hooked six salmon and never got one! However, we did better next day and got five fish. One of them I caught in a pool in which no fish had ever been caught before. Why, I don't know. Some years afterwards I saw the keeper, Johnston, and asked him about this, and he said that as far as he knew no fish had been caught there since.

Most of May I was fishing Bradfield Water on the Pang and Crowood Water on the Kennet.

Then I see there were many days at Nursling. We got quite a number of salmon, but the surprising thing was the number of fish we had on for a few minutes and then they came unstuck. This does happen sometimes and one never knows why; I fancy it is a question of size of fly or being a bit too quick. Probably the latter, as the fish come very slow to the fly on the Test. In June I had many days on Ramsbury and Littlecote Waters. It is uninteresting to my readers to give the numbers and sizes of all the fish caught, but looking through my diary I feel that we shall never see the like of it again on the Kennet—it was really wonderful.

Another day at Nursling on the Test, five fish from twelve to twenty-three pounds. And so it went on most of this summer.

In the autumn, I took the Brander Pass beat on the Awe and asked my brother to fish with me. Anyone who knows this water will agree with me that it is not an easy fishing water from the left bank. Mountains come sheer down almost to the edge of the water, and unless you keep your fly very high the chances of having a barb at the end of your hook are small. But you soon get into the way of avoiding this. The Awe is noted for its large fish and it is a not uncommon sight to see thirty and forty pounders moving about, but one day we saw a fish which eclipsed all fish I have ever seen on the Awe. It was a huge fish, and he came up a number of times in the top pool. I should not be surprised if that fish was sixty pounds—one will never know; he may have been only fifty-five pounds!

We never got him to take an interest in anything. When we got back to the hotel we met a friendly parson, but with a very parsonic manner. He always took a polite interest in the day's sport, which was nice of him as he was not a fisherman. Of course we told him our tale of the big fish. 'Dear me', he said, 'and supposing you had caught this monster from the deep, what would you have done with him?' Not knowing quite what to say to this remark, I said, 'Well, I don't quite know—I think I should have taken him to bed with me'. 'Dear me, dear me', he said, 'What a curious notion'. It was naughty, I know, to pull his leg, and he seemed to take it quite seriously.

We went on to Newburgh from here and had the usual sport with sea trout.

The year 1921 was perhaps one of the greatest fishing years of my life, not on account of the number of salmon I caught, but on account of the wonderful sport I had on the River Aurland in Norway, this river and the Laerdal being the two finest sea trout rivers in Norway. On both these rivers the sea trout run up to twenty pounds, and the majority are caught on dry fly. That's the lovely part of it, because you can generally see what fish there are in the pool before you start at the tail and work up.

I really do not know which river to choose, but I think, given the chance of both, I would go to Aurland.

Unfortunately I lost the records of this trip, but at times the catch was prodigious. One day I caught twenty-seven sea trout, all from three to nine pounds.

The first time I went to Aurland it seemed to be almost impossible to catch these huge fish on a ten-foot rod and the same tackle one uses on the Kennet in May fly time. The river is short and runs out of a lake to the Fjord, a distance of about four to five miles. It is mostly very rapid, with huge boulders and well defined pools. You never know where you are going to get fish, as they lay almost everywhere in those four miles. One day the fish are in one part, the next in another. Certain pools always hold fish. The sport is strenuous, and our usual method was to make three casts with every step. One in front, the next a little more to the right and so on, so covering most of the water in front of you, fishing on the right-hand bank, up stream. It is tiring work, partly as the wading is so bad, some of the worst I have ever struck, and partly on account of the number of casts one has to make, as the river is so rapid. Your *klepper* stays on the bank and can see most of the fish coming up to the fly, if he is a good man.

I found it very hard at first not to strike too quickly. Frankly I was in a blue funk sometimes when I saw a huge fish coming up very slowly to my little fly in perhaps quite a small patch of water, surrounded by big rocks and a tumbling river. On the whole one had very few breaks, the only thing was to give them their head and follow down stream as hard as one could go and keep the rod high and clear the rocks. Many a run of one hundred or two hundred yards I have had—the big ones always wanted to go back to the sea.

The bright days seemed to be the best, and when the sun went down they ceased to take much interest in the dry fly.

The wet fly was very little good in the day time, but when the sun had gone down they took a wet fly well. One method I had which worked well at times fishing down stream, as follows; a wet fly at the tail and a big dry sedge as a dropper about four feet higher up. The wet fly acted as an anchor, and the sedge skidded along the surface, if you held the rod high. I have had big fish follow the sedge right across the water and take almost at my feet.

As a rule I found that a light hackle fly was best in the sun, and a dark hackle when the sun was off the water. A 'Coch y bondhu' or 'Tup' were as good or better than anything. The worst of the 'Coch y bondhu' was that the body made of peacock herl was very tender and was soon destroyed by the sharp teeth of the sea trout. You must have your fly very dry—if it gets 'soggy' it is no use. Mucilin, or similar grease, worked well into the hackles, is far better than oiling the fly.

My friend, Archie Ross, who took me there, was most successful. He had been there once before. It took me quite a week to get accustomed to this style of fishing, so different from the placid chalk streams.

Sometimes the luck favoured one rod, sometimes the other. On one occasion he was on one side of the river and I was on the other—this was at the top of the river. At the end of the evening, I had only three or four. He had about a dozen, all big fish. I was glad he had such a wonderful evening—he was the most generous fisherman I have ever met. He lived to fish many more years with me, and I shall never find a better companion.

The local farmer asked us to supper that evening. It was a most formidable proceeding. We men sat alone at a long table at the end of the room and the women-folk—about six of them—sat at the other end of the room on a bench, with arms folded, looking at us.

It was an odd meal—the thing I remember was a very small leg of mutton, quite black—it had been up the chimney for years. Our host stuck it with his hunting knife and put it down in front of Archie and me. We naturally cut a good thick slice out of it, as one does do with a leg of mutton. Archie chewed, I chewed, but we could not get rid of it. As we chewed we watched the others, and found that they shaved off a piece as thin as paper—this you could get rid of. But how were we to get rid of ours? There was some disturbance at the end of the room and this gave us our chance to get rid of our first mouthful! Whether the ladies saw what was happening at the end of the room, we shall never know. Whisky was prohibited in those days, but our host produced a small bottle which was drunk with many *skolls*, without water.

Such grand hospitality from a simple and charming people.

We spent three weeks in this heavenly fishing place, and returned with sad hearts and many stories to tell.

From Norway I went on to stay with my friend, Charles Burtt, at Southend, Mull of Kintyre. He had a nice bit of shooting and a little sea trout river. The river was very low, but I had seen three or four salmon in a long still pool. One day they were all saying how nice it would be if we could get a salmon—as a change in the food. That evening I came back with a nice fish of twelve pounds—but that is a secret. Brother anglers—have you never done a naughty thing in the whole of your fishing career? I have not often, but there are occasions!

On the return journey I went from Cambelton to Port Glasgow on one of those awful pleasure steamers. It was crowded to overflowing. A small sailing boat with three boys in it somehow or other got in the way. Our boat never slowed down and the poor boys were run down—they were all lost. A more callous proceeding I never saw. It was all in the papers next day— I don't know what happened afterwards.

VIII

TACKLE AND EQUIPMENT

LET us break away from the diary for a bit, in case it may bore the reader.

I find in a number of fishing books that the writer usually has something to say about tackle and equipment. It isn't everybody who wants to know about tackle and equipment, but there may be some who have not had the time, or the inclination to spend much time on this part of fishing, and have relied on what the tackle dealers have told them what is wanted for a particular river. Sometimes they are right—often very wrong. So perhaps a few words of my experience over fifty years may be of help to those who have not been so fortunate as myself in being able to spend the time and experience on tackle.

I will start like this: The old days of sixteen-feet to eighteen-feet rods are gone. Most of my salmon rods in the past were eighteen feet. Now my longest rod is fifteen feet and that is only used on very big rivers where very large flies are wanted. This rod is a 'Leonard' split cane and will cast a very big fly. The line is a heavy 'Filip'. I have not used this rod since I fished the Evanger and Eira Rivers in Norway, before the war.

My next rod is a split cane fourteen feet long. He only comes out in the early spring, in Scotland.

The rods I use constantly and practically always are:

1. A single-handed eleven-feet three-inch Leonard for greased-line fishing when the water is low. This has a removable butt,

six inches long, which I carry in my pocket. When I get a fish I put it on—a matter of seconds. It is much easier to play a fish with this short butt and it keeps the reel away from the body.

2. A twelve-feet six-inch split cane by Hardy, which they christened the John Rennie rod. This is a lovely rod for medium and fine water, and everything that can be desired. A more perfect casting rod you could not wish for.

3. A thirteen-feet split cane by Hardy. I have killed over 400 salmon on this rod. It takes a heavier line than the twelve-feet six-inch and on windy days is a little more powerful and carries a fly up to No. 1. This is the nicest rod I ever had in my hand of this particular length. This rod was in Hardy's shop in Pall Mall when it was 'blitzed' on February 23rd, 1944; it was eventually recovered from the basement, none the worse for its experience.

I have many other salmon rods, but they seldom come out. The above three rods are all that you want in almost any water or with any size of fish. For instance, I have killed two fish of thirty pounds on the eleven-feet three-inch Leonard, and I don't think that I took more time to bring them in than I should have done with the thirteen-feet.

Trout Rods. Many years ago, about 1918, my old friend, Coggeshall, introduced me to the Leonard rod. He had a very fine collection, and was a friend of Mills of New York who made these rods.

One week-end I was going down to the Kennet and he persuaded me to take his eight-feet Leonard. I took it out of politeness, but did not use it the first day. The May fly was on, and I was doing very well with my own rods. On the second day I had a conscience, in the same way as when a man lends you a book. You don't want to read the book, but you feel that you must look at it, for fear that he will ask you questions about it afterwards.

I had the same feeling with this rod. I knew 'Coggy', as we affectionately called him, would ask me all about it. The weight of the rod was about two and three-quarter ounces. There was a line, dressed by himself, as no other person could dress a line—and reel.

The thing felt like a toy. But was not so—I found that I could stretch a line across the Kennet above my house, a matter of twenty-four to twenty-five yards. It fished a short line beautifully. It was as gentle on a fish as any rod could be. That day I killed my limit of three brace, including a four and a quarter and three and a half-pounder, and now you know why I like 'Leonard' trout rods. I have four trout rods, and I love them dearly. 'Coggy' chose all these rods for me in New York. I am not saying for one moment that they are any better than the rods by our leading makers in this country, but that is how I came to be an owner of 'Leonards' and I have never wanted to buy another, as they are as good now as when I bought them twenty-five years ago.

I take the greatest care of my rods. When I have finished fishing I take them down; they are then wiped down with a silk handkerchief, and re-varnished every three or four years. The ferrules are always very clean. Do you know that tip of preventing the ferrules of your rod from sticking? It looks funny, but is most effective. Before you put your rod together, rub the ferrule in your hair. There is always a certain amount of grease in the hair, I suppose. Anyhow, if you do this, your rod won't stick.

Spinning Rods. I was never terribly fond of spinning for salmon —I mean as compared with fly fishing. I think this was partly due to the heavy rods and reels we used to use in the past. I learned to spin on a 'Nottingham'—I think the best education of all. Then I got on to the 'Malloch' which I never liked. Then on to 'Silex' in various patterns. My spinning rods were mostly ten feet six inches to eleven feet, and very powerful.

But still, there are times in the spring when it is pretty well useless to fish with fly; but later in the year when you get into April and May, it always seems to me that it is an insult to the lovely salmon to fish with bait, when there is every chance on a fly.

In the last few years my pleasure in spinning has had a complete revolution since I have taken to a light L.R.X. Hardy rod of nine feet, and Hardy multiplying reel of the 'Elarex' pattern. The reel is placed high up the rod handle, which is a long one, and the butt of the rod tucked up under the arm, the reel being on top. There is no back-breaking stooping, and the multiplier enables you to control your bait in tricky places, far more easily than with the old style of reel. Above all, that boring process of winding in, say, forty yards or more of line at the end of the cast, over useless water, is overcome to the extent of about a quarter of the time by reason of the multiplying gear.

That's how it seems to me. Spinning is now a pleasure. The playing of the fish is much more fun because you can't wind on him, as with the old reels: you have to keep 'on your toes' and 'pump' him in by gathering in line as you walk backwards and forwards on the river bank. I find the accuracy of my casting is much better and I hardly ever have an over-run—perhaps not once in a week, if that, and then only due to my own carelessness. If any of my readers are still troubled with over-runs on the ordinary revolving reel, I recommend him to carry a small button hook. This used to save me a lot of time and much bad language. I have used the fixed-drum type of reel, such as the Illingworth who, I think I am correct in saying, was the originator of this type, but as my spring fishing is now entirely devoted to greased line I have not a great deal of experience in 'Thread line' fishing.

On my multiplier, I use a nine-pound, and sometimes a twelve-pound, line. I never lose a fish by the line breaking. You must remember that the rod is the 'safety valve'. If the rod is too stiff, you lose your safety valve, and so time after time you get broken in fish. Take my advice for what it is worth and avoid a stiff spinning rod as you would the devil, and this applies to all rods.

If you want to know all about spinning I would recommend you to read Balfour-Kinnear's book *Spinning Salmon*. It is a great book and will tell you everything worth knowing about spinning for salmon. There is only one thing he cannot tell you, and that is 'Experience'. We have all got to go through this— some people are quicker than others, some never benefit by experience.

I seem to have got a little bit away from tackle, so must start again.

Flies: I think you will find as you grow older that the enormous number of patterns that we used to carry about with us are quite unnecessary. I must own to taking away with me on a fishing trip of two to four weeks a very large number and many patterns, but I can assure you that this is unnecessary. For instance, on the

Dee last year, I must have taken up fly boxes with quite 400 to 500 flies! Partly, I think, because I love flies and enjoy tying them, but what do I find—that after a fortnight's fishing and having killed over fifty fish in eleven days, I only used about twelve flies—true of different sizes, and the more they were mauled about, the more the fish seemed to like them!

But by all means take plenty of flies. You can spend quite a long time in the evening looking over them or discussing them with your gillie, and this adds much to the pleasure of your fishing. But when it comes to fishing next morning and you get to the river bank, you say to yourself 'Well, yesterday I got eight fish on the Blue Charm, I think I will lead off with this' and it is quite possible that you will only change your fly during the whole day for a larger or smaller pattern of the 'Blue Charm'. As I have said before, I like my flies very slimly dressed, except of course in heavy water, when you want something bulky.

Gut. I found out this about gut. Some years ago I had a small trickle running through my place and by making a dam about sixty feet across I made quite a nice pond, fifty yards long by twenty yards wide. While I was making the dam, I thought it would be fun to put a large window under water. This having been done, I built a hut behind the dam. I got a lot of fun out of this window—I could watch trout, flies, gut and other things. Gut astonished me, for it did not matter whether you dyed it blue, green or any other colour, the flash given off was just the same. Natural gut was just as bad; rather worse. Then I tried the Hewett cast, which is treated with nitrate of silver and 'developed' much the same way as a film. This gave off very little flash, but showed us a black line in the water, much more clearly than natural gut, when it was not flashing.

When the sun is shining down the pool into the fishes' eyes, we all know that the chances of getting a fish are remote. I am of the opinion that gut flashes far worse under these conditions than at any other time, and that it is not that the fish do not see the fly, but that they are put off by the terrific flash from the gut. Under those conditions it might be worth while changing the cast and putting on a Hewett cast, which does not flash. I have tried this with some success.

FISHING THE RIVER AURLAND, NORWAY

Plate 6

The late Mr Nuttall who, I have mentioned before, invented the 'Ballistic Tester', wrote to me in 1939 about knots, and I here quote from him. 'I was interested in what you said after dinner last night, and I believe you are quite correct in thinking that any knot will reduce the effective strength of a rope, cord or wire, regardless of its material or construction. Textile materials of all sorts, when built up into ropes or cords can, when mounted in suitable grips, be loaded to breaking point and if they be skilfully made, each fibre will carry a reasonably fair share of the total load before breaking. The moment a knot is introduced, the internal and external distribution of the load is upset, and the fibres break down one after the other.

'Other factors obtain with gut. Gut is of peculiar construction. It is tough and does not bend easily and is elastic within limits. The circumference is built up of *fillibrae* all stuck together, but because in any knot the gut has to be, or must be, bent round its own diameter, it is thought that the *fillibrae* are cracked or at any rate damaged thereby, and in addition the internal load distribution upset as in textile cords.

'What I have said about gut shows the necessity of soaking. A well-soaked knot will be double the strength of a dry one, and soaked *gut* about sixteen per cent less than dry. I mean if both are tied when well soaked and are dried later.'

I think it worth while quoting these remarks from one who had made a study of this subject.

In these days of limitations, I find it economical to use say a 5/5 cast of about four feet six inches attached to the line, and four feet six inches of lighter gut attached to this. For instance, you may want to use a 9/5 cast if the day is bright and you are using a No. 7 or 8 fly. The afternoon or evening may be dull and you change this end to a 7/5.

Your 6/5 cast may last you two or three weeks, but your finer cast only a few days if you are catching fish.

Lines. I have said before that you must have a line to suit your rod, and you must have a line to suit the fly you are intending to cast. For instance, if you are fishing small fly, No. 6 down to No. 11, you can use a much lighter line than if you are going to cast a fly up to say 3/0, and unless you change your line you will have great difficulty in getting out a large fly, especially if there is a bit of wind against you.

Gaff and Wading Stick. It all depends if you are alone or if you have someone with you as to what type you use. If you have a man, he can carry your gaff and you can let him gaff the fish or do it yourself. Personally I like gaffing my own fish unless the place is a very difficult one and I am sure of my gaffer; but I have to be very sure a man knows how to use a gaff before I care to entrust him with it. The wading staff can be dropped as soon as you get on the bank by means of a quick release clip attached to a ring on the staff.

But if you are alone it is another matter. For some years I used a combined gaff and wading staff. This was a delightful invention of the late Mr Partridge and is made by Farlow. This can either be slung on the back or used for wading. The clever part about it is, that when slung on the back you can release it with one hand in a second.

Now supposing you are using the gaff as a wading stick. It is attached to your person by a strap about two feet long and quick release clip to the ring on the gaff. You are in mid stream—you get a fish, probably you have to use the stick to get ashore. It is when you get ashore that the trouble begins. You may have to run down rocks for fifty or more yards, and your gaff is trailing after you. Sometimes it gets stuck in between rocks and you are pulled up. I know you can tuck it under your arm, but this does not give you complete freedom. After having used this for some years, I have practically given it up when I am alone, and have adopted a new method, as follows:

I always carry a small waterproof bag over my shoulder about nineteen inches by eight inches; this holds a fly box, spare cast pipe and tobacco, etc. On this bag I have a quick release clip this clip holds a telescopic gaff—when shut up it is about fifteen inches long. Then I have a strong bamboo wading staff with a rubber end. This is about five feet long. There is a ring eighteen inches from the top and it is attached to my person by a strap two feet long with quick release clip. As soon as I get ashore release the clip and am not bothered any more with my wading stick. When I come to gaffing my fish, I release the clip on my bag and extend the telescopic gaff—a matter of seconds. I was alone last year and caught the best part of 100 fish, and I found this way of carrying a gaff and wading stick was excellent.

I have explained this at some length as it is possible that others may have had the same trouble when no gillies are to be had.

Waders and Brogues. There is little to be said about waders, except the way in which they are cut. As a rule they do not give you enough room between your backside and your knee, so that when you have to climb a fence or raise your leg to get over a big rock, you find that you can't raise it, or only with great difficulty; so see that they give you plenty of length between these parts.

Messrs Allweather, in the Brompton Road, have made my waders for some years, and they are splendid. I always have a pocket with a zip fastener in front. This is watertight and very handy.

Brogues. These are most important if you are to save yourself from many a ducking. I have used all types of brogues and boots. I gave up boots many years ago—they are heavy and tiring, and I find no advantage in them. Since I have taken to brogues with felt bottoms, leather heels and nails, I have had very few tosses and only one total submersion! On rocks they are wonderful, on slippery grass they do slip but then you use your heels with nails, and then you don't slip. Only once last year did I slip, and that was on a perfectly flat stone in the Dee. I had waited most of the afternoon for the light to be right on this pool and at 5 o'clock stepped in. At 5.5 I was sitting on the bottom of the river with my nose just out of water. When I had regained the bank I could only laugh—it must have looked funny to the people on the opposite bank. I got on to my bicycle and went back to the house. I had to change to my skin, tobacco, cigarettes, watch, everything. Fortunately I had a spare pair of waders. By 6.15 I was in the water again and got a couple of fish before dinner.

Cast Damper. Get a rubber tobacco pouch. Damp the inside and put your casts in the night before. There is something about damp rubber which allows your casts to be kept in it for an indefinite time and does not rot them like a box with damp felt pads. I keep my casts in this the whole time I am fishing, perhaps for two or three weeks and they never go rotten. It is much nicer to carry, and does not 'jingle' against other things. I am indebted to Mr Edward Corbett for this tip given me many years ago.

Otters. If you are spinning, you want an otter to be handy. I have tried a number of these and like the following two examples best.
No. 1, I call the 'Corbett' otter—this again was Mr Edward Corbett's invention, like this:

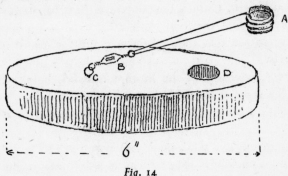

Fig. 14

Get an ordinary net fisherman's cork which is about six or seven inches long and four and a half inches across and one and a half inches thick. At C make a hole through the cork, tie cord B by a piece of strong wire and turn over the ends on the other side. The cord is about six inches long; at A put on a chicken ring or split metal ring.

Hollow out a place in the cork at D so as to house the chicken ring when not in use. This light and efficient 'Otter' will go into the pocket or bag. You have only to attach the chicken ring to your line and it sails out into the stream and does its job in a wonderful way.
No. 2. I get an old chair leg and cut a piece off like this:

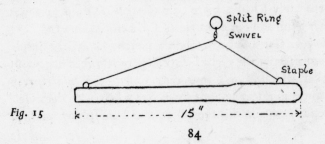

Fig. 15

about twelve inches to fourteen inches long. I drive in two staples and fasten to these a piece of strong cord—a piece of salmon line to which I secure a split ring or chicken ring. Now this is important. You must secure the ring, so that when you suspend the otter by the ring it is one-third the distance from the head end to the tail. This is a wonderful 'Otter' and as far as retrieving the bait is concerned I don't think that there is much in it compared with No.1, but it is not quite so easy to carry.

Most people know all about 'Otters', but I am only mentioning the two which I fancy and which have been the means of rescuing pounds' worth of tackle for me.

Of all the spinning baits I know, there is nothing like the Golden Sprat or Gudgeon, fixed in a 'Scarab',which is a celluloid case to protect it. If fixed properly, this bait will run up the line as soon as a fish is struck. I use a gut mount with two triangles, one at the tail, the other underneath the bait, where the gut enters the celluloid casing.

There is a tapered lead which is inserted into the fish's mouth with a hole through the lead, through which the loop of the gut is passed. This hole usually requires enlarging so as to allow the loop of the gut to go through easily and the bait to run up the trace.

In the spring, when so many kelts are about, this method of encasing a fish in the scarab is an enormous saving of time and baits.

Gudgeon are fine baits at times; I was once on the Sand river in Norway where a gudgeon got a fish every time. We only had one bottle and I think each gudgeon accounted for a fish.

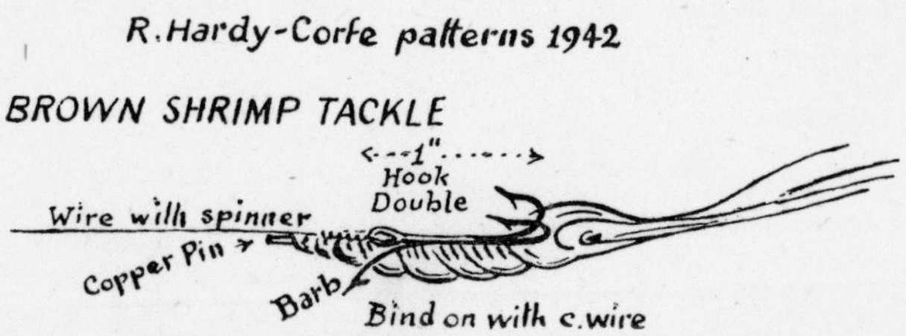

R.Hardy-Corfe patterns 1942

BROWN SHRIMP TACKLE

<--1"...--->
Hook
Double
Wire with spinner
Copper Pin
Barb
Bind on with c.wire

Fig. 16

Prawns. I am a great believer in the artificial prawn, which is mounted with a spinning head and a single triangle in the head of the prawn. I have known this bait kill fish when they refused the natural. It must be a good deep red colour, and spin.

All Other Baits are too well known to comment on. Some suit one river, others suit other rivers.

I am a great believer in small sharp triangles as against the large thick ones. I would not suggest this on big heavy waters for big heavy fish, but such rivers as the Tweed and the Dee.

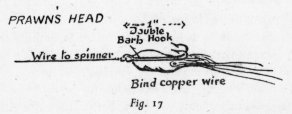

Fig. 17

Some time ago I was staying with a famous salmon fisher, and we were discussing the vexed question of fly and bait, and to support my theory that salmon do not stay in pools as they used to, he told me about a friend of his who owns water on the Welsh Dee. He allows nothing but 'Fly' on his water, with the result that the fish stay in the pools and he catches more fish on his water than most people.

Again—shortly after this I was talking to Mr Law, keeper of Bucklands water on the Usk. Mr Law told me that a few years ago they killed 300 salmon in the season, and practically all on fly. He was also of the opinion that constant prawn and bait fishing made the fish unsettled and drove them out of the pools. I have seen a pool in Norway cleared of fish, when a prawn was spun over them.

IX

DRY FLY FISHING FOR SALMON

THE late Mr Anthony Crossley, when he was writing his book on greased-line fishing, which is a book no beginner should be without, asked me if I would write a chapter on 'Dry Fly Fishing for Salmon'.

I told him that my experience in this way of catching salmon was limited, as the only rivers where I had actually caught salmon on the dry fly were in Iceland.

For those who have not got this book, I will refer to some of the paragraphs:

'I said that it was my belief that salmon could be caught on a dry fly in many other rivers, where these rivers are clear enough, and where the fish are in quantities. Why "quantities"? My answer to this is "I cannot tell you!" But I do think that this has something to do with it, because I have noticed that single fish do not pay much attention to a floating fly; but take more readily when they are there in numbers. I can only think that it is some spirit of competition which enters into it.'

Since writing those words I have been reading the *Bulletin* of the Angler's Club of New York and in their June 1944 number there is a delightful article by that American fisherman, Mr Richard C. Hunt, on 'Salmon in Low Water'.

In this article, Mr Hunt, in describing dry fly fishing for salmon in low water, goes on to say 'If there is but one fish in the pool you are apt to find it hard to catch. From three to seven seem to me to be the ideal number. There seems to be an element of jealousy or competition which will lead salmon to try to get the fly before his brethren. I have put the upper limit at seven purposely because, as the number of fish in the pool increases, it becomes easier—usually, but only usually—to catch at least one of them'. This article by Mr Hunt confirms what I have said in this respect.

Some years ago the Angler's Club of New York very kindly made me a Hon. Life Member. I appreciate it very much and look upon it as a great honour. I constantly receive invitations to go and dine with them and I hope that some day I may have the pleasure of paying them a visit in New York.

Once I saw a film of Mr E. R. Hewett dry fly fishing for salmon—I think it was on a river in Newfoundland. A mass of fish could be seen in the water, and as the floating fly sailed over them, suddenly one fish out of the hundreds would dart up and seize the fly. I met both Mr La Branche and Mr Hewett when they were in this country a good many years ago. They were both very confident that they were going to catch lots of salmon in our Northern rivers, on a dry fly. To the best of my knowledge, neither of them ever caught one in this country, although Mr La Branche, fishing Cairnton with the late Mr Arthur Wood, is credited with having risen no less than twenty-seven salmon on the dry fly, hooked two and caught none.

Later on I shall have some remarks to make about this and the reason why Mr La Branche did not hook his fish.

I think there is a good reason why we don't catch fish in Scotland on the dry fly, the reason being that we hardly ever try it. My opinion is that, given very clear water, a bright day, and plenty of fish, they will rise to the dry fly.

The fact is, when you are catching all the fish you want on greased line, you can't be bothered with experiments in dry fly, when your time is usually limited to two or three weeks' fishing.

I have risen a salmon in Lewis and in Islay. In Norway I am sure that I have risen salmon when fishing for sea trout on a dry fly.

In Iceland we were up against it. Very low water and brilliant sunshine. The fish kept jumping the greased-line and were frightfully shy. We took to ten feet trout rods and ox casts—this worked all right for a time and then they started jumping the line.

One day, I thought of trying a dry fly. I rose and hooked a salmon very soon, but he got off. The next day, one of my fishing partners rose nine salmon and never got one!

That afternoon I rose five fish in a pool which had a high overhanging rock above it, from which one of my fishing companions was looking on. This is what was seen—the salmon rose and took the fly, but before you could count one, the fly was ejected. We had all been giving plenty of time, as one does to big sea trout and Kennet trout. So we changed our ideas, and next day there was a very different story to tell. Fish rose, sometimes head and tail, sometimes a savage plunge, sometimes just a nose. We struck as quickly as we could, and to our surprise hooked the fish and landed them. This added a new lease of life to the river, and a new pleasure in salmon fishing.

Our rods were nine feet six inches and ten feet, our lines the same as you would use in Mayfly season. Casts: tapered to oX. Flies: in sunny pools a large 'Tup'. In shady places: a big hackle black, with two turns of white hackle at the head.

This is where I would like to suggest why Mr La Branche failed to hook his fish. I have heard that he was using quite a big rod, twelve or thirteen feet, and I do not think that with a double-handed rod of this length it is possible to be quick enough. It is only a suggestion on my part, but may account for the failure. I say this with all due respect to him, as he is a magnificent fisher with great experience.

I once fished with him on the Kennet, but that was before all this happened.

I remember once rising two enormous sea trout on the Klep Pool, Aurland River, in Norway. They were both, according to my *klepper*, about fourteen pounds. They both rose to my fly at the same time, and their noses came together. My *klepper*, who could see everything that was going on, said 'Oh!' That made me strike, and of course I missed them, but I doubt if either of them would have had it as they were almost touching each other.

Talking of making noises, it is very hard for the looker-on to keep quiet when he can see everything that is happening; but it is a most fatal thing to utter a sound. Once I was watching the late Bill Ratcliffe fishing on the Wye. I was flat on the ground and I could see his fly coming round. Suddenly, up came a great fish, it might have been thirty-five or forty pounds. I involuntarily made some sort of noise. Bill heard it, and struck too soon. I lost him that fish. He was terribly good about it, and used to chaff me for years afterwards.

But to get back to dry fly salmon fishing. Let me tell you of a 'nightmare' of a day I had in Iceland. An Icelandic acquaintance, having heard of the dry fly successes, asked me over to fish his river, which was about fifteen miles away from ours.

I motored over and met him. The main river was not suitable as it was partly glacier fed, and milky. He told me to walk up the bank for about a mile and then I would find a smaller river running into the main river which was quite clear and full of fish. I had short waders on, and away I went. Just before I started he shouted out 'Mind the banks, they are a bit boggy.' I found the little river: it was deep and sluggish and about twenty-five yards wide. To approach the edge of the river you had to wade through what looked like six inches of water, but when you got to within ten to fifteen feet of the edge of the river you began to sink. I hate bogs, and struggled back to firmer ground. There were fish moving all over the place. I tried other places, but they were just the same, I could not get within ten or fifteen feet of the edge of the river. Out of curiosity I started throwing my dry fly, and after three or four casts I was into a salmon. In a moment or so he had broken me in the reeds, as I could get nowhere near the river. I walked higher up, testing the banks, but nowhere could I find a firm place. I rose and hooked two more salmon, with the same result as the first one. I got bolder, and struggled out nearer the river. Then I began to sink so badly that I thought I was going to stay there for good. I fortunately got my feet out of my brogues and floundered back. After half an hour I recovered my brogues with the gaff. This made me pretty frightened, as there was no one about for miles. So I reeled up and got on to firmer ground. It was a nightmare of the worst kind. Almost every cast a salmon, and no chance of getting him.

The only way to have fished that water would have been to lay down duckboards or hurdles, or to have made a shallow punt. As there is no wood in the island, none of these things was possible.

I walked up the river for quite a mile, but could find no place where I could fish. I shall never forget that horrible feeling of gradually sinking into the mud. This happened in 1936.

In 1939 I went out to Iceland again, and as we were fishing a river not far away from the same river we fished in 1936, the owner asked us over to demonstrate the dry fly. To be frank, I don't think anybody believed us. Thank goodness everything went according to book, and the audience saw two fish hooked and lost, and one fish caught, in about three-quarters of an hour. The river was very low and the sun very hot. Fish generally take in the calm water at the edge of the rough.

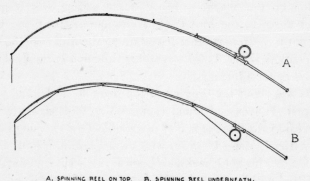

A. SPINNING REEL ON TOP.   B. SPINNING REEL UNDERNEATH.

Fig. 18

I have always found that spinning with the reel on top is a great advantage. Looking at the illustration of the two rods A and B you will see that

A The line lies flat along the rod, when the rod is bent.

B The line forms a series of kinks in between the rings when the rod is bent and the reel is underneath. This makes it harder to reel in a fish and causes more wear on the line.

X

THE NINETEEN-TWENTIES

1922

I AGAIN take up my diary, and find that in April I had a letter from Colonel Baker and General Sir Victor Couper saying 'Why don't you come over here?'—'here' being Killaloe on the Shannon. There was a vacant beat from the Sluices down to the Mill Pool, a distance of about 500 yards. I also got leave from another friend to fish the Mill Pool. So there was plenty of water. I paid something ridiculously small—I think it was £15 for a fortnight.

This was about the time when the 'trouble' in Ireland was at its worst. However, I found everybody in Killaloe quite civil, but occasionally one got a very nasty look. One morning I called on my friend, Major Le Froy, who owned the Mill Pool, and he took me into his house and said 'Look at that'. His smoking-room was pitted with bullet holes. He said it was the Black and Tans, a most unruly lot, and they had fired across the river because he had complained to the Commanding Officer about their conduct in Killaloe.

The only interference I got was one day in the Mill Pool. I think there was some dispute about this bit of water. Anyway, two ruffians started rowing and slinging a bait right across my line. Then a slanging match started between my boatmen and the Sinn Feiners. I told my men to shut up and reeled up my line. Presently the 'Shinners' came ashore. I walked up to them and instead of slanging them I said 'Look here, we seem to be both spoiling each other's sport—is it not rather silly?' This took them aback, and they became quite civil. They said they had no quarrel with me, but only with my boatmen and the owner. So we patched it up with a drink—whisky was cheap in those days, about four shillings and sixpence a bottle—and I never had any more trouble with them.

My boatmen used to draw up at the landing stage at the bridge at 5 p.m. One evening I asked them to go on till 6.30, when the sun was off the water, but they said 'No, they could not, as the "boys" would not let them', the 'boys' evidently being a number of ruffians who collected on the bridge at about 5 o'clock. So I said 'Oh, that's all right, if the boys won't let you go on fishing there is nothing more to be said'. Next day when we drew up at the bridge at 5 p.m. Grimes, the father, said to his son, 'Paddy, get out of the boat, I am going to fish with the gentleman until 6.30'. I said 'No, nothing will induce me to fish—the "Boys" have told you to stop, so we will stop'. Paddy leaped out of the boat and before I could get out we were into the stream again and fishing until 7 p.m. Now I am quite sure that if I had made a fuss and said 'To H—— with the boys' we should have got no fishing after 5 p.m., but because I took the opposite view, I was forced to go on fishing!

I was glad that it turned out like this, as I got several fish during the next few evenings.

But apart from this nobody molested me at all.

It was while I was there that the hotel at Castleconnell was attacked and a battle royal took place between Sinn Feiners, Royal Irish Constabulary and Black and Tans. It was a terrible mix-up—I know the whole story, but it is hardly the place to go into details. The proprietor of the Hotel was shot dead in his backyard, and there were many casualties.

This was my first introduction to the Shannon, and apart from the incident mentioned, I enjoyed it immensely; they were grand fish and some were huge ones. I landed nothing over thirty-three pounds, but had one encounter with a really huge fish which took a gudgeon at the head of the Mill Pool. He came half-way out of the water to take the bait, and I knew I was into a really large fish. The fight went on for the whole length of the pool, which is about 150 yards long. At the tail end he was done. There was a big piece of slack water at the tail and I was towing him in towards the boat. He was on his side and had little kick left in him. When he was within fifteen feet of the boat, the tackle came unstuck and the bait flew past my ear. It is now, almost to a day, twenty-two years ago since this happened, and yet I remember every bit of that fight and the awful feeling when the end came. Nobody said a word—we just paddled back to the head of the pool.

About an hour afterwards, I said to my boatman, 'How big do you think he was, Grimes?' 'I don't know for certain, your honour, but he was well over forty pounds.'

I found at Killaloe that the fish pulled the fly much more readily than they did at Castleconnell. Seventy per cent of my fish were caught on the fly at Killaloe, but not at Castleconnell, which I fished for two seasons afterwards, and where the percentage of fish caught on the fly was very low.

In the *Lonsdale Library* volume on Salmon Fishing, I wrote a chapter on the Shannon and mentioned the above fact. Since the Electric Power Scheme was completed, the river at Killaloe has become a huge lake, right away down to the great Dam, so a wonderful bit of salmon fishing has been lost for ever.

I will quote from a few passages in the article I wrote in the *Lonsdale Library* as follows:

'The great Power Scheme for the Shannon was completed in 1929, and that, you might say, was the end of the salmon fishing although a few salmon are still caught there, but very few as compared with the old days.'

From what I hear, the Free State is now doing what it can to try and improve matters, but it remains to be seen what success it will have. As we all know, salmon are curious creatures and cannot be made to do just as we want.

The Shannon runs approximately from North to South of Ireland, and commences its southern journey through Carrick-on-Shannon and then through Lough Boderg into Lough Ree. At the south end of Lough Ree, the river starts again and flows by Athlone into Lough Derg at Portumna.

At the south end of Lough Derg we find Killaloe. Before 1930 the river commenced again at this point and had an uninterrupted journey to the sea. Now, owing to the Shannon Power Scheme, Lough Derg has been extended for some four miles until you come to the great Dam and head works at Porteen Villa, which is about a mile above O'Brien's Bridge. Six miles below this is Castleconnell.

The total length of the river and lakes is about 250 miles. It has a drainage area of 4,500 square miles, whereas the drainage area of the Tay in Scotland is only 2,500 square miles. In spite of the huge length of this river, the only really good salmon water was at Killaloe and Castleconnell, a matter of only a few miles. As Killaloe is now a lake, the only water left is from Castleconnell down.

It was amusing to watch the fish going up the Salmon Pass and what surprised me was that they took very little notice of one's presence, although we were only a few feet away. I also saw large trout of five and six pounds ascending, but they were much slower than the salmon.

I timed some of the fish and found that they took only fifteen minutes to ascend the thirty-five feet height of the pass.

In those days there were weirs, stake nets, seine nets, drift nets, laxweir cribs, snap nets. No wonder that so few fish got up the Shannon. All this, I understand, has been rectified by the Free State in its endeavour to improve the salmon fishing.

Looking back at old records, I found that in 1865 the beat known as Doonass killed 425 salmon on rod and line and in 1866, 671 salmon and grilse.

After that, the records began to drop so that in 1889 to 1892 the average catch on Doonass was thirty-five salmon up to the end of May. In 1899 only nineteen fish were caught.

In the 'Seventies' 150 to 200 grilse were caught annually. In 1922 and on, there were practically no grilse.

Hermitage and Prospect beats were rented up till 1899 by Mr Cripps, for which he paid £500 per annum. But in that year we find him writing to the Commissioners to say that the fishing had fallen off so much, owing to excessive netting, that he would not pay 500 shillings for the renewal of his lease.

During the last ten years of the life of the fishing, up to the time of the Dam, things had greatly improved, and when I fished at Castleconnell in 1928 on the Newgarden and Prospect beats, I must say that we had magnificent sport and caught and saw a great many fish. 1927 was even better than 1928.

From a sporting point of view, the river below Castleconnell was the finest bit of water you could wish to fish. The betting was always about two to one on the fish. All the fishing was done from a 'cot' which was rather like a slim punt, controlled by two men, one with a pole, the other a paddle. They would take the cot through the most impossible-looking places; but we always got through safely. I never remember an accident, or even heard of one.

I have never been broken and cut by so many fish in my life as I was in those three weeks at Castleconnell. The limestone rocks were very sharp, and the fish had a nasty trick of running down and then up and across one of these sharp rocks, cutting your line as if with a knife.

1930 was the last year I fished at Castleconnell. There were not nearly so many fish as in 1928-9, but still, quite a nice lot. I had taken 'Woodlands' beat, and a very pretty piece of water it was. Starting just below the ferry at Castleconnell, there is a small pool just above some rapids. Even now I feel a bit nervous when I think of this pool. Your cot is poled out to the head of the rapids—if you are good on your feet you stand up. The river is boiling over the rocks all round you. You are told to cast into this bit of wild water, and if you hook a fish, which one always did, to 'Hold on like the Devil!'

The first time I fished there I had not taken half a dozen casts before I was into a fish. Away he went, up and down, then across, round a rock and smash bang! It was all over quicker than I can write.

That fish was between thirty and forty pounds, and they asked me to hold him!

The next time I fished it, more or less the same thing happened. So now you may understand why one is inclined to a feeling of nervousness.

However, with stronger tackle, I managed to hold the next fish and eventually killed five fish in this place up to twenty-five pounds.

Below this pool the river ran into a long, sweeping piece of water which always held a good number of fish, when the water was medium height. This pool took two or three hours to fish

Top. THE FALLS OF THE EVANGER RIVER, NORWAY. I SUPPOSE THAT MORE FISH OF 40 LBS. AND OVER HAVE BEEN CAUGHT ON THIS RIVER THAN ANY OTHER RIVER IN NORWAY.
Bottom. EIRA RIVER, NORWAY. FIFTY-POUND FISH ARE QUITE COMMON IN THIS RIVER. MY FRIEND, THOR THORESEN, IN ONE MORNING TOOK THREE FISH, 50, 46, 40 LBS.

properly. It was here in 1929 that Major Macdonnell caught his great fish of fifty-one pounds. To have caught a fish of that size in such water was a great triumph.

But I will not go into more details of the pools on the Shannon, as full particulars of these can be found in my chapter in the *Lonsdale Library*, and conditions now have entirely altered— many of the pools are pools no longer. Below 'Woodlands' there is a bend in the river with some high rocks and an old ruin. At one time, so I am told, this was the headquarters of the 'Hell Fire Club'. I have never been able to get the correct history of this club, but from what I have picked up, the less said about it the better.

There was a kind of gallery round these rocks and a delightful place to have lunch. Moreck was the name of the pool.

One day in 1929 I was lunching, after a blank morning and no fish showing, when suddenly, owing I suppose to some atmospheric condition, five huge fish started head and tailing. I don't think that one of these fish was under forty pounds, and the largest might have been fifty or sixty pounds.

Other people saw this fish afterwards, and agreed. Lunch was thrown on one side, and away we went in the cot. The big fish came across to my fly and missed. Then I put on a Gold Devon and was soon into one of the big ones. I had him on for about ten minutes, then he stopped, and I felt a grating up the line and guessed he was up against one of the big rocks. I shouted to the boatman to go over to him, but he was slow and I did not give slack line, and we were too late. The line was cut. He was a grand fish—we had seen him twice.

'Moreck' was a great pool. In 1928 the late Col. Maunsell and myself got twelve fish between us in two days. Those fish were mostly thirty pounds, and the best thirty-eight pounds.

There was a small pool below this called 'Poulcoum'. Here Lord Kingston got hold of the fish of his life. I could never get him to say how big he thought he was, and all he would say was that the forty-five pounds fish he had caught the day before was a baby compared with this fish.

The tragic part of the story was that the fish was played out and on his side, when the gillie had a fit of 'megrims' or fright and made a dash with the gaff, caught the cast and broke away the hold. Such things have happened before, and if you will read Bromley Davenport's book on *Sport* you will find what, in my opinion, was the finest article ever written on Salmon fishing, and his description of the loss of a huge fish in Norway under precisely the same conditions as those which happened to Lord Kingston on the Shannon. I have had my tragedies, and many of them, but never in a fish of sixty pounds or more.

Two more anecdotes about the Shannon, and then I have finished telling my lovely experiences on this river.

I remember the first time I went to Castleconnell, I thought my tackle was strong enough for anything. Never shall I forget the day when I was broken in four big fish and lost two others on hooks which straightened out!

My tackle was nearly all gone; my boatman and I were almost in tears. So I told him to row back and we would go home. Before we got to the bank, I had found another tackle, and I said 'Let's have another go'. So we did have another 'go' and I got three fish, twenty, twenty-four and twenty-eight pounds, but these were only small ones.

My other story is of a curious incident at 'Hermitage'. I was fishing on the Doonass side, opposite. The man on the Hermitage side got into a big fish. His rod and tackle were very much on the light side and the fish gradually took him down and broke him. This was not unusual at Hermitage but the point of the story is that, within a very short time, the fisherman was back in the same place and within a very few minutes was into another big fish, hooked in precisely the same spot. The same performance took place and the hold gave way at the same place, but with this difference—he retrieved his minnow and trace from the fish he was broken in half an hour before! Can you beat that? Poor man, he had no luck that day.

I will now leave the Shannon and ask myself 'What did I learn about all those breakages and tragedies?' I have learned this— that the more you 'pull' a big fish, the deeper he will go, and the more chance you have of being cut or broken by a rock— this I have mentioned before and I repeat it. I am sure we were all too hard on our fish in those days, and if we had let the fish have their head more and not pulled so hard, many of those breakings would have been avoided. By all means have strong tackle for big fish in big rivers, but hold your rod high and let them 'go' if they want to, and the chances are that they won't bore down and snag you.

I say this from later experience in life, and have found it pays every time.

When a fish wants to leave a pool and go down into rapids below, if you pull him he will go: if you throw off a lot of line from the reel, he will more than often start coming up again. The line gets below him and starts a pull in the opposite direction.

To take up my diary once more, I find that on 1st July, 1922, I again set sail for Norway. I took all my luggage into my cabin—a small one—and then another passenger turned up to share it. In the course of conversation I mentioned that I was not a very good sailor and wished I could have found a cabin to myself! When I returned at 10.30 I found that I had the cabin to myself!

I was on my way to Aurland again for the sea trout. The voyage was a bad one and there were no fishermen on board to pass the time of day. Two American 'Pussyfoot' enthusiasts bored me to tears at mealtimes with all their stories of prohibition in the States, and I was glad when I got to Bergen and could make my way to Myrdaal and thence by pony-trap to Aurland.

Norway had become a prohibition country, but you could get all the whisky you wanted at about six shillings a bottle. As every hotel in Bergen was full, I had to sleep on board. It rained cats and dogs at Bergen—it always does.

The drive down the steep road from Myrdaal, which is the highest point on the railway, from Bergen to Oslo, is very beautiful, and the road follows a river which ends up in the Sogne Fjord. There is a nice hotel at the head of the fjord, at Flaam, and quite a good salmon and sea trout river. From there to Aurland is about another six miles.

On July 4th I went up the Aurland river, but I found that we were too early this year—very few sea trout had started running. The sport was so poor that I decided to go away for a few days to see the Laerdal, which runs into the same fjord and it takes about four hours to get there by steamer from Aurland.

I got to the hotel at 11.30 p.m.—Lindstrom's Hotel, Laerdalsoren, had a meal and went to bed. Next day I hired a pony and cart and drove up the valley for about twelve miles or more. It is a really lovely valley and river, and in many ways more attractive than Aurland, as the valley is much wider and brighter. In bad weather Aurland is apt to be a bit depressing, as the mountains come sheer down to the river in places.

I spent a very happy day up the valley and arrived back at the hotel at 6 p.m. While I was sitting outside, a man came out with long waders, etc. I said 'Are you going fishing?' which was really not a very intelligent thing to say, but I wanted to get into conversation with him and find out how they were doing. He was a Norwegian, and his friend, who turned up soon after, was a Swiss.

I talked to them about dry fly for sea trout—this they had never heard of: they only fished for salmon. The end of it was, they asked me to come out with them in the evening and show them how to get sea trout on a dry fly. By chance I had brought my nine-foot Leonard dry fly outfit, and a pair of short waders. We had dinner, and got along before 7 p.m. Their beat was at the back of the hotel down to the mouth, perhaps about a mile long. I have never in all my life seen so many sea trout jumping, and some really big ones. I soon got to work and it was most amusing to watch my two friends and the two *kleppers*. They thought I was quite 'crackers', fishing with nine-foot rod and 1X cast and casting upstream. I had not been fishing for three minutes before I had a three-pounder, and in a very short time a nine-pounder. He took me down for about 200 yards. After that the supercilious look came off their faces and they were very interested. Very soon I was left alone, as they went off to catch salmon. At 11.30 p.m. they joined me again. It was still light enough to fish but they had stopped taking the dry fly. In that time I had caught forty-five pounds weight of sea trout, the best nine pounds, next seven pounds and several fours and a five. Then we went home and had some supper and got to bed at 2.30 a.m. It was a wonderful evening.

Years afterwards I met one of my friends again, by the name of A. De-Trey, the Swiss. He told me that the following year he went out equipped with dry fly gear and was so taken with this style of fishing that he had practically given up salmon fishing.

I started off early next morning on my way back to Aurland and determined to go back to the Laerdal again some day, which promise I kept some years afterwards.

The sport did not improve very much at Aurland, as the fish were very late coming up this year on account of the water being so cold. Those that did come lay at the bottom and nothing would move them.

One day I went up to the head of the river on a bicycle and got three good salmon, twenty-two, sixteen, fifteen pounds. It was an awful job getting home on a bicycle and in waders with rods, etc. With the help of a sack, my boy and I managed to get home somehow. It was rather a desolate valley and very few people about, so that I was not a little surprised as I was coming into the road to hear the sound of a real German brass band. It seemed unbelievable, and on turning a corner this is what I saw: About 150 German sailors doing a route march up the valley headed by their band. They looked scruffy and dirty and unpleasant as they ambled on. Their ship lay in the fjord, and that looked unkempt and dirty. Such was Germany in 1922.

Sport did not get much better and we left at the end of the month; so different from the year before.

Beyond fishing the Frome for trout, and a few days on the Wye above Hereford, there seems to have been little more to record for that year. I will just mention this, however. I was fishing Sir Geoffrey Cornewall's water, and was much hampered by bulls on the bank. When I got back to Hereford I told Mr Hatton about it, and he said 'Don't you know how to get rid of a bull?' 'No,' I said, 'How do you do it?' Then he went on to explain how you crouch low down with bended legs, spread out your arms and wave them up and down and make a horrible noise. Advance slowly on the bull and he will turn and run. 'That's all right', I said, 'but supposing he does not run?' 'They always do', replied Hatton.

Well, next day I thought I would try this out. Having found

my bull and divested myself of all my gear and some of my garments, I proceeded to follow out Hatton's instructions. There was a nice strong fence behind me to give me confidence. I advanced slowly on the bull—he did not move—then I gave a little rush forward, making a horrible noise. He turned round and bolted over the skyline and I never saw him again. On one other bull have I tried this performance, and it was equally successful.

In 1923 I see that I was again fishing with Holford Dixon on the Test, at Nursling, in February. However, with much rain and a rising river we did little good. One fish of twenty-five pounds was the only result.

In March I went over to Paris to attend their Annual Casting Tournament. I think this was the first of several trips I made to Paris for these tournaments. Later I will write about tournaments and what I think of them. I had a very jolly time there; the French were very hospitable and we had some gorgeous dinners and much to drink. The Vicomte Henri de France was President that year, a very charming old man who kindly asked me to come and stay with him in his château and fish his water, which was first class, but I could not manage it as I had to be back in town. I see in my diary that I won two First Class and three Second Class prizes in this tournament.

I stayed at the St. James and Albion Hotel, Rue St. Honoré, and my bed and bathroom was only forty francs a night, the exchange being seventy-six francs to the £.

On March 18th I was again down at Nursling, and got a lovely fish of eighteen pounds on a Wilkinson. I remember that fish— he jumped clean out of the water after the fly—a real 'picture postcard' fish. In my life I have had very few fish that have done this—half out of the water, yes. But completely out has happened to me on two occasions only. Then I got a fish of twenty-four pounds. There was nothing more doing that day so I started for home, only a matter of an hour and a half by motor, altogether three fish, eighteen, twenty-three, twenty-four pounds.

Just think of it, salmon fishing within an hour and a half from your house, and about two and a quarter hours from London.

On the 15th April I was going down to Nursling again, but

got a wire from the keeper to say that the river was high and thick. Holford Dixon went down and got three big fish!

On the 22nd April I was again with James Whishaw. He was a grand companion and most entertaining person. He had lived in Russia most of his life and just got away in time. They came for him the day after he had left. He arrived with nothing more than a handbag and a bottle of Vodka, which we drank that night in the Fly Fishers' Club. Although he was a rich man in Russia, on his return to this country he had to live a simple life, as he had lost almost everything. I never heard him complain of his losses. About this time he bought one of those houses in Hungerford with fishing rights, and I think his last years were happy.

We each got a fish at Nursling that day, twenty-six and eighteen pounds, both on a fly. This was Jimmy Whishaw's first salmon, and he was immensely pleased.

Next day was a blank for one reason or another. The only excitement was a fish under a cow bridge. I let down a prawn, felt something touch it, and struck. The fish rushed up and jumped above the bridge, and then rushed down. A good fish of twenty-six or twenty-seven pounds. While we were threading the rod under the bridge, the salmon was running down all the time, and by the time I had got the rod in my hands again a hundred yards of line were out, and the fish round the corner. He must have broken me round a stump or something, as when I reeled up there was no tackle. Very exciting!

On May 3rd I motored down to fish the Wye, with Charles Burtt and Bill Ratcliff. We stayed at the Holme, Eddesleigh—most comfortable quarters, and everything a fisherman could want. Both my friends had rods on Sir Geoffrey Cornewall's water and were allowed to take a guest. I fished a great many times on this water and I think it is quite one of the nicest beats on the Wye, beautiful pools and wading not too bad. Charles Burtt was very lucky and got a fish of forty-five pounds. It was a very long fish and not what I call a 'picture', but Wye fish are long. Soon the river was in high flood and there was nothing to be done except to take a joy ride. The water remained high for two days—Bill Ratcliff decided to go home, Charles and I fished and got two fish, and then I had to depart. Soon after I left, the fish started rising and Charles got into six fish and killed three. He hooked a very large fish, which he said was larger than his forty-five pounder, but parted company. Fishing is a funny game.

In May I had a lot of trout fishing on the Kennet and on many occasions came back with my limit of three brace.

It will be seen in this diary that I have written more about salmon than trout. But how can I write about trout fishing when others have devoted all their time and thought to this subject. I cannot compete with writers like Lord Grey of Falloden, John Hills, Skues, Halford, Taverner, Barton and many others. I am not like Skues and Barton who, I am quite sure, despise the salmon angler: in fact if you have read the latter's most delightful book *Running Water* you will see how little he thinks of the salmon angler.

I remember Skues once saying to me when I asked him if he had ever fished for salmon, 'No, why should I? I don't care about being pulled by a salmon at the other end of my line' or words to this effect. On the other hand, Lord Grey and Major John Hills were, I should say, devoted equally to salmon and trout fishing.

I shall never forget when I went up to Newcastle to see the last of my dear friend Sir Archibald Ross, I went back to the Station Hotel more depressed perhaps than I have ever been, and I met Lord Grey in the smoking room. I made myself known and told him the sad story, for he knew Archie Ross very well. 'Come and sit down with me', he said. Then he began talking about birds and fishing, I am convinced, to try and take my mind away from things, and he succeeded to some extent. For over an hour he talked, and such wonderful talk, and then we went to bed. I never met him again, and I shall never forget his kindness on that occasion.

XI

A VISIT TO NORWAY

BACK to the diary again. I find that I sailed for Norway on 20th July, 1923. I was going to a river new to me, the Sundal, Fahle beat. Archie Ross was to join me a week later, so I thought I would pass the time by seeing a little of the country round Oslo. In a strange country and not knowing the language, I always find it rather difficult to know how to get about and see the country off the beaten track. I stayed at the Grand Hotel, Oslo, spent a day looking round the town. What impressed me very much was the two Viking ships which they have in the Museum. These I believe were dug from a bog. They are wonderfully preserved and set up. To Naval Architects, of which I am one, the lines of these ships are superb. Apparently there was no 'accommodation'—the deck was flush, one mast and sail, and plenty of huge oars. The lines of these boats are so fine that, under favourable conditions, they must have been very fast. When one thinks of the hardships these Vikings must have endured, one feels we are a very 'soft' lot!

Now the crossing to Norway is made in fast twenty-one knot motor vessels, with every luxury and convenience, in about twenty-four hours.

From Oslo I hired a car, with instructions to the driver to take me to Sundrolden, a pretty drive of three hours. I said good-bye to the car and stayed at the hotel, very primitive but delight-fully clean, as are all Norwegian hotels. No such thing as a bath. There was a lovely lake, so I bathed there. But the lake had no fish, neither had the rivers. I think timber was the cause of this—thousands of logs floating down, mills cutting them up, and everything spoiled from the fishing point of view. From there to Honefoss—again logs and pulp mills, but no fish. Then I got on the rail and went to Fagerness, a heavenly place and the terminus of the railway. From here you can take a motor and go to Laerdal, about seventy miles. I tried the river and the lake for trout, they looked so good, but as far as I am concerned, there was nothing there except fish of four or five to the pound.

The hotel is a place not frequented by British, but very much so by Norwegians. After dinner there was a concert, accompanied by a 'zither'. In between the songs, somebody got up and made a speech, then another song and another speech. After about an hour of this I retired to bed; but the concert went on for hours!

Having seen a great deal of country, rivers, and lakes and being very disappointed as far as fishing was concerned, I took the train back to Oslo, a matter of some eight hours.

On arrival at Oslo, I rang up my friend Thor Thoresen, and he suggested that I go off with him that night by sleeper to Opdal, and thence by motor car to my beat on the Sundal.

The valley in the Sundal is terrific—there is no other word that seems to fit it better. Great snow-capped mountains running down to almost the edge of the river.

I think this is the first river of which I have ever been terrified: whirlpools, rocks, torrents, and then a lovely pool, then more of the wild river. I cannot say that I liked this place in spite of its magnificent surroundings, but there are some places which are too grand; they depress one.

At the end of ten days, Archie Ross and I were 'touchy' with each other: we had never been like that before and we neither of us seemed to be able to shake it off.

One morning I said to him 'Let's cut this place out and go and pay a visit to your friend, Thor Thoresen; it is only half a day's journey from here and a change would do us good: the river is in flood and a clay bank has given way below us which prevents the fish coming up'. So after much talk we decided to go.

The next day off we started by car to Sundalsoren, thence by boat to Eidsore, then another car to Eidsvaag, then another boat to Vistal. A more lovely trip you can't imagine. We were welcomed at Vistal by Thor, Mrs Thor and the family.

Here was a delightful and lovely valley, all smiles and sunshine, with a pretty little river and lovely great timber house, furnished and fitted throughout with every comfort.

Everything was now changed, and we were all in the highest of spirits. The fishing, they said, was not much good as the water was too low, but there were some salmon and sea trout about.

Next day we spent in exploring the river, but had little sight of a fish. I only had a ten-foot Leonard trout rod, as we only expected sea trout. One of the girls came with me, I think she was only about twelve or thirteen years old then. Her name was Greta, such a lovely child—she was married about the year 1927 to Lord Glentanar. She was one of the most beautiful women in England, and died suddenly in London in 1941.

Well, she and I started walking up the river until we came to a foss. Here we sat down: she could talk little English and I no Norwegian. We had not sat down for long when we saw a couple of fish jump—salmon of about ten or twelve pounds. I tried them with several small flies, with no result. Then, in hunting through my book I found a 'Terror', particulars of which I have mentioned some way back. Something told me to put it on, as all other flies had failed. Immediately a fish broke the water and made a savage lunge at it, but did not touch. This happened three or four times with various fish. At last one got hold, gave me a good fight and then got off.

This gave me some reason to think that, although I had not been successful, the 'Terror' had risen fish when nothing else would. The next day was Sunday; the party had all gone to church and I was alone. There was a pool just below the house. I went down there with my 'Terror' and small rod, and got a fish of ten pounds and another of seven pounds.

By the time the party had returned from church there were two lovely fresh fish waiting for them. How excited they were. 'How did I get them? What fly?' etc. I told my story and they all looked—shall I say with incredulity?—but later in the evening when I came in with another fish, they were much more excited. Then we all started fishing with 'Terrors' and all got fish. Our time had now come to an end. It was a very sad day when we had to pack up and leave our friends. Moreover it was now raining and the fish would be coming up. We heard from Thor Thoresen afterwards that he had got seven salmon that day and three the next, all on the 'Terrors' I had left him. Some years later I paid a visit to the same house and Thoresen showed me his case of flies—they were all 'Terrors' of every size and colour!

We returned to Sundalsoren and our beat at Fahle—we had some grand baskets of Brown and Sea trout, but the salmon were scarce, so, after staying for another week, we decided to go home.

I can't say that this was a happy river, in fact I think that it is the only place I have ever fished where I was not happy. Yes— there was one river I fished in Scotland many years after where I had the same kind of feeling—what it is I don't know. Of course, on the Sundal things were not very much improved by the mentality of my boatman.

The boats have only one peg for a rowlock. Round this peg they twist a green branch from a tree, and form it into a loop. Through this loop goes the oar. On some rivers they have a piece of reindeer hide, but on this river it was as I describe. It never looked to me very safe, if you were in a tight place. I asked my boatman one day 'Supposing the twig snapped?'—we were in a very nasty place—his answer was 'We should be drowned—a man was drowned in this pool a month ago!'

No, Broghton, for that was his name, did not cheer one up very much.

One day I saw what I think was the largest salmon I had ever seen up to that time. He was huge—he was enormous. I saw him rise in quite an easy place near the bank. I put a fly over him first. After two or three casts I felt the very smallest of touches, like a leaf in the water. I think I tightened a little too soon—I may have, I don't know. I never shall know. I never saw him again. These are the mysteries of the unknown, and that is why fishing keeps its attraction.

And so we leave Sundal. I was not very sorry. On the way back by car to Opdal we stopped to see a friend. He had just caught a fish of forty-two pounds. It was forty-seven inches long and twenty-four and a half inches girth. I never saw such an ugly brute. This fish had such a large protruding jaw that it could not close its mouth. No wonder one misses these sort of fish. It was caught on a four-inch Silver Devon.

So this finishes the season for 1923.

XII

SOME BIG FISH

1924

HAVE you ever fished the Hampshire Avon? I mean the lower part where the salmon are.

My first thought was 'where do I fish?' because in few places, on the Winkton water, are there any defined pools: it all looks very much the same. But after you have fished it for a bit, you find out where the fish lie. To save a lot of time and hard work you should go out with someone who knows the water well. I have had the privilege of fishing this water on many occasions, thanks to the kindness and hospitality of Mr and Mrs Ernest Baker.

The Avon has a great charm of its own. It is similar, only on a much larger scale, to the lower waters of the Test. The fish are larger and are magnificently shaped. Their eating qualities are the best in the world—there is nothing to touch a spring Avon fish. They are very fond of a prawn, but at times they pull a fly quite well. My best fish—thirty-eight pounds—was got on a 'Golden Eagle'. They like yellow flies, and a favourite pattern is dressed with lemon mohair. I have seen enormous fish in this water, but never been connected. There is a certain place called the 'Alder Bush', where one of the rods, a few days before I was there, hooked and was broken by a huge fish—probably in the fifty pound class. He was hooked on the prawn. When I came down to this place a few days later with a prawn, I saw a great disturbance made by a big fish. It then swam higher up. I waited for a bit, walked up to where I thought he was, and put the prawn over him again.

I never saw a fish in such a fright. He turned round and 'hogged' it right down the river, head and tail.

I am convinced that this was the same fish which had been hooked and lost a few days before.

It is wonderful how fish get rid of baits after a few days.

I see that May, 1924, was the coldest and wettest May I can ever remember. However, the fishing on the Kennet was good this year, as I see from my diary. It generally is when there is a lot of rain in the early spring.

I had the good fortune to fish up and down the Kennet from Ramsbury to Hampstead Marshall. Hampstead Marshall was a grand bit of water in those days and I suppose held bigger fish than on any other part of the Kennet. Many of the large fish were on certain reaches of the canal which runs close to the river. When the spent gnat was on, you would see, towards the Kintbury end, a dozen great fish cruising up and down, sucking in spent gnat.

They were some of the most difficult fish to catch that I know. They were never still. You wanted the patience of Job to sit and wait until they took it into their heads to pass your way. It was fatal to follow them up in their cruise. They would suddenly turn and see you.

The towpath is on one side of the canal, and locals would take their evening walks up and down. On one occasion I saw a big fish of about five pounds cruising. There were four people on the towpath watching me on the opposite bank to where I was trying to make myself as small as possible. The ladies had gaudy dresses and one had a red parasol. I saw a May fly settle on my gut about two feet from my fly. The big fish came up and I felt sure he was going for my fly, but he saw the real fly on my floating gut and gulped it. I struck pretty hard and quickly, and was attached to the fish! I saw that the gut must have slipped through his mouth, and my fly was attached on the outside of his mouth on the *other* side. He put up a great fight, and I got out my net. Just at that moment the party on the opposite bank came rushing down, red parasol and all. My fish got the scare of his life and bolted again downstream for fifty yards, and then the hook came away. I did not care about those people very much.

I had a grand day on the Hungerford water on 10th June, securing nine fish of a total weight of twenty-two pounds.

According to my diary, on the next day everything went wrong. Things do happen like this at times. I started by spilling a bottle of varnish over my trousers. Then I dropped my reel and bent it. My rod was standing upright in a hedge, a sharp gust of wind blew it over, and the top broke. A nice beginning for the day! To crown all, I put on too fine a point for May fly, and left the fly in a good fish. I will say no more—we have all had such days as this in our time.

On 14th June I went off to Ramsbury Manor to stay the week-end with the Burdetts. Here the river Kennet forms a large lake close to the house by reason of a dam, known as the Manor Arches. This lake held a large number of very big fish which could be seen quite clearly from the lawn. I have seldom seen so many big fish moving. On one side the lawn runs down to the lake, the other side is shaded with magnificent trees. I chose the tree side. It was well I did, as the fish on that side of the lake were seldom fished for, owing to the difficulty of casting, but as the fish were not far out, it was not too difficult.

This was one of the best days I ever had on the Kennet, and in the evening I found that I had kept seven fish weighing twenty-three pounds, and this considering that I had had to play tennis all the afternoon!

I know no more lovely place than Ramsbury Manor, and I spent many happy days there and met many charming people.

That season I had nine fish of three pounds and over, on the Town water, two of which were four and a half and four pounds.

In the Autumn I took a house at Newburgh. It is extraordinary what a fascination this place has. I think it is the wonderful air and bird life which is a great part of the attraction.

I caught the usual number of sea trout as in previous years.

This was the last visit I paid there—I hear the sport is just as good as it used to be.

1925. In the early spring I paid visits to the Wye with some success. In May I decided to fish Lough Derg for the May fly, stopping a few days at Miss Grace's Hotel, Killaloe. General Sir Victor Couper had been fishing the Shannon, but had got tired of it and passed on his rod to me. It was a bad season on the Shannon, the water was in flood most of the time I was there.

On 23rd May I took a car and went off to Derg Hotel, Mount-shannon, owned by Mr Weatherstone. I found the place packed with fishermen—nowhere to sit in the evening, and baths seemed out of the question, except for a round pan and cold water. I must say that I do depend on a hot bath for my comfort. Even in Central Africa I got my hot bath. I can put up with poor food and poor beds—I have had that in plenty, but hot baths I will have.

This is the first time, and probably the last, that I have tried dapping. I only stuck it for about an hour, and then I told my boatman to take my dapping rod and I put up my dry fly rod. I rose, hooked and caught far more fish than he did, as I was able to cover fish that had escaped his dap. He was rather astonished, as the dap was considered to be far the more killing method. The fact was that in 1925 there were very few dry fly men on the lake; they were mostly dappers. I think there is quite a lot of skill required to be a good dapper, and there must be great concentration on your fly. You must give the fish loads of time. The late Col. George Maunsell, who was an expert 'dapper', gave me the following tip. As you know, you impale a couple of green fly on to your hook and in between these you hook a petal of gorse bloom. He declares that this is most attractive and successful. His delightful book, *The Fisherman's Vade Mecum*, is one that everybody ought to have. Many an hour I spent in making a large number of illustrations for him, such as worms on hooks, etc.

On the following day I found a small bay with high reeds all round it, quite sheltered and free from dappers. I saw what I thought was a big fish rise, so waited quite half an hour in the reeds and saw him come up again. I told my boatman to move very gently to the place and, should I hook the fish, he was to row very gently out into the lake and I would not reel in at all. Well, I rose a fish and hooked him and the boatman did just what I had told him and he was netted—three pounds. But this was not the fish I had seen before, so back we went again and there was my big fish moving.

We got him after three or four casts and the boatman carried out the same performance, the fish following the boat on a steady strain until we had got into safe water. Then the fun began as soon as I started reeling in. He took me a good half hour, and weighed six and a half pounds. The fly was one of Lock's patterns with a French partridge hackle.

This fly I found most successful and was as follows: Partridge hackle dyed yellow, a French partridge for the head hackle about two turns. Straw body ribbed with gold wire.

This is a good May fly for all the Irish lakes I have fished in.

The weather got too atrocious for words—the lake was like a sea and the rain came down in sheets.

An amusing thing happened to me one day. We were obliged to take shelter from a great storm and, seeing a boathouse handy, we rowed for this and found it empty. Within a short time we heard shrieks of laughter, and three boatloads of boys and girls all about the age of seventeen to twenty-one invaded our boat-house. I made apologies, but there was plenty of room for all. They asked me up to their house to have tea—it was very nice of them, and I went.

It was a great big Georgian type of house about 100 yards from the lake. After tea someone said 'We have never drawn the Derby Sweep'. I said 'The race has been run some two hours ago.' 'Oh, that doesn't matter', they said. As I was the stranger they decided that I should draw the sweep, but I asked them to make sure that the same number of names of people corresponded with the number of tickets and blanks in the hat. It was quite a big sweep and amounted to about £15. It took me about three-quarters of an hour to read those terrible unpronounceable Irish names, and when I had got rid of the last name I found that there was still another ticket in the hat. They said 'Of course, you must take the ticket', but this I flatly refused, and lucky I did refuse, as when we opened the ticket we found the name of the horse was 'Manna'. Manna won the Derby in 1925. I never heard what happened afterwards as I soon fled the house. Just fancy if I, an Englishman and a stranger, who had drawn the sweep had gone off with £15 of the local money—I should have been obliged to flee the country!

Next day, a boat hailed me and I found my two cousins, Barbara Vickers and Daphne Wallace, rowing towards me. It appears that they had come from England in a small motor yacht and had come up to Lough Derg by canal. They asked me to stay with them for a few days, but after inspecting the close quarters in the yacht, I thought it best not. I don't like close quarters in any boat.

There is no doubt that I found the dry fly far more deadly than the dap, and if you get still weather, the dappers are then out of action, and you, with the dry fly, can fish all day.

I got home in time for the May fly on the Kennet. My best fish, five and a half pounds, was caught on the Craven water. I was lucky to get this fish. It was a piping hot day and I sat down by the side of one of the locks in the canal. I must have gone to sleep for some time, only to be wakened by the keeper, who gave a whistle. He said there was a big fish in the lock. I crawled and looked over the edge, and there I saw a great trout. I marked the place by a piece of red brick, and then went down to the tail end of the lock, the gates being open. From below the gates I was able to make a cast and the fly actually hit the piece of red brick and tumbled into the water. It was immediately taken by my friend and after a good fight he was netted. A truly lucky piece of fishing.

At the end of July I motored up to Scotland to stay with my friends, the Dunlops, at Dunlossit, Isle of Islay. I left the car on the mainland and took boat to Port Askaig.

Islay is a very sporting island: there is a bit of everything there—a small salmon and sea trout river, several lochs, grouse shooting, deer stalking and wonderful woodcock shooting.

There was little water in the river, but I did rise a salmon on the dry fly. The trout lochs used to be very good, but Dunlop thought that he could improve them by raising the water another two feet. This he did at great expense: the result was heart-breaking. The fish would rise no more, or seldom did. I have heard that the same thing has happened since the height of Lough Derg was raised. One wonders why this should be.

On the night of 11th August, it started to pour with rain. Next morning when Dunlop came down to breakfast he looked perturbed. 'What's the matter?' we said. Then he told us that although it was the 12th August and we were going out shooting, he had told the keeper that we were going fishing instead! Such a thing was unheard of, and he was afraid that the keeper would leave on the spot. But nothing happened, and we had one of the nicest day's fishing you could wish for. I caught a couple of salmon and twenty-three sea trout averaging one pound apiece. All on a ten-foot Leonard. Such delightful days don't often come to one in this unexpected way.

Next day we shot grouse over dogs. They were beautifully trained and it was a great pleasure to work behind them.

From Dunlossit I went on to fish the Awe for a fortnight—had taken the Brander Pass beat. Unfortunately I was called away to London before my first week was up, and there was nothing for it but to go. I stopped on the way back at Loch Awe Hotel and saw Mr Currie, the proprietor. I asked him if he had any guest who would take over my beat for the following week and in ten minutes he found someone and paid me for the last week—it was very good of him.

On 3rd October I see that I went for a few days to stay with cousin at Penlanole, Rhayader, on the upper reach of the Wye. The river was very low, so I tried greased-line fishing and very small flies. Little did I know about greased line in those days, but I got three fish and they weren't too bad for the time of year. rose several others, but I know now that I was too quick. This encouraged me in the greased-line art.

XIII

THE FISH SENSE

I WROTE the following article for the *Fly Fishers' Club Journal* some years ago.

'This heading is for want of a better word. What do I mean by "Fish Sense"? I will do my best to explain.

1. There is the sense of location or direction. This is developed very highly in the African native. I have seen them turn round and make a straight line for the camp after a day's hunting in forest country without any landmarks, and often after it has become dark.

2. The snake charmer has a sense for snakes and the rat catcher for rats. How the latter catches his rats we do not know: but by some mysterious power of mind he is enabled to induce rats to come out from their holes and to capture them with his hands. Of snakes I know nothing.

3. There is the successful huntsman and follower of hounds. He has some sense which the majority of the "field" has not got, which enables him to know instinctively which way the fox is going to break covert.

4. The dog sense. We all know this. For instance, sheep dog trials—the man's mind controls the dog's mind and they work together. Some people have a wonderful way with dogs, others can do nothing with them.

5. The sense of music. Why could Händel, as a child, play with the execution of a grown-up man?

6. The money-making sense. If you ask any successful man how it is that he has been able to achieve a vast fortune from nothing, he will be unable to tell you the secret.

7. We have the card sense: some clever and able people can never play cards however hard they try. The flying and motoring sense are developed very strongly in some people.

'We could go on enumerating all kinds of senses and their peculiarities without any real explanation. I believe that all these phenomena are mental states for which no interpretation can be given. We say to each other "That's very odd, isn't it?'' and let the matter drop. Now let us come to what I term the "Fish Sense".

'I will take as an example a well-known angler, Mr Pashley. We have all heard about him and his wonderful catches on the Wye. I have a great interest in Mr Pashley. I have never seen him fish; but I know many people who have seen him fish and I have cross-questioned them very thoroughly.

'I often say to myself when salmon fishing "Now then, cultivate the 'Fish Sense' which Mr Pashley has developed so strongly", and I think I am rewarded sometimes.

'Let us see what Mr Pashley actually does when salmon fishing. Of course I am only repeating what others have told me. He has an old rod, rather "floppy" from having caught, I understand, over a thousand salmon. Length about eleven feet. He does not cast "a long and beautiful line". His flies are the same as yours and mine. I am told that there is nothing "showy" about his fishing. And yet, when you and I, both good fishermen according to our knowledge, go fishing down a stretch of water, we may perhaps secure one or two fish. Mr Pashley comes along and gets a dozen! Mr Pashley's "Fish Sense" is a very strong one. I know some good fishermen who have never developed this sense and you cannot understand why they do not catch fish. I believe that this sense can be developed to some extent, but not to the extent shown in Mr Pashley. If you say to yourself "It's no good today—thunder, east wind, etc.", it very seldom is any good. On the other hand, if you make up your mind to get one or two before the end of the day, well, it sometimes comes off. Never be despondent in salmon fishing: it does no good and spoils your day.

'So, my readers, don't be depressed. We are not all given the gift of "Fish Sense", but we are all given the blessing of being on the waterside and seeing nature at its best and worst, and we should all be thankful for that.

'If we get a fish or two, so much the better. If not, well, there is so much less to carry home.'

J. R.

I think there is something in what I say, but, of course, knowledge of water is a great thing. I do not know if Mr Pashley is successful in waters other than the Wye—I have never heard.

THE NIGHTMARE

XIV

WALES, IRELAND AND THE TWEED
1926

I WANT to split up this diary as much as possible by including articles on things which may be of interest. A diary gets tedious after a bit, but my idea has been, all through this book, to give fishermen some information where they can go and fish and what to expect. For this reason I go on quoting my diary and the places I have been to.

This year I started off on 31st March for Abergavenny. I fished the water opposite Mardy, which I took from the Angel Hotel. Then I went down to Pontygoitre water, five miles below Abergavenny, and afterwards the water below that. All these waters are good if you hit them off at the right time, but you must be prepared to go down to the Usk at almost a moment's notice. Owing to drainage and the extraction of water, both the Wye and Usk run down far quicker than they used to do. They are up and down in a few hours.

On 3rd May I was fishing the Wye at Eardisley, with my friends, Bill Ratcliff and Charles Burtt. The great General Strike was on, so Bill Ratcliff started for home and Charles and I remained on. The river had been in flood; but on the 3rd May it had cleared. As it cleared the fish began to take, and I got a couple, nineteen and seventeen and a half pounds.

Charles was insistent that we should stop at 2 p.m. and motor home, so there was nothing for it but to obey! But I feel sure that if we had seen the day out we should have had a day long to be remembered.

On May 27th I went off to Ireland to fish Lough Erne from Belleek, Co. Fermanagh. I can't say much for the hotel at Belleek, but since I was there it has been made more up-to-date. I had rooms outside, as the hotel was full. They were beastly!

As a May fly lake, I don't think much of Lough Erne. It has none of the attractions of Arrow, Derg or Sheelin. I suppose there are big fish which come to the May fly, but I never saw anything large. I got a number of fish from one to two pounds, but that was all.

The river Erne is most attractive, and holds some big trout, and I shall have something more to say about this later on, when I fished it for some days. You can get leave to fish this water for trout, if I remember rightly, at two shillings and sixpence a day.

I remember one day going down the river to watch the salmon fishers. Now the gillies will tell you that unless you work your fly with 'The Ballyshannon wobble' you won't get fish. This 'wobble' is brought about by a violent up and down motion of the rod, with the idea of working the fly backwards and forwards. There was an eel weir jutting out below the fisherman, so I walked out on this where I could see his fly—a large one—distinctly. The fly was swinging round quite smoothly, without any 'wobble'. In other words, that violent motion on the rod had no effect on the fly and never reached it! I told the fisherman what I had seen, but he still persisted in his wobble, presumably he wanted exercise with his seventeen-footer. The whole thing is a myth and delusion.

I returned home to the Kennet to fish the May fly and find I was fishing at Ramsbury, Denford and Barton Court.

Lord Burnham had a lease of Barton Court with a fine bit of trout fishing. All his friends knew him as 'Minor'—I fished regularly with him from 1924 to 1943, when he passed away during the May fly season. I never met a more generous and kindly host and no one was more delighted than he when you returned with a good basket. We went to Sweden together one year to fish for the big Em sea trout, which run up to twenty and thirty pounds. There never was a more delightful person to go on a trip with—he was always the life and soul of the party, full of stories of interesting people and up to the end of his days a very keen fisherman, rejoicing in others' success. I looked forward to my annual visits to Barton Court with the same pleasure in each succeeding year. Alas, these things cannot last for ever and nineteen years is a long time without a break.

In August I took a fishing on the Deveron, Inverichnie, near Banff. The Deveron is a pretty river, with nice pools and fine undulating country and lovely trees. There are big sea trout in the Deveron and some of the autumn salmon are very large. A sixty-one pound fish was caught by Mrs Morrison in this water some years afterwards.

It was a very dry season when I was there, and the only time the big sea trout would move was after the sun had gone down.

The best months for this river are March and April, when a fine lot of spring fish run up and the Brown trout fishing is first class. For sea trout July, August and September is the best time.

After leaving Banff I came back by Newburgh, had a nice day's fishing there and got twenty sea trout.

Towards the end of October I went down to the Usk, as I had heard that the Mardy water was for sale. As things turned out I found that the owner had no intention of selling, but he very kindly asked me to share the water with him, which I did for the next three years.

On Thursday, 24th February, 1927, the annual dinner of the Fly Fishers' Club took place. Mr Stanley Baldwin, then Prime Minister, was the guest of the evening. Maj. John Hills, M.P. called me up after the dinner and introduced me to Mr Baldwin. He was no fisherman and not the slightest bit interested in fishing or in water pollution and other matters connected with rivers. So we ended up by talking about Waterloo Bridge, which was designed and built by my great grandfather, John Rennie. He told me that he was doing his best to save it and had that day appointed a Royal Commission. At the mention of 'Royal Commission' my heart sank. We all know too well the results of these commissions—in other words, marking time for the politician. However, in spite of the Royal Commission's report, it was pulled down some years later and an ugly modern concrete erection takes its place.

Mr Baldwin, in spite of knowing nothing about fishing, gave

us a good speech, lit his pipe and said he had enjoyed himself.

On 1st March I went up to the Tweed to fish the Lees beat, which belonged to Sir John Marjoribanks. The Tweed here takes a semi-circle round the town of Coldstream. The fishing is first class in the spring, and in the autumn some of the largest fish have been caught in this reach. The Abbey pool is one of the best. My host, Carlton-Cross, and I did pretty well; but mostly spinning. The weather was very cold indeed and the fish came poorly to the fly. I got two salmon and a big sea trout on my 'Terror' of which I have spoken before. We did not seem to know about Golden Sprats in that year, and I don't think they came into 'fashion' much before 1930.

On Sunday, 6th March, we motored up to have lunch with Sir George Douglas at Springfield, Kelso. His father was an old friend of my mother's, and she used to tell us the following story.

My mother was a girl in those days living in Gibraltar and Sir George sailed out in his yacht and spent some time there. There were two beautiful Spanish girls of very good birth, but very little money—so little had they, that when there was a ball, there was only one ball dress between the two of them, so one went and the other stayed at home. When Sir George arrived he attended a ball at the Governor's house and was very much struck by one of the beautiful Spanish girls. He asked to be introduced, and to cut matters short, he fell violently in love and asked her to marry him. In due course he sailed back to England, and the poor girl was chaffed unmercifully 'You will never see your Sir George again'; but not many months afterwards Sir George returned in his yacht with a trousseau and everything complete. The marriage took place at Gibraltar.

When I lunched at Springfield, I asked the late Sir George, his son, about this story. He said it was quite true, and that his father's and mother's marriage was quite ideal during the whole of their lives. He took me in and showed me a picture of his mother, and so struck was I with her beautiful face that he gave me a print of the picture. It was a pretty story.

The Tweed is a lovely river, so calm and silvery and peaceful. Some years afterwards I fished Carham water for four years in succession. At Carham, the river is much rougher and swifter, as compared with Lees, six miles below. After this I went home and amused myself at week-ends alternately on the Usk and Kennet.

To me, one of the attractions of the Usk was the easy way one could get down there for odd days when the water was in order. I used to rise at 5 a.m., make some breakfast and leave soon after 6. A run of three hours in the early morning, with no traffic about, got me to Abergavenny at 9 a.m. Then I had another breakfast, and at 10 a.m. went off fishing. I usually got two or three salmon during the week-end and sometimes a nice lot of trout, then returned home to Newbury either on Sunday night or early Monday morning. This was in 1927, not 1947! This year the Usk was not fishable any more for salmon until the end of June—there was no water.

June 4th—a lovely day with Geoff Turner on the Avington water on the river Kennet—six fish all from two to two and a half pounds. I saw no big fish.

June 6th—fishing on the Craven water, Kennet, a day spoiled by gales of wind and showers. It is a curious thing how often this seems to happen in the May fly time and then, when the fly is over, we get the most wonderful days of sunshine without wind. For the last ten years these conditions have been prevalent, much to our disappointment and disgust. I see in my notes that I saw a huge fish that day, and put him at nine to ten pounds. This sounds a preposterous statement to make, but you do occasionally come across these fish in the Kennet.

On 11th June I fished with that very charming American, George La Branche. Most people—fishermen, I mean—have read some of his writings. I found him a delightful companion on the river bank and a most skilful angler. We had a nice day together on the Ramsbury water. I got five fish from one and a half to two and a half pounds.

Shortly after this he gave a dinner in London to his English fishing friends. He very kindly asked me to join his party at the Savoy. I turned up at the appointed time, white tie and all, and then I waited. I must have been there for the best part of forty minutes, making every enquiry about the dinner, but nobody seemed to know anything about it. So I gave it up and went back to the Fly Fishers' Club and had a modest meal. The next thing I heard was, that the dinner had been held at the Ritz! Poor La Branche, he was full of apologies.

On the 25th June and up to the 10th July I went down to the Usk. The water was generally out of order, that is the worst of the Usk unless you live on the bank, but I managed to pick up a few fish to take home, just to show that I had been trying. On my next visit there the river rose eight feet, so that was no good.

Sweden. On 20th August I left England to go and fish that famous river the Em, in Sweden, where I never saw a sea trout under eight to ten pounds, and the average is about sixteen pounds. The late Anthony Crossley wrote a lot about the Em. I think that 1928 was the first year he went there, and was then almost a beginner in fishing. But he was extraordinarily quick in the uptake and for the next ten years until the time of his death in 1939, when he insisted on flying out to Sweden and the plane crashed, he had picked up more about fishing than most people do in a lifetime.

I had some difference of opinion with Crossley with regard to the catching of these big sea trout, as compared to the dry fly fishing for sea trout on the Laerdal and Aurland in Norway. He wrote a letter to the *Times*—I think it was early in 1938— which I quote with my reply. Mr Campbell Muir also wrote giving his opinion.

Great Sea Trout. A Twenty-nine-pounder.

To the Editor of the *Times*.

'Sir,—The accompanying photographs may possibly interest you, as I remember that some years ago you published correspondence on the great sea trout of the river Em, in Sweden. The single fish is the world's record sea trout, twenty-nine pounds two ounces. It was caught on a fly in the dusk of September 8th this year by Mr Gavin Clegg. This fish, which was thirty-nine inches long, was probably, according to Mr G. H. Nall's reading, nine and a half years old, during which it was coming up river to spawn for the fifth time. There have been several larger ones taken in the traps (which are down only till the fishermen arrive in August), the biggest, several years ago, scaling thirty-six pounds. The largest rod-caught fishes previously taken there were three, each of twenty-eight pounds, one of which is now over the mantelpiece of the Fly Fishers' Club.

'The other photograph shows my morning's catch on September 7th. The largest weighed twenty-six pounds, and the four big ones (weighing ninety-two and a half pounds) were caught in one hour of bright moonlight with a greased line. The two small ones were taken after breakfast. Our river is quiet and gracious, but the bottom is too dark to see where the fish are lying, so we do not use the dry fly. Is it heresy to suggest that greased-line fishing for sea trout is much more difficult than dry fly fishing as practised in the Laerdal?'

I am, Sir, etc.,

ANTHONY CROSSLEY.

Great Sea Trout. Methods of Fishing.

To the Editor of the *Times*.

'Sir,—I noticed with interest Mr Crossley's letter in the *Times* of November 7th.

'For many years I fished the Laerdal and Aurland rivers in Norway: I have also fished the Em river in Sweden, which produces these big trout.

'Mr Crossley says "Is it heresy to suggest that greased-line fishing for sea trout is much more difficult than dry fly fishing in the Laerdal?" I am of the opinion that it is "heresy" even to contemplate this or compare the two methods. The greased line is "blind" fishing, whereas the floating fly is usually placed over fish, which can be seen in these clear waters, and to my mind is far more difficult.

'Perhaps Mr Crossley has used the word "heresy" in order to get a rise. If so, he has succeeded!'

Your obedient servant,

JOHN RENNIE.

Great Sea Trout.

To the Editor of the *Times*.

'Sir,—Mr Anthony Crossley asks if it is heresy to suggest that greased-line fishing for sea trout is much more difficult than dry fly fishing as practised in the Laerdal. I understand the record sea trout of twenty-nine pounds, which he refers to, was caught on a 4/o salmon fly at night. Surely there cannot be any comparison between this method and that of catching sea trout in the daytime with dry fly and 2X trout cast, which is the method used on rivers in Norway, where I have seen sea trout caught up to sixteen pounds weight.

'He may describe it as greased-line fishing, but not exactly trout fishing.'

I am, etc.,

D. E. CAMPBELL MUIR.

Anthony Crossley wrote a great deal about this river in his book *The Floating Line for Salmon and Sea Trout*, quite one of the best books of its kind.

When he finished there, youth was on his side, but when you get to a 'certain age', one's inclination and ability to fish through the night and early morning is not the same, and becomes a drudgery instead of a pleasure. From what I have gathered, most of his sport was done between the hours of 11 p.m. and 4 a.m.

Lord Burnham, Walter Barrett and I, were content to fish up to 10 and 11 p.m. There is no doubt that night fishing for these big sea trout was more successful than daytime fishing, but I shall never think that fishing in the dark is nearly so enjoyable as fishing when there is some light and you can see what your fly is doing. However, every man his own choice.

The day after I arrived at Em, I went out for a short time, really to see the river, and before very long found myself very busy in a heavy fish. The fish put up a good fight and to my surprise when he came to the gaff, I found he was a very beautiful specimen of a brown trout of twelve pounds. He was so lovely and so much like the Kennet trout, that I spent the afternoon painting a picture of him.

This was my first fish on the Em river—not a bad beginning.

The smallest sea trout I got on this river was eight pounds, most of them were about twelve to sixteen pounds.

My impressions of this river are delightful. The house, a large one, built of timber, as all houses are in this country, was very comfortable and within fifty yards of the river. Our host and hostess were charming, and the food and wine good. There were little drawbacks in the 'accommodation', for instance, the bathroom led out into the drawing room. The other 'conveniences' were very familiar, but apart from this, which one soon got used to, everything was just what a fisherman wanted.

The fishing was more like salmon fishing than trout fishing, and one fished with tackle accordingly. The flies used were large, mostly about No. 1. I feel that with another season's experience, one would have done much better. Crossley went there many times and with the experience behind him, caught more fish on each visit.

Taking it on the whole, we did pretty well and never had a blank day. In twelve days' fishing I got seventeen big trout of an average of fourteen pounds. My best sea trout was twenty-one pounds.

XV

NORTHERN IRELAND
Season 1928

IN the early part of this season I went down on several occasions to the Wye and the Usk. Both these waters fished very well in March and April, but most of the fish were caught on bait of some sort. I always dislike fishing with a spoon, but on several occasions I found that a two-inch spoon of silver and copper was very deadly at times. On one occasion on the Usk, I finished up with three fish on the spoon after I had been fishing all day unsuccessfully with fly and other baits. If you are fishing bait, it is as well to remember this.

In a previous chapter I have given a full description of the Shannon and the fishing we had in 1928, so that I will not now repeat myself.

The late Col. Maunsell and I had the Newgarden and Prospect beats from 1st to 15th May, and I here show a photograph of one day's bag. There were three fish over the thirty pounds. The best fish thirty-eight pounds. The average weight was twenty and a half pounds.

This was the last really good year of the Shannon. Mrs O'Donovan of the Shannon Hotel, Castleconnell, made us very comfortable, and more obliging people you could not imagine. Her husband, poor man, was shot in the hotel during the 'bad times'.

The Kennet during this season seems to have gone off badly. I fished on several stretches, but the Avington and Denford waters were lacking in good fish. At Barton Court and Ramsbury I noticed a great falling off in the size of the fish and, from this time on, the fishing was never the same as in previous years.

Furunculosis was undoubtedly the cause of the loss of the big fish, but I cannot help thinking that if new blood had been imported into these waters, this disease would never have got the hold on the fish as it did in these years. One can only conclude this from the experience gained in the years from 1896 to 1925, when furunculosis was little known and new blood was put into the water. I know there are many who will not agree with this theory, but I shall always believe that the want of new blood has been the cause of the falling off of the Kennet.

In my diary I conclude by saying 'What has happened to all the good fish? I never remember such a poor year'.

After this I had several trips to the Usk on the Mardy water, and found that the fish came well to the fly.

On 21st July I find that I went down to Glanusk Park on the Usk to take part in the Casting Tournament, and was lucky enough to win the 'Championship of the Usk' both for trout and salmon. We were casting with 'fishing' rods in those days, and had not developed into 'Tournament' rods and lines—these came later.

In August I made a trip to Donegal and Tyrone. I had never seen this country: it is very fine, but I found little fishing of consequence. The nicest place was Gweedore. The hotel was excellent and has a pretty little river, but you must be there earlier in the year, when the salmon fishing is quite good.

One awful place I shall never forget, and I won't mention the name of it now, as it may have changed. I was fishing the Mourne and found what I thought to be quite a nice hotel of the commercial class. It had an A.A. sign and I thought all was safe. When I went to bed, as a matter of precaution I turned down the bed, and found it simply alive with bugs. I raised 'Cain' and had the household up. Of course it was the usual story—'Never been known before', etc. I changed my room to one with an iron bedstead and smothered it all with Keatings and Farlow's Midge lotion. Little sleep did I get from the thought of that horrible room, and I left next day. I have never had this trouble

n Southern Ireland, but I am told that it not unusual in Northern
reland. So, if you go there, be prepared with all the necessary
rmament.

I think it is time we had a little rest from the diary, and write
bout something else. So let me conclude this chapter by
elating a story which a friend of mine told me in the Fly Fishers'
Club one night. I hope he will not mind me repeating it.

It was a big function at the Fishmonger's Hall and there were
ome two hundred people present. My friend found himself
itting between two learned professors with long beards. One
aid to him, 'Do you know that the oyster is the only living
pecies that we know of, that can change his sex at will?'

My friend thought that this professor was being humorous
nd replied, 'How very awkward for him, he would never know
whether to go to Ladies' or Gentlemen's lavatory'.

The professor said nothing but remarked to his neighbour,
'The fellar must be a damned fool!'

XVI

ODDS AND ENDS

THIS is a chapter of odds and ends from cuttings and reports.

1. I wonder if the majority of people know the amount of strain you can put on your gut. It seems almost impossible that you should be able to break in a salmon when you know that with all the strain you can put on a big seventeen-foot salmon rod you will not pull more than two and a half to three pounds. Now let us look at the breaking strain of salmon gut from the heaviest down to 9/5.

0/5	-	32 pounds	5/5	-	$10\frac{1}{2}$ pounds
1/5	-	24 ,,	6/5	-	$8\frac{3}{4}$,,
2/5	-	19 ,,	7/5	-	7 ,,
3/5	-	$15\frac{1}{2}$,,	8/5	-	$4\frac{3}{8}$,,
4/5	-	$12\frac{1}{4}$,,	9/5	-	$3\frac{1}{2}$,,

These tests were made with dry gut and presumably before any knots were tied. Soaked gut does not give such good results. It is interesting to note that even the 9/5 gut taking a strain of three and a half pounds is more than equal to all the strain you can put on a seventeen-foot rod. How is it, then, that one can get broken by a big fish when using gut of nineteen to twenty-four pounds breaking strain.

I think the answer must be, the weakening of the cast by reason of the knots: this will account for some fifteen to twenty per cent and the sudden 'jerk' which a salmon is liable to make from time to time. This 'jerk' may come when he takes you, it may come in a jump and it may come just as you are bringing him up to the gaff and he makes a sudden twisting plunge. These have all happened to me. I am more cautious now. But apart from this, it seems almost impossible that this sudden 'jerk' can be sufficient to exert this strain on the gut and yet your rod does not suffer. If I am careless, it will happen to me again.

2. 'Sometimes I think that Catchment Boards go mad. This country is running out of water, so we are told, and we are urged to ration ourselves, and yet we are doing our best to hurry every drop to the sea as soon as possible. Every ditch and river is being cleaned at great cost, with the result that many wells are going dry, and if we get a hot summer the crops will probably suffer.' The above remarks were written to me by a large landowner in Norfolk.

I sat on the enquiry of the Catchment Board of the Wye in October, 1934, representing 'The British Field Sports'. The enquiry was long and tedious and lasted three days. The original idea was to dredge and remove all obstacles right up the river beyond Hereford. Thank goodness in the end it was not carried out and was mostly confined to the water below Monmouth. Here is a letter which was published in the *Times* in July, 1937. There was not much response.

THE RIVER WYE

To the Editor of the *Times*.

'Sir,—Might I draw the attention of your readers and all interested in the preservation of the natural beauties of our countryside to a flagrant piece of vandalism which is now being perpetrated on the River Wye.

'From Monmouth down, trees are being felled and excavating machines are tearing away the banks, making them into a uniform level to an angle of forty-five degrees to the river. When completed, this glorious stretch of the Wye will resemble the Manchester Ship Canal.

'I venture to assert that if the Thames Conservancy were to announce a plan to treat the banks and trees at, say, Cliveden in the same way that the Wye is being treated, public opinion would force them to hold their hand before a tree had been felled or a yard of earth removed, but whereas Cliveden Woods are within easy reach of London, the Wye is 120 miles away.

'Nevertheless, its beauties are far-famed, and I suggest that if ever there was a case which required the attention of the Council for the Preservation of Rural England which has done so much to conserve the fast vanishing beauties of our countryside, this is an outstanding one, and if the publication of this letter

can do anything to draw public attention to this matter before it is too late I
shall feel that its object has been attained.'

Yours faithfully, etc.,
JOHN RENNIE.

I remember they made a great fuss about a few houses which
very occasionally get flooded on the flat ground just outside the
town of Monmouth. It was the Monmow which overflowed its
banks and piled up the water in the Wye, owing to obstructions,
as it could not get away quickly enough. The scheme as drawn
up by the engineer was to cost over a million pounds and when
he was asked if, after doing this work the Wye would be free
from flooding, he replied 'I can no more guarantee this than a
doctor can guarantee his patient getting well!' Rather a weak
reply, I thought. These dredging operations are carried out by
grabs, and the soil is heaped on the banks of the river; in the
case of one small river I know, these banks are five to six feet
high, thus ruining any chance of fishing. Instead, they should
distribute the soil evenly over the ground. I believe the lovely
river Wylye has been ruined in this way. What with the water
being tapped and the bottoms being dredged, to say nothing of
pollution which is turning our rivers into open sewers, I feel
very much for the anglers of the future. There may come a day
when a little more caution and sense will be exercised by some
of our authorities. Let us hope so.

Our new fear is the electrification of a large number of rivers
in Scotland. The Severn barrage scheme has also come into
prominence again. If this does take place, then I think you can
say 'goodbye' to the Wye as a salmon river. The plans show
the barrage just below the mouth of the Wye.

And so we shall have many examples of the 'Shannon' scheme
and we know what that has done.

3. *Vibrations in water*. I once wrote an article on this subject
some years ago. I will not quote the whole article, but the idea
was this. In about the year 1919 I was taking a cure at Harrogate
and part of that cure was to immerse my whole body in the
water. One day I totally submerged, stopping up my ears with
my fingers. To my surprise I heard sounds which I could not
hear when my head was above water. For instance, I heard a tap

running next door—I could hear nothing when my head was above. Then I made scratchings on the bath with my feet. I could hear nothing with my head up, but when immersed I could hear every movement. And so I tried a number of other experiments of this nature, with the same result. There was a reply to my article in *Game and Gun* which I attach. Mr Rogerson had the same experience as myself.

Vibrations in Water.

To the Editor of *Game and Gun.*

'Sir,—I was most interested in Mr John Rennie's letter on "Vibrations in Water".

'I first noticed the amazing way sound carried under water when I was bathing at Deal.

'Quite by chance, while "duck diving" one calm day, I thought I heard the "chug-chug" of paddles. I immediately came up expecting to see the round-coast steamer. To my astonishment the only sign of the boat was a tiny smudge of smoke on the horizon, and while my head was above water I could hear nothing of her!

'Putting my head under water, I again heard paddles quite plainly, but it was not until fifteen minutes later that I could hear the paddles with my head above water, although the day was fine and there was no wind.'

W. T. C. ROGERSON.

Brandon Rectory, Suffolk.

This led me to think about fishing and the noise one makes when wading a rocky river with nailed brogues and metal-ended wading staff. The vibrations of the 'click' of the reel I am sure frighten a fish as they are conveyed down the line to the fish. I tried this out in Norway; the experiment was as near as one could get it.

I hooked a good fish on the fly in a famous Norwegian river. My reel had a powerful and noisy 'click'. That fish was very wild, and took me twenty-five minutes. It was twenty-five pounds.

I went back to the same place and got a fish of the same weight on the same fly but—and here is the difference—I switched off the check of my reel and applied a break which gave out no noise. I killed the second fish in half the time. These two fish were identical: you could not tell 'one from t'other'. I now wear felt bottoms to my brogues and fit a rubber end to my wading staff.

Do I scare less fish? Perhaps I do, but I do know this—that felt soles to your brogues seldom let you down.

4. Letter from A. H. Wood of Cairnton. I once had a little joke with Mr Wood. I tied three flies which I christened The Forest, The Wood and The Spinney. These were tied on enormous hooks, the largest being three and a half inches and the smallest two and a half inches. The body and wing were diminutive. It was a huge exaggeration of Wood's patterns. Here is his reply:

Dear Mr Rennie,

'Many thanks for your letter and also for the collection of flies. I like the names. When I received the original you sent through Bostock I thought for fun I would try it. Before I had got my full length of line out I had a pull. But as the water is so low and not much room for other rods I am not fishing now until we get some more water. In fact the fish are so stiff that no one is getting more than one occasionally by fair means: sorry to say a great many are being got by the ribs, in fact practically all. Some cannot help it, but I am afraid a great many are intentional. I find some interesting things with the fish in this clear water.

'Your fly is no exaggeration, in fact there is too much on some of them, as I find the fish will go for the bare hook in summer time and clear water. The only trouble is to get the cast fine enough so that the hook does not look like part of the cast. There is one of my ripe March Brown's illustrated in the Lonsdale book and I have caught a lot of fish on that fly. Plate 50 shows the illustration. I have got some others much thinner and more lightly dressed than that, which are good killers.

'I am so awfully sorry I did not meet you when you were stopping with the Slades. I am afraid we are not likely to see Alice and her brother up here now that the old lady has gone, but if you ever come up this way please let me know, I should like to meet you.

'Many thanks for these flies which are very interesting and I hope to prove useful.

'There are any amount of fish in the river, far more than usual for this time of year, but they will not take anything and are only being got by foul means.

Yours,

A. H. E. WOOD.

5. Here is a cutting from some paper on a lecture I gave in London on behalf of the 'British Field Sports Society'.

I took a great deal of trouble in preparing this lecture for the young angler, but I was sadly disappointed to find that there were more grown-ups than young. I did not want to lecture to grown-ups; but I did want to say a few words to the young people and start them in the right way of thinking. I had prepared a cinema film on casting and lantern slides on tying flies and making knots, also a rod or two to illustrate what I was saying to them. I was 'reported' as follows:

Chancellor's Six-pound Trout. Described in Fly Fishing Lecture.

Expert's Advice on Casting.

'A six-pound trout which was caught in the river Test by Mr Neville Chamberlain, Chancellor of the Exchequer, was mentioned by Mr John Rennie in his lecture on "Fly Fishing for Beginners" at the Grotrian Hall, W., yesterday.

'Mr Rennie, who is Chairman of the Fisheries Committee, gave the third in the series of Christmas Holidays Sporting Lectures "for the Young of all ages" arranged by the British Field Sports Society.

'Equipped with fishing rods, which he dexterously wielded on the platform, and aided by lantern slides and films, he gave a comprehensive survey of his subject. He gave hints for the novice on, among other things,

How to make a fly:

'Stages of dry-fly tying;

'Four kinds of knots, and

'Casting.

'He advised his listeners to practise casting on the lawn with half-a-crown and then a saucer as the objectives.

'*How to Strike.* Casting should be done with wrist action, he added, the elbows close to the sides and the body kept steady.

'The beginner usually made the mistake of bringing the rod right back when it should only go slightly beyond the perpendicular. The full force of the drive should be made at the start of the cast. Wrong casting meant arriving home worn out.

'The fisherman should count "one-two-three" before striking. The big fish were slow, and many were lost because the angler struck too soon.

'Referring to the increasing popularity of greased-line fishing, Mr Rennie said it was undoubtedly more successful than the old-fashioned method.'

By looking at the heading of the report you would think the lecture was about Mr Chamberlain's six-pound trout, but in point of fact I was only showing a photograph of the Test where I had fished with Sir Joseph Ball and I remarked to my audience 'And it was at this spot that the Chancellor recently caught a six-pound trout'. This little remark was seized on by the reporter, hence the headline. It only shows how careful one should be with reporters about.

I hope my lecture was of interest to the few young ones that were there. I now repeat this lecture in case some young angler should get hold of this book.

XVII

TEACHING THE YOUNG TO FISH

*A Lecture to boys and girls, given 4th January, 1937, to members of
the British Field Sports Society*

'BOYS AND GIRLS,—When I was asked to give a lecture
on behalf of the British Field Sports Society, I was told
by the Secretary that it was to be composed for "Young
People".

Now I see that there are a number of people present who can
hardly be described as "Young People", and this has rather
frightened me, because there is probably nothing in my talk
which they do not know and I would not presume to teach them
in any way, as they probably know just as much as I do about
"Fly Fishing".

So, it is to the "Young People" I address my remarks this
afternoon, and I can only hope that the "grown-ups" will not
be bored.

I will open my remarks by saying that anything I tell you has
been picked up during my experience of over forty years. But
I am not saying that my views are any better than others who
have had the same experience.

If I can hand on to you some of the things I have learned from
this experience and the experience of others, then I shall be
satisfied. Such things as holding the rod, joining gut, tying on
flies and generally how to treat your tackle and throw a line,
these things I shall tell you. I shall show you a few photographs
and a cinema film, which will help you.

I propose to talk on the following headlines:

(a) A few words on the general behaviour and the spirit in which fly fishing should be approached.

(b) Rods and Tackle.

(c) Casting.

(d) Wet and dry fly fishing for trout.

(e) Fly fishing for salmon.

I am a great believer in teaching the young to start in the right way, whether it is fishing, shooting, hunting, tennis or any other sport.

I want you to have the right spirit of the sport. I am now talking of fishing. Don't go out with the one idea to catch fish.

To get the right idea, you should study the habits of fish, the water you are going to fish, and the conditions of the weather.

For it does not matter how well you may learn to cast a fly, if you do not know the habits of the fish and watch the water, you will most certainly not catch as many fish as the man who has made this study and who may cast a more indifferent line than you do. Secondly, you will not get the same interest out of the sport.

Then I would impress upon you not to be "jealous" of another man's take. You should congratulate him and try and find out from him how it was that he was more successful than you were. You will not only learn quicker; but you may make a lasting fishing friend.

Don't be afraid *to ask questions* of a fisherman older or more experienced than yourself. You will always find that the older the man, the more flattered he is at being asked questions from the young.

When you get on the river bank, *don't be in too much of a hurry* when you see a fish rise. Watch him for a bit and see what his habits are. He may be a cruiser—that is, one who wanders up and down a certain beat, and you want to find out where is the bottom of his beat instead of hurrying after him, in which case you will probably meet face to face and that will be the end of him.

I feel sure I need not tell you not to hurry away to the best place. If you are acting host, you must always give your friend the first chance.

This does not always work out quite as you wish, as I remember on one occasion I put my friend on the two best pools on a salmon river and went down to an indifferent part of the water where I had never caught a fish. That morning I caught two, and went back to my friend to find that he had caught none. But he was the best of sportsmen and he laughed over the matter.

Don't load yourself up with *too much tackle* when you go out on a day's fishing. I have so often found that when I have gone out salmon fishing with just a rod, a spare cast and a few flies, I have had some of my best days. Whereas on other days when I have taken two rods and any amount of tackle, the result has been nothing.

See that your *waders* are in good order and when you get back, turn them inside out in a warm place. They are expensive things and last a very short time. I have found the best brogues are those with the *soles made of felt* and the heels leather with nails. In rocky rivers, felt is the only thing which does not slip.

Take my advice and *don't wade too deep*. It is a horrid experience to get carried off your feet and have to swim for it. I think the best way, if you have long waders on, is to turn over on your back and swim.

Keep your *fish nice and roll them up* in a *damp cloth* and don't bring them back in a string like a lot of red herrings. I like to see a beautiful basket of fish brought back in perfect order and colour. When you get home and lay them on a dish, a little salt sprinkled over them will bring back the colour.

If you get *caught in a snag* or branch, don't go tugging away with your rod. You will only strain it and probably spoil it. A rod is a delicate and beautiful thing and if properly treated will last a lifetime. I have rods I have used for thirty or more years, and they are as good today as the day I bought them. If you get caught up, or snagged, put your rod down and catch hold of the line and if a break is necessary, do it in this way.

Dry your lines carefully when you have finished your day's fishing, also your flies, and take your casts out of the damper.

The great thing is to *start with a good rod*, whether trout or salmon. And get a rod that suits you. Some rods suit some people, some suit others. Get someone of experience to help you.

Rod-making nowadays has advanced so much that most of the rods are good to start with; but I have found that the more expensive rods from the best makers are the cheapest in the end, as they never go out of shape and they last a very long time if properly handled. So, if you can get a kind relation, get him to take you to one of the best shops and tell him what I have told you!

Here is an eight-foot rod I have had for over twenty years. It is very light, somewhere about three ounces, but it is very strong and will cast a line of twenty-five yards. It has killed a great many fish up to five and six pounds. It is as good as the day I got it, and it is a delight to cast with. But here again, you must have *the right line to suit a rod*. Many a time I have been told that a rod is of no use, only to find that it was the line that was no use, and as soon as a line was put on which suited the rod it became a different thing, and became a good rod.

You must pay great attention to your lines. After a day's fishing, I take the line off the reel and hang it up in loose coils. Personally, I like this better than a line winder.

Before going out next morning I *rub it down with* a silk handkerchief. This removes any dirt and if I am fishing dry fly I put a little mucilin on my fingers and rub this into the line. As a rule, except on very hot days, the line will float all day long. When you are fishing large rivers and where there are big fish, then I recommend a rod of nine feet or nine feet six inches. I now hardly ever use a rod over nine feet unless it is that I want to occasionally give my old friends, the ten-footers, a day's outing. I always feel that my rod is rather human and likes a day on the river occasionally!

I don't suggest that you should buy *a large number of rods*, reels and tackle to start off with. But start making a collection when you are young, and you will get to love your tackle.

Now about flies and how to make them. Presently I shall give you an idea of how a fly is made. It is really not at all difficult to make flies to kill fish; but it is difficult to tie the imitation of natural flies found on our chalk streams. You can start making your collection of feathers and wools and furs in quite a small way. There are several good books on how to make flies, but your quickest way is to get a friend to show you how it is done. Then you want a vice, and some pliers, scissors, etc.

With this small equipment you will be surprised how quickly you will learn to make a fly.

To show you the use of being able to make your own flies and the great amount of satisfaction to be had out of it, I will tell you a short story.

I had a nephew, then at Eton. He and I were both asked down for a day's fishing on the Itchen, which is, as you know, one of out two greatest chalk streams, and the fish are very shy and difficult. We were walking along the bank with our host when we came to a spot where a good fish had defied capture, but was a very free riser. There he was rising away. Our host threw two or three flies over him. Then I did the same, without an offer. So our host said, 'Oh, that fish is no good. We had better leave him to the boy.' So we left the fish and the boy. About twenty minutes after we heard shouts. 'I've got him, Uncle John!' And sure enough he had. We ran up and found that he had got a fine fish of two and a quarter pounds—the first thing our host said was, 'What did you get him on?'

"Oh," said the boy, "a fly I tied myself!"

We looked at it. Oh! What a fly. Nothing on God's earth like it—and the fish had certainly never seen anything like it. Still he had caught the fish and became a very good fly tyer.

Many a time I have been away fishing in Norway, Sweden, Iceland and other places, where some particular fly was more attractive than any other. And it is a curious thing, but fish are always more attracted by one single pattern you have in your book, rather than all the others put together.

This year I was in Iceland and I don't think that I am exaggerating when I say that our bag would have been smaller by thirty or forty salmon, but for the fact that I was able to copy a very small, silver, blue and teal fly.

Practice makes perfect, and I can only tell you this, that if I have not been tying flies for two or three months, it takes me several days to get back to my old form.

Now we will talk a little about *Knots*.

I was once told by an expert in knots that whatever knot you

made, you reduced the strength of your line or cast from anything between thirty and fifty per cent of its strength, according
to the type of knot you made.

This information was arrived at after long experiments with
a machine, which I believe is called a 'ballistic tester'. So you
see you must be very careful not to put any more knots in your
cast, other than those by which the cast is made. There are
numerous knots, some favoured by one fisherman, some by
others, but I shall only show you three or four, and if you learn
these you can carry on quite well.

1. Tying small-eyed flies to gut.
2. Tying large flies to gut.
3. The double blood knot for joining casts together or adding
   a point to your cast.
4. Loop knot.

No. 1. We will now take No. 1. Tying small flies to fine gut.
This knot is generally known as the "*Turle*" knot. I have used it all
my life. It is simple to tie, and once you have threaded the eye
of the fly, you can do the rest with your eyes shut.

No. 2. *Tying large flies* to gut or tying your line to the loop of
your cast. Generally known as the "*Figure of Eight*".

It is a very safe attachment knot and quickly tied.

No. 3. *Double Blood*. It was only a few years ago when Mr Chaytor
published that splendid book *Letters to a Salmon Fisher's Sons*, that
this knot became generally known. It has been a boon to all
fishermen. It is the strongest and best knot known. I will try
and show it to you on the screen and explain its method.

No. 4. This is for making a loop in your cast. It is stronger than
any other loop.

For all these knots I advise you to get a copy of Mr Chaytor's
book and a little book called *Fishermen's Knots and Wrinkles* by the
late W. A. Hunter. This latter book will show you how to make
all kinds of knots, the whip finish and other things. Take a piece
of string and steal a skewer from the cook and practice all these
knots.

Always put on your flies yourself and fix up your rod and
tackle. If anything goes wrong, you have *only yourself to blame*.

There is another thing. If you do all these things yourself and if you make your own flies, the gillie will think a lot more of you. You will *go up 100 per cent* in his estimation.

CASTING

Now, having touched very lightly on rods and tackle, because time is pressing, I want to say a few words on casting.

Casting is a very simple thing, like all other things, if only you know how.

It will save you endless time and trouble if you know a really good fisherman, and if you don't, go to one of the gentlemen who teach casting and in two or three lessons they will teach you more than you can learn by yourself in months of practice. This is the same with any other game, cricket, tennis, etc.

Half the pleasure of fishing is to know that you have perfect control of your line no matter which way the wind is, and land your fly in the right place. To cheat the wind and cut a fly into it with the minimum of effort gives one great satisfaction. Of course, it is impossible to demonstrate this to you on the platform. In the first place, there is no wind. In the second place, I might get into trouble with my audience.

When you have had your lesson, take your rod on to the tennis lawn or some suitable grass plot. Get your uncle to put down half-a-crown at, say, ten yards distance. When you hit it with your fly, the half-crown is yours. Then another half-crown, fifteen yards away, and do the same thing, and so on.

I don't know where the uncle comes in; but they are always supposed to be benevolent persons, so perhaps he won't mind.

Failing the uncle, put down a saucer or small plate.

When you can do this quite easily, you are a fit person to go to the Itchen or Test and not disgrace yourself.

I will now show you, as far as I can, the correct motion and poise of the fly fisher, both for salmon and trout.

You must learn good style in this, as in anything else. Bad style is horrible to look at in any form of sport.

Casting with a trout and salmon rod is very much the same thing.

First, I will take up a *trout rod*. Mind you, I am only talking to those who have had little or no experience, as I said at the beginning of this talk. Watch my grip on the rod with my four fingers and the thumb uppermost.

Whether you are casting dry or wet fly, the theory is the same. But as you know, when you are casting dry fly you give two or three casts in the air, for the purpose of drying your fly. Like this.

Whereas in wet fly you do not do so.

When you have made your cast and gone over your fish, do not snatch your fly off the water, but recover your fly gently and raise your rod.

The beginner nearly always takes his rod too far back, in the fear that he will not recover his line. Don't take the rod beyond or much beyond the perpendicular. If you have a lot of slack line out, gather it in with your left hand and then shoot your line at the next cast. You must always try and get your line straight out behind you, parallel with the land. Then when your line is fully extended at the back, give a drive forward. If your line is not straight behind, it will not be straight forward. Remember to keep your body steady and your elbows in.

Very often it is a mistake to drive your line in too straight a direction forward as this may develop into a drag on your fly, which in dry fly is hopeless. You can overcome this by giving a slight check to the forward cast. This will allow the fly to land quietly on the water with a little slack line which will overcome the drag.

CASTING SALMON ROD

Casting a salmon fly is much the same as casting a trout fly.

I will show you on the screen six positions of a salmon fisher on a river in Norway.

No. 1. You will notice the way the rod is held preparatory to lifting the line off the water. Note position of hands. Stand upright and don't bend forward.

No. 2. Here you will see the rod being raised and lifting the line off the water, before driving the line backward. Never snatch the line off the water. Lift it gently and smoothly.

No. 3. Shows the backward cast and you will note the position of the rod, not very much beyond the perpendicular. This is what it should be, and if you do this your line will not fall behind you and you will not lose your flies. And salmon flies, if you buy them, are very expensive things. If you feel the smallest touch behind you, gather in your line and examine your fly. It is very likely that you will find the barb broken off. That, I need hardly say, will cost you a fish if you happen to rise one and have not examined your hook.

When you start the forward drive don't "creep" forward with your rod. This is a bad trick and you must watch it.

When there is a wind against you, finish your cast like this (see photograph). For some reason or another if you finish your cast in this way, you can drive a fly right into the wind, whereas in the ordinary way the fly turns back on you.

If you cast in the right way, there is no effort, but if you do it in the wrong way you will come back tired out. Let me once more say what are the things to beware of.

1. Snatching the fly too quickly off the water.
2. Trying to pick up too long a line, with the result that you take the rod too far back.
3. *Creeping.* That is to say, when the rod is taken back to the perpendicular, the tendency is to let it creep forward, before the forward drive is made.

If you have a long line out, whether for salmon or trout, and the water is rather slack, pull in four or five yards of the line, then make a switch cast downstream and as soon as the line touches the water, make your overhead cast and shoot the four or five yards of line you have in your hand. By this way, you will avoid lifting a heavy, sunk line and so save both yourself and your rod.

Never use rods which are too heavy for you. If you do, the rod will become the master, not you.

WET FLY TROUT FISHING

Having told you a little about rods and casting we will now have a few words about how to fish the water.

So much has been said and written on this subject that I approach the matter with diffidence.

Fishing can only be learned by practice and the study of fish habits and rivers.

Supposing you are going alone to a strange river. Go and have a talk with the local tackle man if there is one, but don't rely on him entirely; think for yourself. You will certainly learn something from the locals, but very often they are dogmatic on the kind of flies they will choose for you.

Many people are good casters, but they do not catch fish because they are deficient in knowledge of insect life, and have a lack of observation. Whereas the poor caster, who is more observant, may come back with a fine basket.

The novice should make it his first duty to study the insect life on the river and not merely rely on the local angler for the choice of his flies. To find out what the trout are taking is a great help. One way is to find out what the fish has in his stomach; but to do this you must catch one first.

You can do this by cutting the trout open or, as Mr Skues advises, by running one of those marrow scoops down his throat, then give it a twist and withdraw it. Put the contents into a glass of water and you will very soon see what the trout have been feeding on.

Fly fishing, as you know, is practised in two ways. Wet and dry.

We will deal with wet fly first.

You might ask me, "Why do we use wet fly in some rivers and dry fly in others?"

The reason is probably this. That whereas the North Country and Welsh rivers are rapid, many of the insects which rise from the bed of the river before hatching out are carried downstream under water, or perhaps the water is too rough and they cannot get rid of their "nymphal" cases, or in other words, get hopelessly shipwrecked before they get to the surface.

So, in this type of river, the trout get used to taking their food under water. Under these circumstances, we use the wet fly.

You can use your wet fly upstream or down. You can do this in several ways. The usual method is to cast downstream and let the flies swing round with the current. In this way, which is the popular way, you will, at times, get good baskets.

But there is another method of downstream fishing. This method is to cast more across or slightly upstream. In this way the flies are carried for a short distance downstream without a drag and it is best not to cast too straight a line.

The angler wades downstream a yard at a time.

In this *second method* you require more observation, as very little of the rise is seen, the striking of the fish becomes more of an instinct. In the first method the fish hooks himself.

When there is a good hatch of fly coming on, it is often advisable to give up the downstream method and fish upstream with a wet fly. This is much more difficult than the downstream way, as you will miss many rises at first, but it is far more fascinating and has many advantages.

Upstream wet fly fishing is anything but "Chuck and chance it". You wade upstream very slowly, casting not necessarily at rising fish but dropping your fly or flies into all the little eddies and behind rocks.

Fish, as you know, always lie with their heads upstream, so the chances of being seen when you are wading right behind them are small as compared with the downstream method.

You must remember that trout have wonderful eyesight and are very sensitive to vibrations under water. So go slowly and do not stumble about and you will be surprised how near you can get to them.

Fishing downstream does not require so much skill, and many fish are pricked and lost. When you are fishing upstream there is no necessity to use a long line. When you are wading you can get quite close to your fish, and a long line floating downstream rapidly is difficult to recover and makes it difficult to see the rise and strike. So use a short line. In many cases a line not much longer than your rod is sufficient. If you will do this you will save yourself a lot of trouble.

In striking do not raise your rod overhead. I have always found, whether fishing wet or dry, that the sideway strike or movement of the rod, either right or left according to which bank you are on, is far better than the overhead.

Now let us have a few words about "Dry Fly" fishing. Dry fly fishing is practised on all our chalk streams, such as the Test, Itchen, Kennet, etc. Here you have a steady flow of unbroken water and the natural fly comes sailing down in "battalions".

is very beautiful to watch, as you can in these clear rivers, a rising trout feeding here and there on the flies floating over him.

First of all you must find out what he is feeding on, as a chalk stream trout will, as a rule, refuse all flies which are not a good imitation of what is floating over him. And it is here that your observation will come in.

The flies you fish with in dry fly fishing are tied in a different way to those in wet fly fishing. They are tied to float. Some flies are tied with wings and some with hackles only. It is a matter of choice, not only of the fish, but the fishermen!

When you go to a dry fly river you will probably be given a stretch of water and you must not go wandering about too much and if you do, keep a long way from the bank, just so far as you can see the water or hear a rise. Watch for any sign of a rise, and when you see one, don't hurry up to cast a fly over him, but see if he rises again and try to find out what he took. Sometimes you may have to wait for hours before the rise is on, and you must never "fish" the water as you do in wet fly fishing, but wait for your fish to rise.

If you see your fish rise again, crawl up very carefully behind him and take your distance. It may be ten yards or fifteen or more yards. Notice very carefully how the flies or any other objects come over him and see what the eddies are.

What you must try and avoid at all costs is *drag*. This is fatal and will put your fish down. This is caused by the current being swifter in one part than in another, which pulls your line and so drags your fly faster than the water would really take it if it were swimming down naturally.

Having made your observations and not scared your fish, proceed to get out your line, yard by yard at a time, always keeping your fly in the air and not letting it touch the water.

When you have got out what you think is the right length of line to cover your fish with the fly, if you are very clever, you will drop your fly just a little bit ahead of your fish, but if you are not quite confident, make a false cast a foot or two behind your fish and then give the next cast a little longer. Try not to let the cast float over the fish. If you are terribly clever you will make a "shepherd's crook" in the last yard of your cast so that only the fly floats over him, before any gut. But there are not many who can do this. It is done by giving a slight check to the line in the forward cast.

I will repeat here. Don't be too anxious to cast a very straight line. If you do, you will get drag. There was once a fisherman who cast such a perfectly straight line on the water that he caught no fish! So he gave up fishing and took to golf.

Well, supposing you have dropped your floating fly over the fish correctly. If he is a big one, he will swim up and take it very slowly. Now is the time to see if your nerves are in good order. You must not strike when you see him open his mouth and take in your fly. If you do, you will probably lose him. With a big fish, count 1, 2, 3. Then strike—*I* say sideways, others may disagree; but if you are lucky you will be in him.

Having hooked him, it is hard to tell you just what to do, as you never know what a fish is going to do. But I have always found that, on a chalk stream river, where there are usually banks of heavy weeds, the best thing to do is to try and turn his head and lead him downstream. By pulling him downstream you are far less likely to get weeded.

Having got him on the run downstream, keep him going, and you will be surprised how soon you will get him into your net.

Now supposing that he insists on going upstream, and sometimes he does—I had a four-pounder this year on the Kennet which took me quite eighty yards upstream. Well, supposing he does this and then dives into a bank of weeds and holds on there with his mouth as I have seen them do, my experience is that as long as you keep a strain on him he will never come out but if you lay your rod down and give him a slack line, he will very often come out after a few minutes. It is well worth trying and I have found it very successful.

I think I have already told you the way to keep your line and fly floating. Let me repeat what I said. If your line starts sinking stretch it out on the grass. Rub it down with a dry handkerchief and then rub in a little more "Mucilin" or some such preparation for this purpose.

Now, I could go on talking to you for a long time about dry fly fishing, but time is getting on and I have not yet touched on salmon fishing; but before I stop, I should like to say a few words about dry fly fishing for sea trout.

DRY FLY SEA TROUT

I first started this in a Scottish loch in 1911—when very little was known about it in those days.

I went to fish in Harris. There were three or four lochs practically joined together. The lowest loch was tidal. It was very hot weather, the lochs were so low that the sea trout could not run up. But the semi-tidal and tidal lochs were full of fish. I remember that I had a very 'dour' gillie who said that it was no good fishing. I said that I had come a very long way, and I intended to have a try.

We went out in the boat and I fished for an hour with a wet fly and although the sea trout were rising and jumping all over the place, I could not get a rise.

Then I said, "Have you ever tried a dry fly?" and he said, "No, it was no good here."

However, I put up what is known as a "Variant". "Variants" are things you must always keep in your box. There are all kinds of "Variants" and they are very useful. If you don't know what to fish with, try a "*Variant*". In a very few casts I was into a fish of three pounds and so it went on for about three hours. Fish after fish rose and by the end of the day I had twenty-eight pounds weight of sea trout.

All this time the gillie had been quite silent and at the end of the day I said, "Well, what do you think of the dry fly now?" and his remark was, "*I dinna care about it at all*." It was something he did not know and for that reason disliked it. This was the start of my career on dry fly for sea trout.

My method on the Loch was to cast the fly where I had seen a fish move and let the fly remain on the water, for sometimes more than a minute. Now I always fish dry fly for sea trout when I get a chance.

You may want to know what is the best dry fly for sea trout. In my experience, almost anything that floats well and will sit up in rough water will catch sea trout. My preference is a "*Tup*" in bright weather, which has a light red hackle and pinkish body.

When the sun is not on the water, then I have found that a badger hackle and all black hackle fly is the best.

DRY FLY SALMON

Some years ago Mr La Branche and Mr Hewett startled the fishing world by telling us how to catch salmon on the dry fly, but all his experience had been confined to rivers in the U.S.A., Canada and Newfoundland. Then he came over to this country and fished with Mr Wood on the Dee. I understand that he rose twenty-eight fish, hooked one and caught none.

Both he and Mr Hewett tried various other rivers in this country, but I never heard that they were successful.

I have tried it in Norway, Scotland and Ireland, but I never had any captures. I have only found one place where the salmon take a dry fly readily and then only in very low water. That was in Iceland.

We also found out this, that whereas you must give the large sea trout plenty of time between the rise of the fish and the strike—count 1, 2, 3—we found with the salmon that you had to strike just as *quickly* as you could. The first morning we tried, I think we lost eleven fish by giving them too much time. When we found this out and struck quickly we got into fish after fish. I often wonder if this was the reason why Mr La Branche did not hook the fish he rose on the Dee.

SALMON FISHING

Now, I have told you a very little about trout fishing, but nothing about salmon fishing, except dry fly, so that for my last few minutes I will just skim over this subject.

I hope you will all learn to trout-fish first, because if you don't, I feel sure that you will be spoiled for trout if you start too early after salmon. Also having once mastered the art of casting a trout rod, you will soon get into casting with a salmon rod.

We will start with the *ordinary* way of fishing for salmon with a fly. I should advise a rod of *thirteen* feet or *fourteen* feet at the most. In the old days we used to use rods of seventeen and eighteen feet, but now there is no need for these, as rods have improved so much that it is only on exceptional rivers and where there are very large fish that rods of sixteen feet are used. With a rod of thirteen or fourteen feet you can now throw with ease thirty yards of line, which is all you want in fishing. This rod I am holding is fourteen feet split cane. The line is forty-five yards long and there is sixty or more yards of fine backing behind it.

The thickness of your cast (which I prefer to be not less than nine feet in length) and the size of your fly, must be according to the time of year and state of the water. In the early spring, we use very large flies. You cannot use a large fly with safety on a fine cast. Broadly speaking, there are two ways of catching salmon with a wet fly.

1. The old-fashioned method of casting the fly downstream and across at an angle of forty-five to fifty degrees, and this is the method which has been used for 100 years, and the majority of salmon fishers still continue to fish in this way.
2. The new-fashioned way, invented by the late Mr Wood, of Cairnton on the Dee, and generally known as "greased-line fishing".

Naturally, there is not much time to go into the respective methods. My feeling is that on certain rivers it pays you to fish one way and on other rivers the other way.

On heavy, rather clouded rivers, I fancy the old style. Whereas on bright, clear waters there is no doubt that *the greased line* is far and away the best, and to me, much more attractive. But you cannot lay down any hard and fast rule.

No. 1. We will first consider No. 1. The old-fashioned. Let us go to the head or top end of the pool and cast the fly, beginning with a short line, down and across the river. Let the fly come round quite steadily, without moving the top of the rod up and down, which is really quite useless. I have stopped doing this for many years and caught more fish. It really gives no motion to the fly and the fly gets plenty of motion from the currents of the stream.

When your fly has come round under your own bank, do not be in a hurry to pull it up out of the water. A fish will often follow it right across the river and take it just as you are raising your rod. I usually pull in three or four yards by hand. Then raise your rod quite slowly and when your fly is leaving the water, deliver your back cast. In driving forward let go your three or four yards which shoots out and lands your fly more lightly. By gathering in your line, there is not so much effort required for your cast. When you want to get out a longish line and the water on your side is sluggish and the line sunk, raise the rod and give a switch downstream, and as soon as the line touches the water, take it back overhead and deliver your cast as before. In other words, make a false cast. If you try this you will be surprised what a lot of effort it saves. Unless there is quite a hard pull from the current on the line I always fish in this way.

When a fish takes you, don't drive into him hard with a sudden backward strike. In heavy water he will hook himself; you have only to move your rod to right or left, the point of which is near the water. If you strike violently, you will probably leave the fly in your fish.

Now look out for fireworks. As a rule a fish does not make off at once when he is hooked. He generally gives you time to collect yourself. But sometimes he is off in a flash and I find this more so with Norwegian fish and Iceland fish.

Hold the top of your rod high and if you are wading, get out of the water as soon as you can, because you may have to run for it.

Personally, I always like keeping abreast of my fish when I can, and it is often fatal to let a fish get a long way below you. Keep a good strain on the rod and keep your hand off the reel when he is running. Never try to stop a running fish, he will break you like cotton.

I always keep *my finger* on the underside of the reel, just touching the line. By doing this you steady the reel and don't get an overrun.

When he is tired of running and you have steadied him down, then begin to reel in. Sometimes he will come in slowly, a yard at a time. If he refuses to come in, put a side strain on your rod and that generally moves him. If he sulks, which I hardly ever find if you keep him on the move, a few taps on your rod butt may start him moving.

Now you have the fish, say, within fifteen or twenty feet from your bank and if you have a gillie to gaff him, walk back a few paces if you can, as this does not put such a strain on your rod and tackle.

Never be in a hurry to gaff your fish. As a rule, wait until he is on his side. I have seen so many fish lost by being in a hurry. Also make your gillie keep still. Some like to jump about and follow the fish. This is fatal and only frightens them.

If you gaff your own fish, it is more difficult, and you must take your rod in your left hand, keeping your arm well behind you. Keep a yard of slack line under your forefinger and when you gaff your fish, let this go, otherwise you may break the top of your rod.

Having gaffed your fish, hit it on the head immediately. For this purpose, keep what is known as a "Priest"—a small metal rod with a "blob" at the end. Keep this in your pocket. It is horrid to see a fish jumping about on the bank. That is all the time I have to tell you about this style of fishing.

Before I leave this I might just mention the question of flies. Personally, I suppose I have well over a thousand flies, because I like making them, but in practice I use very few.

If you have a *Jock Scott*, *Silver Doctor*, *Black Doctor*, *Thunder and Lightning*, *Blue Charm*, *Logie*, in various sizes from small to large, then you won't go far wrong. But it is hardly for me to tell you that!

A few words about greased-line fishing. When Mr Wood invented this style of fishing he broke almost every rule and upset all the theories and traditions of the old school. So you can imagine the controversy that went on when he gave this to the fishing world. But there was no answer against it, as he succeeded in catching more fish on the Dee than, I suppose, anyone else, and under conditions when the old method was hopeless.

If you want to study this, and I am sure you will—then you must read those two excellent books *Greased Line Fishing*, by Jock Scott and *The Floating Line for Salmon and Sea Trout*, by Crossley. These will tell you far more than I am able to tell you, and put Mr Wood's methods in a very clear way, and both books deserve great credit to the authors. One of my great regrets is that I have never had the opportunity of meeting Mr Wood, although we corresponded and he kindly asked me to come and see him. I was unable to accept his invitation at the time.

To be very brief, as there is no time for much more, Mr Wood's idea was to allow the fly to swim naturally down with the stream, without any form of drag. Except in very heavy water and when the temperature was low, he used very small flies, with hardly any dressing, on fine gut and an eleven-foot rod.

His method of casting was with a single-handed rod, more up-stream, or across, than down. His line was slack, with no pull on the fly. He would mend his line when the current was in-clined to pull his fly. By mending the line, he threw a loop of slack line upstream, or down, according to the eddies or current, always for the purpose of avoiding drag on the fly. He greased his line, so as to make it float and not sink and drag.

To mend your line without disturbing your fly, is not easy. Sometimes he would mend his line three times in a cast. Some-times he would pull off three or four yards of line and let it all go slack.

When you start fishing in this way, it seems almost incredible that a salmon will rise up and take it. But the point is that they *do*. It is a delightful form of fishing. For one thing, you are not encumbered with a heavy rod, and your fish more often than not makes a head and tail rise, which is so nice to see.

But when he does this, don't strike, give him plenty of time and see your greased line being taken away. When you have given him plenty of time, strike sideways, not a sudden strike, more of a sweep of the rod, and you will find he is well hooked.

In clear water, it is surprising what a small fly a salmon will take. Flies must be dressed very lightly. That is to say, very little wing and hackle.

I often fish greased line with a single-handed rod of eleven feet, but if you feel that this is too much single handed, then use a double-handed rod twelve or thirteen feet. It is surprising how quickly you can kill your fish on an eleven-foot rod. You require plenty of line, about 140 yards.

Now, as time is short, this is all I can tell you on greased-line fishing. Buy your book and study it carefully, and you will have some very happy days.

SPINNING

I am not going to touch on this branch of fishing for salmon. Not because I don't spin, but for one thing, this is a talk on *fly fishing*; and another, I don't want you to start spinning too early in life. In the last few years there has been far too much spinning both for trout and salmon on many of our rivers. I have seen so many cases where good fly water has been spoiled, having been over fished with minnow and prawn. By all means spin, when it is out of the question to do otherwise, but leave your spinning alone until the fly is found to be quite useless.

Fly fishing for salmon is an art and a game and should be treated as such. We know that we can get salmon out of a river in various ways, but it is not merely the catching of fish we are after. It is the SPORT of catching them on a fly, which, in my opinion, is far more attractive than any other method.

So, let me say this: don't be too eager to get out your spinning rod, because, after a time, you will find it becomes an obsession and, for the sake of your conscience, you will merely run over a pool lightly with your fly, the whole time "itching" to get at your spinning rod, with which you have grown to have more faith.

So, don't let this get hold of you, otherwise it will spoil your days. You may not catch so many fish, but what does that matter. So that is all that you will hear from me about spinning.

And now, boys and girls, I must finish my talk on "Fly Fishing".

I have tried to cover a lot of ground in a very short time, and I hope that I have not bored you or been telling you all the time about things which you know quite well. But, as you know, I was asked to lecture to the young and inexperienced, and if you have picked up a few things which you did not know before, I shall be well satisfied.

If there is anyone who would like to come up and ask me a few questions, I shall be very happy to answer them.

To the rest of my audience, I say "Good night and tight lines".'

KEEP OUT OF SIGHT.

XVIII

CASTING

I HERE reproduce an article which I wrote some years ago for *The Salmon and Trout Magazine.*

Casting—The Advantage of Combining Theory and Practice,
by John Rennie

'In the above title I purposely left out the word "Tournaments", as it produces a peculiar effect on some fishermen! My aim is to interest fishermen in this form of sport and to point out the benefits that have been derived from competitions and the influence they have had on present-day fishing rods.

'May I take my own experience which dates back some good many years, when my friend, Mr Campbell Muir, asked me to come to the Crystal Palace Tournament, in the year 1907. In those days I was a moderate caster and a day's fishing with an eighteen-feet salmon rod was a very hard day's work, and a cast of twenty-five to thirty yards was a great effort. At the Crystal Palace I saw prodigious casts of thirty-eight to forty yards with a salmon rod, and twenty-seven yards with a trout rod.

'My next experience was at the White City Tournament, in 1908. I had then begun to take a little interest and had ordered a Castleconnell rod from John Enright. What a rod it was! It nearly threw me into the water. For some reason or other, the judges refused to accept it as a fishing rod, and I was thankful to hand it back to Enright. Someone lent me a rod, and after cracking off a fly or two and hitting the ground at the back several times, I think I was credited with twenty-eight yards!

'After this the British Amateur Fly and Bait Casting Club was formed in about the year 1909 or 1910. I became a member, and, from that time on, I began to take a greater interest in casting, partly for the fun of the game, but more especially to learn about rods and lines, so that in actual fishing my casting should be a pleasure with the least possible effort. My casting improved out of all knowledge, and so did my fishing. I am certain that with a fourteen-feet split-cane rod I can cast with ease a line which I could never have done with my seventeen-feet or eighteen-feet rods. At the end of the day I am not tired, no matter what length of line I have been casting.

'In 1910 I found that my length of salmon line had increased to thirty-five yards, and on one occasion I nearly touched the forty yards mark. In 1911, I think, the Club closed its doors, and it was not until 1922 that I started again to take an interest in casting and attended the Paris Tournament.

'I was greatly struck by the pleasant surroundings and the hospitality and "bonhomie" which prevailed: the "Casting Club de France" was really more than hospitable. In a short time we were all friends, and I was much impressed with the way in which our French friends cast, and their keenness. I learned quite a lot in Paris in 1922 and 1923, and at the same time found my length with a salmon rod had increased to thirty-eight yards. Beyond this I could not go, and I felt it was a question of studying rods and lines more intimately if I was to achieve a throw of forty yards.

'I found that by trying various lines of different weights and taper I could increase my cast quite appreciably. The difficulty was that without a proper stretch of water I could not carry out these experiments, so I made a pond forty yards long and marked it out in feet and yards. I thought that forty yards would be quite long enough, but this pond has now become too short for myself and for some of my friends. In fact we have increased our casting capacity to forty-four and forty-six yards simply by the attention we have paid to our tackle, and we have made a few casts up to fifty yards.

'Messrs Hardy and Farlow, who have taken a great interest in our sport, have been most kind in sending down rods to try, and on one occasion Mr Marston, of the *Fishing Gazette*, came down with six beautiful rods made by Hardy, and all built on different principles, so that we could try out each one. The results were very interesting.

'These two makers have now revolutionized casting and added greatly to the pleasure it gives to the caster.

'Most people probably know that atmosphere plays a great part in casting: that is one of the reasons why the Americans are credited with such long casts. In heavy, dull weather the line will not go out in the same way that it does on a dry day and in a light atmosphere. Let the Americans come over here and try their long casts and they will be surprised. I believe one did go over to Paris, and was astounded at the difference.*

'I wonder how many people have considered this point. A man, or a woman can, with a nine-feet rod weighing five ounces, put out a line from twenty-eight to thirty yards, but to get out another ten yards of line will require a very strong and heavy rod of some sixteen or seventeen feet and about ten horse-power behind it. Why is this?

'For an answer I would refer the reader to some articles which came out in that excellent paper *Game and Gun* and *The Anglers' Monthly* in the early

---

*Since these words were written, the Americans came over here before the war and showed us some wonderful casting; but they never equalled the casting records made in America.

part of 1930. These articles were written by Professor Borchgrevink, of Norway, and he went into the whole question from the mathematical point of view. As far as I can remember, he explains that the forces which stop the line in its passage through the air are air resistance and friction. It follows that the smaller the "entrance" a line has in coming forward the less the resistance. In order to obtain a small entrance, the line should point horizontally backward at the moment when the forward cast is made. If the line falls below the horizontal, then a belly will be formed when the forward cast is made, and so the resistance increases enormously. This full extension of the line horizontally on the back cast is most important, and it will be seen that to obtain it, timing to a fraction of a second is necessary.

'Professor Borchgrevink has pointed out that the line velocities are very great and correspond to a speed of sixty-eight miles per hour, so that when you have thirty-five to thirty-eight yards in the air and have to maintain this speed, the power required to do so is very considerable.

'In order to overcome wind resistance, the line should be as thin as is possible in relation to the rod. A thin line heavily dressed is the ideal.

'Perhaps I have said enough on this subject, but I merely wish to point out the interest which can be obtained from the study of casting.

'At Tournaments a few years ago a cast of forty yards with a salmon rod was generally a winner. Now you have to do forty-four or forty-six yards to have any hope of winning. In a few years' time, I think it will need fifty yards. There are quite a number of casters now who can cast forty yards, and fifty yards and more have now been obtained.

'I do not mean to say that the rods are not rather "special" rods. In the same way, you require a "special" car if you want to win the Tourist Trophy race, and we should never have seen our touring cars reach their present state of perfection and speed if it had not been for the influence of motor racing. So I think the same thing can be said of our fishing rods. Tournaments have done what nothing else would have done.

'A good comfortable fishing rod can cast thirty-nine yards, but something a little stronger and stiffer is needed to get forty-four to forty-six yards. The ordinary fishing rod will not lift and provide the extra velocity to the line which gives those few coveted extra yards. Apart from this, tournaments bring a lot of nice fishermen together, and we have lots of fun and plenty to talk about. I wish there were private casting tournaments as there are lawn-tennis tournaments, but, of course, there is always the difficulty of water, whereas for tennis there are plenty of courts available.

'Finally, I should like to see some sporting person provide a really handsome trophy and run it on the "Schneider Trophy" principle, the trophy to be competed for by any club in the world, each club being represented by three members. We might get the London clubs to join in, and one can imagine the Athenaeum competing with the Fly Fishers' Club and Whites having a great battle with the Royal Air Force! The foreign clubs would join in and make an international interest.

'The first thing is to find some public-spirited person to provide the Cup, and then I am sure there would be no lack of interest or entries.

'Will someone please come forward!'

You will see at the end of the article I asked for some public-spirited person to come along and provide a trophy. The following year the Duke of Westminster presented a very handsome cup to the 'British Field Sports' for this purpose and we held a most excellent and enjoyable Tournament at Denham. Various Clubs were represented, and two Regiments. The Cup was won by the Bath Club, the team being Laurie Dunne, Dickie and myself.

I also reproduce an article written by Dr Barton for the *Fly Fishers' Club Journal*, of which he is the popular Editor.

A Fly Casting Competition

'The late W. D. Coggeshall used to relate how that on one occasion when fishing in Scotland an American in the same hotel approached him expressing a wish actually to see a salmon caught, and asking Coggeshall if he might accompany him on the morrow. In the well-known kindness of his heart he agreed to take him out on the following day. After casting fruitlessly for some time, Coggeshall was surprised by the stranger asking him if he might try the rod. The rod was passed over to him with some misgiving, and much to Coggeshall's wonder the stranger cast a beautiful line, straighter and farther than he himself could do. On the stranger handing back the rod, Coggeshall said to him, "But you tell me that you have never fished. How is it that you cast so well?" To which the stranger replied, "I have never caught a fish nor seen a salmon caught, but I am a casting champion in America."

'Therefore and for other reasons, it was that when I had my orders from W. E. to cover the Fly Casting Competition at Thorney Weir, in June last, I jumped at the change from my usual work, slung my camera over my shoulder and found myself amongst a number of the Members of the Club. The day was ideal with no wind, the curse of such gatherings.

'The object of such tourneys is not only competitive as to the casting, but no less to discover the vices and virtues of rods of different make: just as in flying competitions the principal object is the elimination of inferior engines and the resulting triumph of the best manufacturer. Consequently there are many small differences between casting long distances and casting in actual angling.

'The line used in long-distance casting is never greased; indeed it is highly polished, the better to run easily through the rings in shooting the last few yards. Also the line is pulled off on the staging from which the competitor makes his cast in order that it may be picked up quickly during the extension of the line before the final cast is made. The fly is a large one, often a "coachman'', for it is important that the marker should be able to record the exact spot on the marking-board alongside which the fly falls. The action in long distance casting is quite distinct from that used in ordinary angling, for the arm is outstretched to its utmost in order to give some security against touching the water behind, such a touch behind the caster disqualifying the cast. Then, too, the caster looks behind him as he recovers his line, and keeps his eye on the fly as it passes behind him to observe whether he has enough clearance from the water.

'I have ventured to depict the nice action of Mr Rennie, both in salmon and small-rod casting. It will be seen that the coils of the line on the staging are being taken up as the cast lengthens. Though he did not win the trout-rod casting, he might have done so had he not just touched the water behind him in a final cast. His picture shows him casting twenty-nine yards two feet.'

These two articles give some idea of what we aim at. It is not fishing, but it is a sport and helps you a great deal in the knowledge of rods and lines and how to use them, and brings a lot of fishing friends together and helps to spend a jolly day talking about fishing with all its arts and wonders.

For many years I held a casting tournament at my home in Berkshire. The programme was as follows:

1. Accuracy. This consisted of a number of floating hoops placed about the pond in various difficult places. Each competitor had three shots with a dry fly at each hoop. If you got in at the first shot it counted three, the second shot two and the third shot one. A possible six points for each hoop, or a maximum of thirty points for the round. It was really extraordinary the small number of points that were scored. Looking up my records I find that the winners scored only nine to eleven points, and many of them were good dry fly fishermen!

After 'Accuracy' we generally had lunch, and lunch was lunch in those days—looking at the menu, which is now before me, I can hardly imagine that these things really existed. Of course I am writing of 1944 when there was a war on. I say this, as in five or ten years hence there are many who may have forgotten what the war was about, but I can remind them that in 1944 there were not many chickens, tongues, hams and rounds of beef, and glasses of port to talk about!

After an hour and a half of good fishing gossip, we went forth to try our skill and strength in casting a trout fly as far as we

Plates 9-10

Top. RIVER DEE, CAIRNTON. THIS IS TAKEN JUST BELOW THE LODGE. THE POOLS BELOW THIS
ARE SOME OF THE BEST ON THE CAIRNTON WATER. ON THE OPPOSITE BANK IS BLACKHALL.
Bottom. WOODEND, RIVER DEE. THIS IS ONE OF THE BEST STRETCHES ON THE DEE. IN THE
DISTANCE THE GARDEN POOL AND BLUE CHAIR CAN BE SEEN, WHILE JUST BELOW IS THE BOAT
POOL AND THE LEAP.

could. This was a handicap event and the handicaps were made up the night before by myself and those staying in the house. 'Bogey' was set at thirty yards. Then we discussed the casters— we were very frank, and the conversation ran like this. 'What about Mr J.?' 'Oh, he is a rotten caster. Of course he can catch fish, but he can't cast more than twenty yards', so he got ten points to bring him up to Bogey thirty points. Then there was Mr K. 'He is a dashed good caster, he got twenty-five yards last year, we will give him five points'.

The difficulty was that, when it came to handicapping, those who were staying in the house always thought that I had under-handicapped them, and wanted me to give them a few more points. But I was very stern and looked up their past records. My handicapping became so good that on one occasion there was only a yard separating the first four.

Finally we finished up with salmon-fly distance. The pond was originally forty yards long, but eventually I had to increase it to fifty yards. There were only two people who ever touched this, and those casts were not in tournament.

So much for casting tournaments, and I hope this chapter will give some idea of their importance to fishing to those who have never attended one.

BARTON COURT R. KENNET

XIX

A MIXED BAG

Season 1929

I SEE that the spring of 1929 was most unusual. In February down south we had thirty degrees of frost lasting for three weeks, and there had been no rain since December. Rivers were running at summer level and the Wye and Usk were unfishable. At Easter, on the Usk there was no water and no fish. This continued into April. I was due to leave for the Shannon on 21st April. On 18th April I heard the cuckoo for the first time. Year after year we hear him at the same date almost to a day.

On 22nd April I went to Castleconnell. The fishing was disappointing this year and my best fish was thirty-two pounds.

I went over to see the Maigue, at Adair, one Sunday. I had heard much about it as a trout river. The May fly was just coming on and many nice trout were moving. By staying at the Dunraven Arms, Adair, you have the privilege of fishing quite a long stretch of water. It is a very comfortable and nice hotel.

The Kennet, this year, was very low, but I had some good days on the Craven water, Littlecote, Barton Court and Denford, and Avington. Altogether I got thirty fish of sixty pounds weight, but nothing over three pounds.

In June I made a trip to Norway. This was more in the nature of a voyage of discovery than a fishing trip: I wanted to find out about the rivers in the Trondhjem district, and what possibilities there were for fishing in the future. The expedition, as far as fishing was concerned, was disappointing. From Trondhjem I went by car to the Gula Hotel on the Surendal River, a nice little place and a grand river. But alas! it has a history of the past. Owing to overnetting and trapping there was hardly a fish in the river. One guest in the hotel had been fishing for a month and had only got two small fish. The river may have improved in later years—I hope so.

I was told that there was good trout fishing in a small river up in the mountains, a six-hour climb. So off I went. I am not particularly fond of mountain climbing, but I really did enjoy this, although at the end of the journey I found that there were no trout in the stream and the mosquitoes were simply awful. I spent the night in the woodcutters' hut with three Norwegians. As I could speak no Norwegian and they no English, the conversation was limited. We lit a wood fire and smoked the place out to try and get rid of the mosquitoes but with little result. Next day I trudged back again, and I came to the conclusion that rivers and lakes at the top of mountains are, for the most part, entirely in the imagination of the locals. I have never yet found one and my friend, Archie Ross, who was always looking for these wonderful places, never found one. Now I leave those little excursions to the very young and hopeful.

On the way back to Trondhjem I passed those two great salmon rivers, the Goula and Orkla. At one time these two rivers ranked as two of the finest rivers in Norway. When I was there, they were almost fishless. Unlimited sea netting all along the coast, and trapping in the river, had entirely spoiled them.

It was short-sighted policy on the part of the farmer-owners. They received very high rents and much money was spent by the fishing tenants. Many built themselves houses. Unless things have improved in recent years, and I doubt it, these rivers are of little use to the fishermen. I was offered a beat in 1936, but the records were so bad I did not think it worth while.

Before I left Trondhjem I was given two days' fishing on the Nid, a fine river that runs through the town. Just above the town, there is a grand waterfall and hydro-electric plant, and I fancy that few fish get above this. There are big fish in this water and plenty of sea trout, and a few days' fishing here are well spent. From here I went on to Oslo and so home.

I had learned quite a lot of this part of Norway, and came to the conclusion that it would be waste of time to go to this district for a fishing trip until some curtailment had been made on the netting rights and traps.

Season 1930

I had often heard of that famous little river, the Leannan, Ramelton, Co. Donegal. I had known several people who had fished there, and the salmon catches were prodigious at times. There is really only one pool about a quarter of a mile long, then there is a weir and traps and a small pool below—after that, tidal water. At the top of the Long Pool there is a waterfall and no ladder. Consequently, of the hundreds of fish that run into the pool, only a very few manage to get above the falls and into Lough Fern until later in the season. I am told that during the last few years, some sort of ladder has been built which enables the fish to run straight through the pool and into the lake some two or three miles above. But the Ramelton Pool is no longer the fishing it used to be, and takes are now quite moderate to what they were in former years.

Before this the fish could not, or would not, negotiate the obstruction before May.

Some years after this I fished the upper river and Lough Fern in May, and I was surprised at the number of fish. It was no uncommon thing to get two or three fish in a day from the boat. An eleven-feet rod and fine tackle with No. 8, 9 and 10 flies was all you required, but plenty of line on your reel, as they are great runners. The upper river and lake are free fishing, and it is probably some of the best free salmon fishing in Ireland.

In 1930 I was not very fortunate with the weather at Ramelton. I arrived on 18th March in a snow storm: it was bitterly cold. I found George Maunsell just departing. He had had a rotten time and only got two or three fish in ten days. Few fish were up, and no rain. Next day the water was in flood and very thick with six inches of snow on the ground. The only thing was to put up a bait and I got a nice fish of eighteen pounds. For the next two days the water was unfishable, and so it went on until the end of the month, but I picked up quite a number of fish one way and another.

On 30th March the water was steady, but nothing moving until 12 noon, when suddenly the fish started taking and I got three good fish, seventeen, fifteen and twelve pounds, in an hour. I thought I was now in for one of those great 'Ramelton' days, and looked forward to another six or eight fish at least. Then suddenly there was a storm, and not another fish moved.

It rained all night, and next day was a sight I shall never forget. There were hundreds and hundreds of fish slithering up and over the weir—I say 'slithering' because that was what they were doing—not jumping—there was not enough water to cover them. When they got into the pool, they were rising head and tail everywhere. I worked my hardest and tried my best. I felt an awful 'mug' and went home without a fish. I suppose the reason was that they had just arrived in fresh water and took a little time to settle down.

With a little more kindness on the part of the weather I might have had a great time. The rods that followed after me did have a good time in April, and got between 100 and 200 fish. The late Col. Claude Beddington and Col. Bowles and another rod were the lucky ones.

Ramelton was a dirty little town and everything looked impoverished and tumbledown. Goodwin's Hotel was quite passable and the people most obliging and civil. Mr Goodwin was an Essex man, which accounted for the cleanness and good plain food. I believe it has changed hands since 1930, but if it is still going, I can recommend it as a centre for fishing the Upper Leannan and Lough Fern, and you will have a cheap and enjoyable holiday with some sport and, if you are lucky, good sport. May is the month, and June is also good.

I used to write funny things in my diary—for instance at the end of this trip I find the following—why I put it down I don't know—'No human being has ever appeared to another as he appears to himself, and that the only hope of having a "personality" is being unconscious of it yourself.' Quite true, I am sure, but what has that got to do with fishing?

11th April. I shall always remember this trip to my friend, J. Arthur Hutton, at his famous fishing on the Wye. I have seldom spent a more enjoyable week-end. Hutton is a great conversationalist and a most interesting one and not only that, he is a good listener to anything of interest you have to say. This makes conversation agreeable, but it keeps you up very late at night when the day's work is done. Hutton told me many things, but what impressed me more than anything was his statistics. Nothing was left undone—temperatures of air, water, density of water, height of water, etc., size and colour of bait or fly under all these conditions. These records covered a long number of years, so that one came to the conclusion that at a certain height of water at a certain density and at a certain temperature, if you put on, say, a two-inch Silver Devon, you caught fish. If you did not catch a fish, it was the fish's fault and not yours.

I am very glad that I had the opportunity of seeing this water, and when the other day I read Arthur Hutton's latest book on the history of this water, it made it all the more interesting.

On the 25th April I went down to fish the Wye again with my friend, Bill Ratcliffe: he was fishing Sir Geoffrey Cornewall's water. I always enjoyed these trips—Bill was a perfect fishing companion.

I got a nice fish of twenty-three pounds and then a flood started coming down. That so often happens when you are fishing the Wye. The river is always up and down, owing to the drainage. Formerly this did not happen and the river was much steadier. I suppose these Catchment Boards do some good, but I rather doubt it myself and, from what I hear, the farmers are not too pleased.

To fish the Wye with any success, you now have to live on the water. On the last three occasions I went down there I never unpacked my rods. As I can't live down there, I have now given it up, and prefer to take my chance in Scotland for three or four weeks when, if there is a flood, you will know that you will probably be fishing the next day.

On the 9th of May, I started off to Ireland to fish the Shannon for the last time before it was ruined as a salmon river by the Hydro-Electric Scheme.

I had taken Woodlands Beat. Although I got a fair number of fish one could see that the 'Works' had already done harm to the fishing. There was nothing like the number of fish in the river, and I presume they had already started to go up the 'Tail race' and were not too keen to face the salmon ladder.

On Sunday, 11th May, I did not fish, as I went to inspect the salmon ladder with the Engineer-in-Charge, Mr Hansard. It certainly looked to me to be a beautiful ladder and very easy to negotiate. The interesting thing was seeing the fish going up in the various stages. At each stage they would take a rest, then go up another step and take another rest, and so on until they got to the top. I saw great fish of twenty and thirty pounds waddling up, quite unconcerned at my presence, only a yard or so away, and big trout of four or five pounds doing the same thing. Why were they not frightened?—in the river they would have been terrified.

From the Shannon I went on to Lough Arrow to fish the May fly. I got there on 19th May and found that I was a bit early for the May fly. I was staying with Frank Gethin at Ballindoon House. This is a delightful place, standing well up on a hill over-looking the Lough and only five minutes' walk down to the boathouse. The whole of the hill down to the boathouse was one mass of bluebells; a more ideal spot for a fishing centre on Lough Arrow you could not wish for. With a pair of glasses—and you want these on Lough Arrow—you could scan a great part of the lake and see if the fly was up and what bays were sheltered and free of fishermen. There was always a certain amount of jealousy about these fishing bays and some fishermen used to think that their particular bay really belonged to them. I remember one man whose boat was hauled up on the shore and who was not fishing at the time, hurled abuse at me when I entered the bay. So I said to him, 'If your fishing is as bad as your language, it must be pretty rotten!' He danced up and down and was so funny that my boatman and I could do nothing but roar with laughter. But this sort of thing does not often happen, and most of the folk are quite friendly.

I have always had a strong feeling that those outboard motors were spoiling the fishing on these Loughs. On Lough Sheelin I told the Committee who used to have an Annual Meeting on one of the Islands, that I felt sure of this from what I had seen. If an outboard is used with discretion, there is little harm, but so many of the owners have not the slightest regard for others and come motoring into a bay at full steam, and put every fish down.

I will give one example of an experience I had. It was a perfect evening for the dry fly man—not a ripple on the water, and the spent gnat falling in nice numbers all over the lake. My luck was in. Big trout were rising all round my boat. I got a six-and-a-half-pounder, followed by four and a half pounds, three pounds, and a couple of two-pounders. And so it would have gone on, but! there was a boat with an outboard about 100 yards from me. Whether he was hungry or could not catch the fish I don't know, but the occupant started up his outboard, which was a particularly noisy one, and away he went. The result was that every feeding fish, as far as I could see, was put down, and the rise was over. These vibrations in the water can be felt by the fish over a very great distance. One thing more in support of this theory—since the war, petrol has often been *non est* for motor-boats. I hear from Lough Arrow that last year was one of the best they have ever had!

I myself own an outboard on Lough Arrow, but I use it only if I want to get to a particular spot on the Lough, and cut off the motor before I get into the bays. In this I do not think that there is much harm done, but I would prefer to see a rule made by the Associations on the various Loughs prohibiting the use of motor-boats, say between the hours of 10.30 and 6 p.m. This gives time to people to get to their fishing places and get back home in time for dinner. In the meantime, if they want to change their fishing ground, let them row the boat.

I think that the most suitable rod is nine feet six inches to ten feet. I am speaking only for dry fly fishermen. A reel with quite seventy to eighty yards of line and backing. Nothing finer than 2X cast for May fly and 1X cast in the evening. Anything less means disaster with the big fish. There was a well-known chalkstream fisherman who fished Lough Arrow once and who would persist in using 3X and 4X tapered casts, against all advice. He was broken up time after time in big fish.

Although I have seen very big trout at Lough Arrow, up to nine and ten pounds, the largest trout I ever saw were on Lough

Sheelin. There I saw a fish which I put down at anything between fourteen and seventeen pounds. I actually rose him after a chase of half a mile: he was feeding on spent gnat and never stopped moving. Eventually when I did rise him, I was too quick and I put him down. My nephew, who was fishing the same place the following night, rose him again. When I asked him afterwards what size he thought he was, he said seventeen pounds; and he is a good judge and a first-class fisherman.

On 30th May I had to leave Lough Arrow and went out in the morning with an old fishing friend. There was practically no rise of fly, so my friend produced from a box a large number of Green Drake, caught the day before, and let them go in twos and threes on the water, so creating an artificial rise. The response was immediate: fish came up and started rising round the boat, and in half an hour I got four fish, all from two and a quarter to two and a half pounds. The question is—was this 'cricket'? I think so. Another tip is to shake the trees overhanging the water. This often brings down a lot of flies and as they drift away the fish start coming up. I have followed a drift like this for quite a long way and picked up an odd fish.

In dry fly fishing on a lake there are two schools of thought as to the best method to adopt. One is to sit still in your boat all day long and not paddle about. The other is to paddle about and hunt for feeding fish. If you know your Lough well and the way the fish are likely to feed according to the wind, then the first method seems to be equally good as the second.

On the other hand, I feel that sitting still in a boat all day is mighty tedious, and I prefer to move about slowly from place to place. I have often missed good fishing by leaving the bay I had intended to fish, from the boredom of sitting still; but I have often been rewarded by moving on to another point or bay and found fish moving.

As to flies, I never know which pattern I think best. When the green fly first comes on, I think Lock's pattern is as good as any. Then a little later on I like a fly tied with four blue hackle points for wings. A yellowish-greenish hackle and straw body of a yellowish colour. Tail—three whiskers from a hare. These hare whiskers make the fly sit up well and don't get sodden. I think a little Mucilin grease rubbed between the fingers and then over the hackles and tail keeps the fly floating longer than oil.

There is a great temptation in following a feeding trout and a more exciting hunt I do not know. Sometimes he will feed for a quarter of an hour or more. You can back your boat very gently after him and follow in his track, doing your best to keep to the side of him and not directly behind him. Sometimes this is very successful, but sometimes he will turn round and swim right at your boat, and then 'goodbye'. It is most exciting, but you want a good boatman. A clumsy splash of the oar, and your fish is gone.

I remember once on Lough Sheelin going out very early in the morning before the sun was up. I had an idea that the big trout fed in the middle of the Lough early in the morning on the spent gnat which had fallen the night before. I was quite right in my theory. The trouble was that I could not get a boatman to come out so early. I think it must have been about 4 a.m. (G.M.T.) when I got into the boat alone. It was a big clumsy boat and difficult to handle quickly. Sure enough, in the half light I could hear the 'plop' 'plop' of big trout in the distance. Then I came upon a couple of huge fish swimming side by side in the water and taking every fly within reach. They never stopped for a second, but just as I had laid down my oars, got my rod and lengthened my line to twenty yards, the fish were out of reach. The chase went on for a long time and I never got on terms with them. Then suddenly the sun tipped the hills and shone down on the water. Every fish went down and I saw no more of them. If only I had had a companion in the boat I should have had some of those trout.

So much for the May fly fishing on Irish Loughs. It is great fun, and I hope to get back there some day.

On my return in June I fished the Kennet, and had fair sport.

In August I motored up to Loch Awe. I left my home at 3.30 a.m. and got to Carlisle in the afternoon. The early morning is a lovely time to motor. No traffic, lovely air and the world is your own. It is the only time I ever enjoy on the road.

I fished the Awe for a fortnight and got a few salmon and good sea trout. But August is always a poor month on the Awe.

XX

THE CLUB DINNER

ON 16th March, 1931, my dear friend and fishing companion, Sir Archibald Ross, died after a long illness. We had fished together in many places and a better companion no one could wish for. I never tire of thinking of him.

This year I had to take the chair at the Fly Fishers' Club Dinner. This is a bit of an ordeal to anyone who has had little practice in the art of after-dinner speaking. I really was in a blue funk! I took the precaution beforehand to write out my speech very carefully. Then I went and had a few lessons and picked up a few tips.

The awful day arrived and there were about 160 people to dinner. I had to follow after one of the best after-dinner speakers in London, Lord Macmillan. Of course he made a most excellent speech, but knew nothing about fishing. I got through mine, and I hope not too badly—anyway, I got a few laughs and 'hear, hears', which is always encouraging.

On March 20th I went down to the Hampshire Avon for a couple of days to the Winkton fishery, about three miles from Christchurch. It was always a great pleasure to go and stay with my friends, the Ernest Bakers, and the Avon has many attractions in the early spring. One appreciates this after having spent so many dreary weeks running up and down to London.

I got a fish of thirty pounds on the fly: as a rule they don't take the fly very much before late April and May. What lovely shaped fish these Avon fish are, and the best eating fish in the world.

In May I went over to Ireland to try the upper part of the Leannan river at Ramelton. As I have said before, this is one of the best 'free fishing' lakes and river waters in Ireland. I found that in the river the salmon like a small prawn or large fresh shrimp, fished with a single hook and very fine tackle; they were shy at pulling the fly; but on the lake they rise well to the fly.

From Ramelton I went on to Lough Arrow, but I need say no more about this, as I have already said quite a lot in the previous year. After that a few nice days on the Kennet and Test, and then nothing more until 28th July, when I left for the Laerdal in Norway.

Incidentally, I had never lost an umbrella in my life, but somehow or other I managed to lose mine at Kings Cross. I was much upset at this and tipped all kinds of porters and guards in the hope of finding it. However, the train went and there was nothing more I could do.

On arrival at Newcastle one of my travelling companions saw the guard walking down the train with an umbrella. I dashed out and found it was mine. So another five bob went!

From Newcastle we travelled on the new ship *Venus*—most luxurious and comfortable, with a speed of over twenty knots. Hot and cold water in the cabins, cocktail bar and wonderful food. On the first night they always have a great assortment of lobsters, smoked salmon, prawns, caviare, etc. It's just as well to make the best of these good things while you can, as later on you may not care about them. When I think of these things nowadays, it makes me feel horribly greedy. We got to Bergen next day at 5 p.m., having taken only twenty-two hours in the crossing: I wish it had been longer. It is a longish day from Bergen to Laerdal, but a very beautiful journey. We caught the 8 a.m. train to Myrdaal, which is the highest point on the Bergen-Oslo railway. The line from Bergen to Myrdaal follows that wonderful river, the Evanger, where the average weight of the fish is over thirty pounds. I had not fished it then, but in later years I had the pleasure of fishing it on two occasions.

From the station at Myrdaal you get into a pony trap and go down from a long winding pass to Fretheim which is at the head of the Sogne fjord. There is a nice little river which holds very big salmon and sea trout, and there is quite a good hotel in the Norwegian style. At Fretheim you get into a small fjord steamer which calls on its way at Aurland. I jumped out and ran ashore to have a look at the Aurland river and to see my old friend at the hotel, but soon I heard the whistle sounding and I had to run for the boat.

We got to Lindstrom's Hotel, Laerdal, late that night, had some supper and went to bed. We stayed in the annexe of the hotel and were not troubled by all the tourists who go through. Next day was spent in unpacking and getting things straight, with a walk up the river to see if there are many sea trout about. The river was very low and incredibly clear, but we saw quite a number of sea trout. I have often wondered which of these two sea trout rivers I liked the best, the Aurland or the Laerdal, and I have never been able to make up my mind. They hold equally large numbers of sea trout, both of which rise well to the dry fly. The Laerdal has the advantage of not being so closely shut in by the mountains, but I shall never be able to decide. The fact is, they are equally nice, each in its own way.

We had wonderful sport both with sea trout and salmon, but we were rather on the late side. July is better than August, and the fish take more freely.

The great thing in this type of dry fly fishing is to have a fly which floats well. The water is rough in places, and you must have something which will keep afloat. If the fly gets 'soggy' you do no good. A large Tup, Coch y bondhu or black hackle fly we found the best. Also a fly dressed with badger fur is very good at times. It was John Henderson on Lough Arrow who invented this fly, thirty years ago. Don't have it overdressed with fur, otherwise you will get plenty of rises but few fish. If you have a longish walk to take between pools, take off your cast and put it in your damper—for preference a rubber tobacco pouch, slightly wet inside. The dry atmosphere, together with the constant drying of the fly, makes the cast very brittle in warm weather. It is very little trouble and well worth it, and will save you quite a lot in flies left in the fish's mouth!

In the evening I always used to fish for salmon, often getting three in one evening. When the light had gone, I would put on a large white-winged Ackroyd, about three inches. It was very amusing when my *klepper* used to say every evening, 'Oh, Mr Rennie, not so big—much too big', to which I would answer, 'Well, Hoveland, we caught two on it last night, why not again tonight?' and sure enough, the next night, two or three fish. But Hoveland never liked the fly.

A curious thing happened to me one night. I got into a good fish, something in the twenty or thirty-pounder type: he gave me a great fight and at last I managed to get the best of him and when, within twenty yards of me, I suddenly saw my heavy casting line disappearing through the rings, I made a grab at it, but it was gone, and so was the fish. I examined the line and it was cut perfectly clean in the middle of the thickest part of the taper, just as if it had been cut with a knife. I have never been able to discover the mystery of this. I was fishing a pool where there were no rocks, and there was nothing to touch me behind.

I remember another funny thing happening, and in the same pool. I was fishing with a big two-and-a-half-inch fly and got into a good fish. After a quarter of an hour the fight was over and he was coming in. Suddenly the rod top went up and my fish was gone. I naturally thought that the hold had given way, but on looking at the fly I found that the iron had broken in half in the straight part and not in the bend.

On another occasion on this pool I was fishing in a gale of wind, and, as does happen sometimes, the line caught on the handle of the reel. This is quite an ordinary thing to happen and instinctively one clears it, but I did not do so on this occasion and a fish took me almost immediately after the fly had hit the water. There was a terrific bang and a break. The treble gut broke, and not the single. Soon after that my feet gave way, and I was entirely submerged! I stripped off everything and we made a fire and dried the clothes as much as we could, started fishing again and was rewarded with a good fish of twenty-three pounds. It was now time to go home. I always feel that there was a 'Hoodoo' on that pool.

We were only fishing fly for salmon, but the last evening I said that I was going to try a prawn, as I wanted some fish for smoking. I got up to the 'Hoodoo' pool at 5 p.m. and the *klepper* and I counted thirty-six salmon. He thought it would be better to fish it a little later on, owing to the light, so we went up above, where I rose and hooked a very large sea trout on a floating March Brown, but he got the best of me. When I came back to the pool about one and a half hours afterwards, there was not a single salmon to be seen in the pool. I got one small fish lower down, and that was all. Now, if I had only followed my own inclination I feel sure I should have got two or three fish. But what made them all suddenly move? That evening, rain started to come down, so I think it must have been that.

The mixture of salmon and sea trout fishing was great fun, but although the salmon were beginning to turn a bit red, they put up a magnificent fight in most cases.

It was now the 21st August, and we had to leave the next day.

July is a better month for sea trout, but we could not complain, we had done very well.

On 4th September I went over to Lough Arrow on a visit to my friend, Lord Kingston. There is always a chance of getting a few big fish in September, but the big ones were not moving much. It was lovely weather, and a nice finish up for the season. One day we went over to see Kingston's house, Kilronan Castle, which was shut up. He had one of the finest collections of African heads I have ever seen. These were all hung in a huge hall which showed them off well. The Sinn Feiners took charge of the place at one time and did a little big game shooting in the hall, but not much damage was done. I regret to say that Lord Kingston died in January, 1946. He was a great sportsman.

I find that on my return I went for a day's fishing with General Madocks, who had water on the Avon at Woodford. What pretty water this is, and what a nice lot of free-rising fish.

On the whole, 1931 was a grand year, crammed full with all kinds of fishing, and all kinds of rivers and country.

XXI

A MIGHTY SALMON

I TOOK the lower Clytha water on the Usk for the 1932 season. This water can be very good in some years, as many as 199 fish have been caught on this beat in the season. But you must have plenty of water if you are going to catch salmon on the Usk, and you must be prepared to go there at a moment's notice after a flood. As neither of these things happened, we did not catch a great number of fish. The trout fishing is good here, but it is always difficult to mix trout with salmon fishing. When you have a trout rod, the salmon seem to be on the move, and when you have a salmon rod, the trout always rise like mad! You may say 'Well, why don't you take a trout rod out with your salmon rod?'—the answer is, as I always fish alone, I find that a spinning rod, a fly rod, long waders, tackle, lunch and probably sketching things, are quite enough without carrying a trout rod and net.

On 26th May I went over again to Lough Arrow to stay with Kingston, but I had only been there for three days when I got a wire from London which called me back on some business. It was a pity, as they had a good year. Owing to these urgent business matters, I was unable to go abroad this year and was obliged to content myself with days on the Usk and Kennet.

A poor fishing season with no outstanding events.

In 1933 I have again taken a beat, but this time on the Upper Clytha water of the river Usk. This is nicer water than the Lower Clytha and we had plenty of rain in the spring, and some really nice fishing.

On 11th March I went down for a day on the Avon—Winkton Water. The whole river was out in flood, but the water was clear

THE FLY FISHERS' CLUB MASCOT

I DESIGNED AND MADE THIS MODEL OF A SALMON FROM A 45-LB. SHANNON FISH CAUGHT BY THE LATE LORD KINGSTON. SEVERAL MEMBERS OF THIS CLUB WERE KIND ENOUGH TO ADMIRE IT, SO I PRESENTED IT TO THE CLUB AS A MODEL FOR A CAR MASCOT.

AT KIMBRIDGE HOUSE. RIVER TEST, MAY 1939

MR NEVILLE CHAMBERLAIN AND SIR JOSEPH BALL. IT WAS A GREAT WEEK-END FISHING.

enough for a big fly. I put on a No. 1/0 fly with a light brown Turkey wing, yellow seal's fur body and yellow hackle. These Avon fish like yellow. A great fish made a huge wave after my fly and I guessed he had missed it. Against all rules of the game, I raised my rod and to my astonishment I found that I was in him. After thirty minutes hard fighting, Ernest Baker gaffed him for me. It was now time for lunch at the hut and we had to wade a good half mile through flooded meadows up to our knees. The fish got heavier and heavier. I said to Ernest, 'I am sure this fish is nearly forty pounds'. He said, 'Yes, I quite agree, John'. He was thirty-eight pounds.

Now, I am quite sure that fish did not mean to take my fly and if I had not raised my rod I should not have caught him where I did—in the underside of the lower jaw! So it pays sometimes to do the wrong thing.

There is a nice little river in Sligo, the Ballysadare. A friend of mine, Captain Percival, had a lease of it. On 25th May he asked me to go over and fish with him.

There was a tidal water below the falls up to which the nets worked, and above this there were three miles of rocky water with a number of nice pools.

One day I was fishing below the falls and there was hardly a fish showing. Presently the boats and the nets came up and made a sweep in the pool where I had been fishing: it was not a large pool. Out came between thirty and forty salmon. It's a horrid sight seeing these beautiful fish knocked on the head with a policeman's truncheon and pitched ashore. It makes you feel rather sick—I would not see it again.

On Sunday we went over to lunch at Templehouse, owned by some cousins of Percival—a fine big Georgian house. We could get no one to answer the bell, so Percival walked in and we went into the drawing room. There I saw the most wonderful collection of Chinese jade I have ever seen. Most of it in glass cupboards with the long windows of the room all open and there was this priceless collection, worth many thousands of pounds, open to the world. I heard afterwards that the collection was sent to the Exhibition of Chinese Art in London and attracted remarkable attention.

So finished a very pleasant little fishing trip.

A day at Littlecote on the Kennet on 7th June with Sir Ernest Wills. The Duke of Beaufort was the other rod. We got a number of small fish, but nothing of much size. There was a great rise of May fly. Several other days on the Kennet fishing with Geoffrey Turner and the late Lord Burnham. The May fly was pretty well over by 10th June this year.

This year, on 8th July, at the British Fly and Bait Casting Tournament, I won the Open Salmon event, also the Amateur Salmon and Trout events.

By August I had tired of the Usk and decided to go and fish the Laerdal. We were a party of three and took a motor-car with us to Oslo and arrived there on 21st August, 1933. That night we got to Farganess, about 120 miles from Oslo. The road was none too good and we got badly ditched at one place, with no means of getting un-ditched. There we remained for an hour or so, when along came a motor-bus. They kindly stopped, took out a tow rope, and had us out in a few minutes. The rest of the journey was uneventful but slow. Next morning we got going again and made the run to Laerdal. At the head of the river there is a gorge and a narrow road leading down to the valley. This road is only passable for one vehicle at a time, so there is a notice at the top and bottom, 'Cars going down are only allowed between the hours of 12 and 1 p.m., cars coming up between the hours of 1 and 2 p.m.', and so on. If anyone had disregarded this rule, I don't know what would have happened.

On the high ground above the river we stopped at an Inn and got some lunch, of sorts. There was a lovely lake and stream. We asked if there were any trout. The owner took us to the kitchen and showed us a basket of trout caught the night before. There were twenty to thirty trout, all about one to one and a half pounds. How they were caught, we could not discover, probably on 'otters' or night lines. There must have been plenty of trout in the loch. I found Lindstrom's Hotel just the same as in previous years, and I had the same rooms in the annexe as before. There was time to go out in the evening and have a quick 'angle'—we came back with three salmon, not a bad beginning.

It was getting a bit late in the year for the Laerdal, but there were a lot of salmon about and a fair number of sea trout.

The salmon were very sulky about taking a fly, so as we were offending nobody, we fished bait part of the time. Salmon, in these clear rivers, get very scared of a prawn. The first day or so, they will grab it—after that they get scared and you have to be careful.

Altogether on this trip we got 150 sea trout and thirty salmon in a fortnight's fishing. Not so bad considering it was so late in the season. The average weight of the sea trout was just two pounds, and salmon fourteen pounds. My best fish was thirty-three pounds.

After this trip I had a few days on the Usk, but the fish were getting red by this time.

Season 1934

I find this note. 'This has been another extraordinarily dry year and a very hot summer. All rivers have been dead low and, except for a short time at Easter, the Wye and Usk have been useless.'

I took no fishing this year on the Wye and Usk, and just as well, as it would have been money wasted. I picked up a few fish on these rivers and fished at Broadlands on the Test one day. The latter place is rather dull fishing to my mind.

In May I went to the Porth Hotel, Llandyssil, a comfortable little place with some mile or so of river.

I spent a couple of days fishing farther down the river with a friend. The Teifi lower down is one of the most lovely little salmon rivers that you could want to see, but the trouble is that there are very few big fish, owing to the excessive netting of the coracle fishermen. So intense is this that very few fish get through. If it were not for that, what a perfect little salmon river it would be. Various attempts, I understand, have been made to curtail the coracle rights, but I believe only to this extent, that those rights die out with the present generation, but that will take some time, as they appeared to be mostly young men.

From Porth I motored to Fishguard on my way to Ireland to fish Lough Sheelin with the May fly. It is a lovely drive to Fishguard and a very nice hotel at the end of the journey. On arrival I saw the A.A. man and I found that I had somehow or other lost all the necessary papers to allow me to land and drive a car in Ireland. This was a pretty state of affairs. The A.A. man told me it was quite useless to put my car on board, they would not allow me to land it. However, I did put it on board and trusted to luck at the other end. I arrived at Rosslare early in the morning, went ashore and saw an official-looking person walking about. I talked to him and found he was a fisherman—he was also the man I had to deal with about the car. I said to him, 'I am sorry I brought a car over here, there is such a bother about the whole thing I wish I had left it behind.' He said, 'But what's the bother?—you just bring it ashore and I will see that there is no bother.' So it went ashore and he passed me through without any licence or anything. I did not waste a minute, but started up before he could ask any more questions. For a fortnight I drove about in Ireland and it was not until the day I left that all the necessary papers turned up. I have always found people most obliging and helpful in Ireland, far more so than in any other country. Here is a thing I have always noticed in Ireland. You are motoring along a road and you see a number of bicycles ahead of you. You blow your horn. Now, in England, when you do that, everybody turn their heads and swerve out into the road; but Irish men and women—no. They never turn their heads, but drop into single file at the side of the road. The thing was so marked that it remained in my memory.

The drive from Rosslare to Lough Sheelin is quite lovely in the spring. The road to Dublin runs along the river Slaney—a river I have always wanted to fish but never have. There are so many places where one would like to stop and fish if only one had the time.

From Dublin I went north-west to Mount Nugent and then to Sheelin. In the back of the car I had an outboard motor, not that it is really necessary on Sheelin, as the best of the fishing was quite close to the house. Although I saw the largest trout I have ever seen on Lough Sheelin, I do not like this lough as much as Arrow. There are not so many bays and islands to get shelter from the wind, which always seems to blow at this time of the year. What is more, the fish do not seem to frequent the bays as they do in Arrow. I think this is due in some respects to the motor-boats which come at full speed into the bays, make a great wash, and drive the fish out into the middle of the lough. Anyway, that is what I found.

I had a few lovely days' sport with the dry fly when the wind was not blowing, and I was sorry to leave the comfortable hospitality of my host, Captain Phipps.

It would appear to me that in all these lakes where there is May fly, you must go early when the rise starts and you can get fishing most of the day, or you must wait until the fly has been on some time and then you get a heavy fall of spent gnat. That only lasts for a few hours in the evening. After a few days, the fish seem to tire of the green fly and the big ones come up and feed almost entirely on the spent gnat. But to have a really good evening on the spent gnat, you must have perfect calm.

I arrived home in time for a few days on the Kennet, but the river was low and most of the fishing was over by 9th June. Everybody was complaining and saying what a bad year it had been.

July 21st I took part in the British Fly and Bait Casting Tournament. I find that I retained my amateur status in the Salmon, but had to take a Second in the Open Salmon as my best cast of forty-seven yards just touched behind. I was beaten by two feet by Captain Edwards, who was a professional caster. We always ran each other pretty close.

In August I paid another visit to the Aurland River in Norway, much of which I have written about before.

We started fishing on 20th August: this was a bit late in the year for the best of the fishing, but we managed to get 140 sea trout, averaging over two pounds. The best fish were sixteen, fourteen and a half, and nine and a half pounds. We did not bother much about the salmon and there were not many in the water.

In October I went to Monmouth to attend the Catchment Board Enquiry. I happened to be the representative of the British Field Sports Society. We had two or three days on this enquiry, much of it boring and much of it interesting. As I have written about this in a previous chapter, I will say no more.

While sitting on this enquiry I had the pleasure of meeting many well-known men in the fishing world, Hutton, Calderwood, Pashley and Beddington, to mention only a few of them.

Calderwood told me the story of the great salmon which was caught by a poacher on the River Earn in Scotland some years before this. The legend of this great fish, which was reputed to have weighed 102 pounds, is roughly as follows: It was caught by a poacher—how it was caught is not related, but we can assume that it was caught by unfair means. It was so large that the man was afraid to sell it as a whole, so cut it up in pieces. But, before cutting it up he took it to a neighbouring farmhouse and had it weighed there; it scaled 102 pounds. Calderwood went to the farmhouse as soon as he heard the report and testified that the scales were correct, and was satisfied in his own mind that the recorded weight was correct. I must say I would have liked to have met that man. Little did he know that he was making history. Willingly would any of us have paid the fine which might have been inflicted. It was a tragedy which can never be repaired.

As far as I can remember, the case for the Catchment Board on the Wye collapsed on the second day and they were told by Mr Dobson, the President, that he was not prepared to listen to a further enquiry unless they put forward a scheme which had the approval of the Wye Board. I made this note in my diary, 'This is all very satisfactory and will be a lesson to Catchment Boards in the future, that they have to study fishing interests'.

I see that after the enquiry was over, I motored to the Usk and got a twelve-pound fish on an Ackroyd, which must have been a pleasant relaxation after sitting on an enquiry for two days!

This was the finish of the 1934 season.

XXII

A CURIOUS LAW CASE

1935

MY first trip this year was to the River Tay, Grantully Castle water. This is almost the top beat and starts below Aberfeldy. I like this part of the river very much: it is fast and rocky, with some grand pools. Unfortunately most of the Tay fishing is from a boat, which I never care for so much as fishing from the bank, especially in the cold and windy weather one generally has in January and February.

The Grantully Castle water is divided into two beats. One day the left bank will fish the lower beat and the right bank the top beat, and change over next day. This arrangement is very good as you get no interference from the opposite bank fishermen, which, if people will not stick to the rules of the game, can be very awkward at times. For instance, the opposite bank man, or lady, may be fishing the head of the pool. You sit down and wait until he or she has worked down some distance and you can then step in. But sometimes they stick at the head of the pool and won't budge, and it is then difficult to know what to do. One has a perfect right, if they won't move, to go in and start ahead of those people, and then it makes unpleasantness. I have heard them say to their gillie, 'That man got in and started fishing in front of me', when really the poor man had been waiting half an hour for the wretched person on the opposite bank to move on! Personally, I usually call out, 'Are you moving down, or if not do you mind me going in ahead of you?' This usually makes them move on. But a request like this should not be necessary.

If you are fishing bait and the man opposite is using fly, you should always give him the chance of going down first, even supposing that you have arrived on the pool before him.

Going back to the Grantully water; one does a little harling but not much: most of our fish were caught casting from the boat.

I see on 8th February we got four fish, twenty-four, twenty-four, twenty-one, and eighteen and a half pounds, all beautiful fish and just up. The cold was intense. The river was moving up and down most days, which spoiled our sport, but it was an early season and the fish were running in great numbers. The water temperature was very low, and the majority of fish were caught on bait.

I left on 20th February and arrived home just in time to attend the Annual Dinner of the Fly Fishers' Club. I always enjoy these dinners, as one meets a host of fishing friends and acquaintances.

I see that on 25th February I had to attend the Law Courts. I was the principal witness in the case of Hedley *versus* McCowan. I was on the side of Hedley—he was an old friend of mine and I had fished with him for some years. It was a curious case and as far as I remember was, in the main, as follows: McCowan owned a stretch of the Usk. He sold one side of the river to Hedley. They quarrelled over something, and the upshot of it was that McCowan tried to restrain Hedley from casting his fly or bait beyond the centre line of the bed of the river, the *medium filiam* as it is called. The question was—what was the centre line of the river? In summer the centre line was high and dry! Further, had anyone ever heard in the course of his fishing career a fisherman who did not cast his fly as far as he could over to the other bank when fish were lying there.

When I was called I gave a list of all the rivers I had fished in all parts of the world and stated that I had never heard of any instance or met anybody who did not cast his fly as far as he wanted to. What the law is I don't know, and I don't think that any legal decision has ever been made on this point, but if there is a law against this, I know that nobody has ever observed it. The end of it was, the judge told counsel that they had better get together and arrive at a settlement. The settlement was, that McCowan paid Hedley back what he had paid for the river and, in addition, all his costs. Hedley was very glad to settle it in this way, and I think he was well out of it. He vowed that he would never take a fishing again unless he had both banks. He afterwards took Upper Carham water on the Tweed, which had both banks.

After this was over I went down to the Winkton water on the Avon and got two fish, twenty-two and twenty-one pounds, a most enjoyable visit after the atmosphere in the Law Courts.

On Monday, 6th May, I had a jolly party at the Fly Fishers' Club to drink cocktails and afterwards to see the illuminations for the Jubilee of King George. I never saw such an orderly and well-behaved crowd. No drunks at all—very different from the 1897 Jubilee of Queen Victoria, but whisky in those days was three shillings a bottle!

In May I went over to my favourite fishing ground for big trout on Lough Arrow, Ireland. This sport of May fly fishing has always a great attraction for me. I caught several fish of four pounds and a fair number of two and a half and three pounds. The excitement of stalking these fish from a boat is great, and this lovely lough has many attractions.

When I got back on 8th June I had a grand day's fishing with Lord Burnham on the Kennet. There was a large crowd there but we all managed to get in somewhere—Walter de Winton, Selby Lowndes, Robert Ward and Lady Mary Ward, Lord Dalhousie, and several others. Walter de Winton was a good salmon fisher but no dry-fly man. He wanted to come with me and see how the game was played. I dislike people crawling behind me, but there was nothing for it. Thank goodness I got a good fish and everything went right, but usually it doesn't on these occasions.

On one occasion I was fishing the Kennet and a big fish was rising. I was conscious of someone behind me; it was my old friend, Mr B. Presently he said, 'You heard of my great loss, Mr Rennie?' I was busy casting, and said, 'No—was it a big one?' 'No', he said, 'I lost my wife!' What can one say on those occasions?

Here is another story about poor old Mr B. I must explain that Mr B. had a huge white beard reaching down to the fourth button of his waistcoat. One night I was trudging home along the banks of the Kennet and there was a place with a barbed wire fence which you had to crawl through. To my astonishment I found someone so tied up in the barbed wire that he could not move. It was nearly dark at the time. When I got up to him, there was my old friend Mr B. His beard, his coat, his net and everything that belonged to him was securely fixed in the barbed wire and he could not move. With much patience and help with my scissors, I cut away large pieces of his beard and clothes and managed to set him free. If I had not passed that way, he might have been there all night.

And that reminds me of another occasion, when I was fishing on the Usk for salmon. 'Do you mind me coming and watching you catch a salmon?' said a perfect stranger. I said 'No, but you may have to wait quite a long time.' Well, he didn't have to wait a long time, for at the second cast with a gudgeon, which I was spinning, I hooked a fish and in ten minutes he was on the bank—sixteen pounds. My friend said, 'That looks very easy.' I said 'Yes' and he walked away! I often wonder what he thought about salmon fishing afterwards.

Again, I am reminded of a meeting with the late King Alphonso of Spain. I was at Laerdal and he had just arrived off a pleasure cruiser. He was standing outside the hotel with a bag of cherries which he was eating and spitting the stones into the road. He said 'Good morning' to me and asked about the fishing. He said that he would like to become a salmon fisher. I was afterwards told that he went off to see someone salmon fishing, and having watched him for twenty minutes said, 'When are you going to catch a salmon?' The salmon were not obliging that morning, and the man said, 'Well, you never know, Sir, you may go a whole day and fail to get one.' The King said, 'Oh, that's no good to me: I can't wait all that time', and away he went. I gather that he was rather an impetuous and impatient person!

There is a lovely little bystream, a branch of the Kennet, below Newbury. You can see it following the railway as you go to London. This is known as the Moor Stream and was owned by Mr Currie. I have had several delightful days on this water and the fish run large, which is surprising considering the size and depth of the water. There are a few May fly at the end of May, and the fish seem to prefer a large 'Variant' to the imitation May. But they are very free risers, or I should say 'were', as this water was badly polluted in 1943 and every fish below Newbury was killed. Another case of all our rivers being turned into open sewers.

I have to thank Mr Currie for many a pleasant day on his water.

On 22nd June the British Field Sports Society held a Casting Tournament, which I have mentioned in another part of this book. It was a most successful meeting and much enjoyed by the crowd, which included a large number of 'film stars', as Denham is the headquarters of the film industry. I was introduced to a well-known producer and others, and they seemed to think us quite mad! I had the same feeling about them.

On 5th July I went down to fish the Monkswood water on the Usk, through the kind invitation of a friend, and on the 9th I had a day on the Wysham water below Monmouth on the Wye. I think those four days were about the hottest I ever remember.

I saw one huge fish on Colmans Pool, on the Wye, which came up repeatedly and showed himself. It was a difficult place, as he had taken up his home in between two rocks. I was fishing with No. 7 flies and greased line. Twice he came after me, but there must have been a drag which he did not like and he would not take hold. The keeper told me the following year that this great fish remained in the same place for the rest of the season and that he eventually caught him in September, when he was forty-three pounds. I wonder what he weighed in May or June.

I rose seven fish that day and never got one. I put it down to the temperature of the water, which was very high.

On 13th and 14th July I was fishing the Test with my friend, Sir Joseph Ball. He had a very nice stretch of the water below Kimbridge, and a farmhouse. We were very comfortable, very thirsty, and we enjoyed ourselves very much. We could only fish in the evenings as in the daytime it was too hot for words— or rather for fishing!

I left for Norway on 12th August to fish with a party on the Aurland. We first stayed at Leylands Hotel, Bolken, which is near Voss. The hotel has the upper portion of the Evanger River which runs out of the Great Lake at Voss. It was a clean and rather primitive kind of hotel, much frequented by Norwegians. For a quiet and cheap holiday with a little fishing thrown in, you might do worse. There were quite a number of sea trout and a few odd salmon. It is one of the few hotels in Norway that have fishing rights: I can't think why there are not more of them. Board and Lodging, six shillings and sixpence a day, how wonderful to think of it in these days!

Having spent a pleasant week at this place we journeyed on to Aurland by motor-coach and boat on the Fjord. At Aurland, although rather late in the season, we caught 261 sea trout, mostly on the dry fly, and a fair number of salmon, but we did not fish much for the latter. I have always noticed how quickly fish turn red in the waters of Norway and Iceland. One week you will be catching beautiful bright fish, and a week or ten days afterwards they are all on the turn and going off colour.

I don't think the change is so quick in our country.

1936

I seem to have had quite a lot of fishing this year. So that I could have something to run down to fish at weekends, I took two days a week on the Wysham water of the Wye, just below Monmouth Bridge and going down for about two and a half to three miles. In spite of its being mostly casting from a boat I must say that I enjoyed this beat on the Wye very much. Some of the pools are first class, with a nice run of water, and the fish fight much better down that way than they do higher up the river. The best fish I got was thirty pounds, and we caught quite a number between twenty and thirty pounds. I never stuck in anything really large.

On 11th May I took a run up to Scotland to fish the Carham beat on the Tweed. I am very fond of this stretch: it is much more rocky and quick-running than other stretches I have fished on the Tweed. Another thing I always find, the Tweed fish are exceptionally free risers—at least they are at Carham, and if there are fish showing, you get fish, which is not the case on every river by any means. In my five days I caught a large number of fish, all on greased line and flies No. 7 to 9. Fifty per cent of these fish were caught on a dropper. That bogey about the tail fly getting caught up when a fish takes your dropper has no terror for me, but I know many people think that it is a great danger in a rocky river. Most of the fish I got on a Blue Charm and Teal and silver.

On 29th May I went down to Kimbridge House to fish with Colonel Adderley Cradock, and from there to the Island House, Percy Tarbutt's. The May fly was on in fair numbers, but nothing like the rise one gets on the Kennet. I saw no big fish feeding, but plenty of fish of two pounds.

There were very few fish in Tarbutt's water. He would not stock his water, so gradually the fish got eliminated, or the rising fish did; anyway, one saw very few. I am a firm believer in stocking, if you stock with new blood. I don't mean to say that you should stock with heavy fish, born and bred in the same water.

Then I had some good days with Lord Burnham on the Barton Court water, with one good fish of four and a half pounds. After that I continued my visits to Wysham on the Wye, with very fair success.

I think this is about the only occasion when I lost a big fish through the swivel breaking in the trace. Of course one must have these accidents at times, but how very seldom they happen.

Iceland

Not being able to find anything suitable in Norway this year, I decided to go to Iceland and make up a party. The unknown is always a great attraction in fishing, and Iceland was quite unknown to me except for the little I had read about it and the few people I had met who had been there.

I may say right away that fishing in Iceland is no easy matter unless you are prepared to ride ponies over the roughest country I ever rode over. It is decidedly a place for the young or active middle-aged. I was told on all sides that unless one was prepared to use the worm—a thing I abominate—one would never get any great number of fish. Well, we did take a box of worms, and I fished one morning with these horrid things. I caught three fish in about half an hour and said 'never again'. The worm was taken right down their throats and had to be cut out. After all, there was no necessity to use a worm, unless you wanted to slaughter a large number of fish. The salmon were very free risers to small fly and greased line, and, later on, to the dry fly, and if you are not content with six or eight fish in a day, you had better give up salmon fishing.

I have described in an earlier part of this book how we discovered that the fish would take a dry fly, and how we caught them after several failures.

The ship we went out in was a small boat of 1,200 tons, and the voyage not too good. It took four days to get to Reykjavik, the capital of Iceland. There is quite a good hotel there—I might say the only hotel in Iceland worth calling by that name. It even had bathrooms attached to some of the bedrooms, and the food was good. Iceland was a prohibitionist country in those days, and you had to take your own liquor with you. On the other hand, I remember going to a race meeting, which was more in the nature of a gathering of all the Icelanders, and which lasted for three days. At this Meeting I saw more 'drunks' than I have seen anywhere. What they drank and where they got it from, I don't know.

The Borg Hotel was quite reasonable in its charges, about fifteen shillings a day all in. I am told the charges went up to £4 a day after the occupation in 1940. Our agent, Mr Zoega, arrived, and with his help we got all our sundry baggage, tackle, food, drinks, etc., safely through the customs.

If we had gone to our destination by boat, we should have waited three days, so we decided to charter a motor-bus which would take all the gear. If I had known what the road was like and what the bus was like, I think I should have waited the entire three days in Reykjavik. They weren't roads at all in some places, and the bus broke down. But all things have a finish, and at last, after ten hours, we arrived at our tin house. It was a nice little house and I should say that it was probably the best fishing lodge in Iceland. The great charm about it was that it was cheerful and on the banks of the river. There was room for ponies and room for gillies and one could dispose of one's fish through the grocer in the village four miles away: he allowed us groceries against the fish. It was a good arrangement and worked well because one can't catch fish and then find no home for them—I would rather not fish. We had arrived a little early for the fish—or the fish had arrived a little late—I don't know which: anyway there were very few fish in the river and we only succeeded in getting a modest four or five a day.

At the mouth of the river there is a foss (waterfall) which tumbles into the long tidal arm of the river. One day soon after we had arrived we went down to the mouth, and we saw what we thought were great masses of green weed floating towards the foss, but when it came nearer we saw to our astonishment and delight that what we thought was weed, was actually a huge mass of salmon. So then we knew that the salmon *had* arrived. They can only get up the foss when the tides are very high. That night, masses of fish came up, and the pools became nicely stocked. Half a mile higher up there is a very big foss, and one wonders how the salmon could possibly get up. But they do get up by getting into pockets at various stages in the falls. Underneath the falls you can see large numbers of fish waiting to get up, but they are so busy thinking about how they are to get up that they will not look at a fly. It says much for the self-control of the party that no member ever attempted to sink his fly amongst these fish and draw it quickly away.

There was a pool above this foss which was called the Rest Pool. I think this was the most attractive pool on the river, rapid water at the head, and then widening out into a calm nice flow of water. It was ideal for greased-line fishing, and we got most of our fish on the dry fly in this pool.

A salmon would take you at the head and then you had to scramble over the rough rocks and keep your line from drowning and fouling the rocks in the river. At the end of the pool there was a sheet of calm water, like a lake, and as often as not a fish would run right down to this calm water and take off seventy or eighty yards of line. With a little persuasion and gentle handling, as we were fishing 1X casts, we usually got him back again.

The Rest Pool will always remain in my memory as one of the most outstanding joys I have ever had in salmon fishing: moreover, it was only ten minutes' walk from the house.

The scenery is beautiful here, with a beauty unknown in Scotland or Norway. There is not a tree on the island, but it makes up for this in other ways. Such lights and colouring it is impossible to describe. At one moment the huge mountains opposite look like mountains of coal, but shortly afterwards they turn into shimmering gold, then red, purple and every other colour the artist may have in his paint box. I made many attempts to reproduce in water colour these wonderful effects, but I fear that I failed miserably.

There were days when the wind blew from the glaciers; so it was as well to have warm clothes to wear in the morning, as the wind would change at a moment's notice. You might be very hot at one pool and shed your coat and waistcoat, but an hour later you might want all these things on again.

We had a grand cook and maid; but when she got any sleep I don't know. She never seemed to turn in until midnight, and at 4 a.m. she was scrubbing every floor in the house. I was told she had a bad temper; I am not surprised, considering the unearthly hours she kept.

One drawback to this river was the long distance between pools. Apart from the three or four pools near the house the other pools were a long way. This meant a pony. Now ponies are all right in their way, but apt to be capricious at times. After half an hour or an hour's ride, loaded with rods, bags, waders, etc., one hobbles one's pony and lets it go. Often as not the pony strays in some mysterious way and you can't find it on your return owing to the rough country and scrub which is six feet high.

I remember one day in particular: I had ridden about four or five miles, hobbled the pony and started fishing. I caught three fish and thought this was enough as it was getting late. Could I find my pony? No, he had entirely disappeared and here was I in long waders with three salmon, a rod, gaff, etc., and a walk of four or five miles over the roughest of country. There was nothing for it but to start on the long trek. The progress was slow and the salmon increased in weight every mile. At one place I had to ford the river: this was not easy. I think it took me a good two hours to get home, and I was done to the world. When I got to the lodge, there was my pony comfortably grazing with the others. I said to myself, 'This is a young man's game'. By next morning all this was forgotten and off one started again. On another occasion I was away up at the head of the river, a matter of five hours' riding. All went well for the first day—we were staying a night in a small hut—but the following day my pony got bored, broke through the wire fence and started for home.

I followed him on foot for a long way, but as soon as I got near him, off he went. I started to return to the hut with little prospect of being able to return home when, by all good fortune, I suddenly saw a small boy riding a pony. I hailed him and after much difficulty in explaining to him what had happened, he cantered off over the country and eventually got my pony. I can't say how thankful I was to that boy, and I loaded him up with cigarettes and chocolates. Where the boy came from I don't know, as there was no habitation within sight. He just dropped from Heaven!

Those were the sort of little things which constantly happened. One day a pony returned to the Lodge festooned with salmon: salmon attached to every part of the saddle. Both the pony and the fish arrived safely—the rider turned up some hours later.

For greased-line fishing, those Icelandic waters were ideal. The waters are very clear and the river not too deep. The fish rise to the small fly very readily. Size 7 to 9, dressing very skimpy, Teal and silver with blue hackle, was the favourite, with only a couple of turns of hackle. Most of the time I used my single-handed eleven-feet Leonard rod, but if a double-handed rod is preferred, a twelve-feet or twelve feet six inches is ample. You want plenty of line in your reel, as the fish run like 'scalded cats': long waders and felt on your brogues, as felt slips far less than any other material. Beware of long rubber boots—they are awful. A gaff is not often necessary. You can beach most of your fish providing you can walk back far enough. For those who do not know this delightful way of landing your fish, let me explain.

You reel up your fish to within about twenty to thirty feet. Then start walking backwards without reeling in any more line. Presently the fish will come slithering over the shingle, in fact it will crawl up on its own providing you keep a steady pressure and keep walking backwards, but don't try and reel in. When the fish has crawled three or four yards up the bank, lay down your rod carefully with the handle of the reel up, and then walk down below your fish and tail him or give him a knock on the head.

I have beached salmon of over twenty pounds weight in this way on a 7/5 cast. It is much nicer than putting a gaff into him. Seldom have I lost a fish in this way.

There was hardly a spot of rain the whole time we were in Iceland, and the weather for the most part was glorious. As the river got lower, so the fishing got more difficult, and it was then that we took to the dry fly, which I have described in another chapter.

One day I ran into two members of the Fly Fishers' Club. We gave them lunch and showed them our dry fly methods. Whether they tried it I don't know. They were fishing a river about twenty miles away. We have not met since.

Once again, in 1939, I paid a short visit to this river: it was the end of August, on the verge of war, and for my part I found no pleasure in fishing. We were all waiting to get a boat home, as war might be declared at any moment.

So ended my first trip to Iceland.

Just one thing more: when we returned to Reykjavik we all wanted to see the famous geyser, which spouted once in twenty-four hours. We chartered a car and off we went, a matter of some twenty miles from the town. Apparently we had struck a day when everybody else wanted to see the same thing, and there were 200 to 300 people there, including the Prime Minister, the Mayor and corporation, etc.

This geyser is a very peculiar person: if you leave him alone he will spout to some hundreds of feet high at regular intervals of twenty-four hours, but he does not spout at just the time you want him to, so you have to use methods of persuasion. On arriving at the spot we found a lorry loaded with bars of soap—there must have been some hundredweights. Who paid for the soap I don't know. Men started pitching soap into the crater, I should say about twenty to thirty feet in diameter. It was then about 12 o'clock. We were told he would start spouting at 2 p.m. We gathered round the crater and watched. At 1.50 I said to the Prime Minister or the Mayor, 'I don't think your geyser is going to play the game'. He said, 'Oh yes, at 2 p.m. you will see.' Sure enough at 2 o'clock there was a most terrifying rumble and everybody started running away like rabbits to about 100 yards from the crater. Then up went the most magnificent spout of water. I believe it is the highest spouter in the world. The wind caught it and it drenched the folk on the wrong side. We were left dry. This lasted for about ten minutes and all the time there was a roaring, terrifying noise like that of some caged animal. It was a beautiful sight; one always to be remembered.

There is a little river quite near Reykjavik which used to be a first-class salmon river. People wanted electric light so a dam was thrown across. The fish could not get up the dam as there was no provision, so now they net the fish below the dam, put them into great lorry-borne tanks and dump them above the dam. So they swim up into the lake and into the river above. I have never heard of this in any other part of the world.

EIRA. NORWAY

XXIII

A WET SEASON

IN my diary, February, 1937, I say, 'This has been the wettest season I have ever known. Raining almost every day since November. Very little snow and not very cold.'

I opened the season on 14th February by going to the Tweed to stay at Carham with my friend, Percy Hedley. During my stay the river was mostly in flood, so a golden sprat was the only possible thing. In spite of this I see that on 15th February I got eight fish. On 16th four fish, 17th no fishing, 18th five fish, 19th eight fish, 20th a gale, six fish. Thirty-one fish in five days, averaging ten and a half pounds. Considering the weather this was not so bad. Our fishing hours were not long: we would start at 10.30, fish until 1 p.m., start again at 2.30 and fish until 4 p.m. Hedley liked fishing in this comfortable way, and I don't blame him. His house was on the river bank and he was there all the season, and he was getting on in years. Fishing for the market was a thing he hated, and there I am with him every time.

I had often heard of Bracken Bank and the Cumberland Eden, so on my way back from the Tweed I thought I would stop for a few days and see what it was like. There were no other guests and the place was more like a country house than an hotel. They had a nice stretch of water on the Eden about five miles away. If the river had been in order I am sure one would have caught a fair number of fish, but after catching one the water came down in flood and then big flood, so fishing was out of the question.

It then started to snow, and in Cumberland it really can snow.

By the morning there was deep snow and drifts. I started for the station, ten miles or so, got stuck in a drift and had to dig out the car: got to Penrith and the trains were snowed up. Decided to stay the night, and next morning got away. There was no more fishing for some time.

February, March and April were all very wet months and several times I went down to the Usk and Wye without unpacking my rods. This is so often the case on these rivers.

In May I had a very pleasant little trip to Ireland with a party. We stayed at Bundoran at a most comfortable hotel. From here you can fish all kinds of rivers and lakes. The nice little Bundroes river runs quite near the hotel. It is full of small trout, to one pound, and there is a fine hatch of fly. Quite a number of salmon come up and go into Lough Melvin. I had often heard of the 'Gillaroo' trout in Melvin, but I did not come across any.

The River Earn is only a few miles away and you can get first-class dry fly fishing there. When the May fly is on you can get some very big fish. I was too early for the May fly, but every day there was a fine hatch of Olives and Iron Blue Duns, and we had some very pretty fishing. I have never fished this river for salmon—it can be very good at times.

As one crossed the bridge at Ballyshannon one could see large numbers of salmon coming up, some very big. We called on Major Moore, of Cliff House. The Free State took away all his netting rights, which meant anything up to £8,000 a year to him. He fought the case through all the courts and it cost him, so he told us, about £40,000, and in the end they took all, except his rights on the river. In the bad times he once had to swim the river in front of his house and so escape from his would-be assassins. But he was very cheerful and gave us a most amusing account of his experiences.

From Bundoran we went on to Lough Arrow, and stayed at the hotel. It was full of fishermen, but all 'dappers'. The fly was up and large baskets were being made. I had a new boat this year and still kept to my outboard motor, an 'Evinrude' which I have now had for fifteen years. It has never given me one bit of bother all this time.

The weather was shocking at Lough Arrow this year—gales of

wind and rain. In consequence the fish would not show up, the fly was driven off the water, and the spent gnat died in the trees. So goodbye to Lough Arrow on 3rd June: the May fly fishing was over for this year.

I got back home in time to fish the Kennet, the Moorstream, Barton Court, Benham, Denford, an odd day or so on the Test. I remember one good fish I got at Benham. I watched him rising for some time and then put a fly over him on his left. He took no notice. Then I watched him, and he appeared to take everything on his right. I put a fly on his right, and he immediately had it. I looked at his left eye: it appeared in perfect order. He was feeding on the right, and right only.

I decided to go up to the Eira river in Norway this year. I had always heard of it as a 'big fish' river, where some of the largest fish in Norway have been caught. Like all Norwegian trips, it takes a long time to get there, but the coast of Norway is so beautiful that if one can relax and say to oneself, 'Now I am on a pleasure cruise; I have nothing to bother me—I am away from the office and all tiresome business, the scenery is beautiful, the weather is calm, and there is nothing to complain about; not even because the boat is a bit slow and stops every few hours to take on a passenger or a calf or something of that sort.' If one can philosophize in this way, the time passes very pleasantly. After two or three days from Bergen you arrive at Molde. Molde, which was totally destroyed by the Germans in 1940, was one of the prettiest little towns on the coast.

The Hotel Alexandra was very good and looked out towards the Romsdal Fjord, with its wonderful range of mountains. There were numerous smart little yachts sailing about, and all was peace and beauty. Now it is a heap of ruins. The hotel was shot up and burned. All the houses were of wood and were consumed in a few hours.

And how cheap it was. My bedroom and bath attached was eight kroner (eight shillings and sixpence) a day. I had a balcony overlooking the fjord. I could have stayed there several days with pleasure, but fishing, of course, was what we had come for, so next morning we chartered a bus and piled ourselves and our luggage aboard. The journey to the Eira river takes two and a half hours, and the single journey cost £2 10s. That's how things were in those days. We took over the house and fishing from Percy Tarbutt. They had not had much of a time, but one of his party got a fifty-five-pound fish just before we had arrived.

We soon found out that August is a bit too late for this river. One has to learn these things from experience. The fish were beginning to turn in colour; at least the large ones were. June and July are the best months. The party that left were not very reassuring: they had not got many fish themselves, and they did not think our chances were very good. We did get into a few big fish and we did have some accidents with them, but on the whole we had a lovely time and lovely weather on a beautiful river.

The river was divided up into beats, each beat having its boat and *klepper*. As the boats were collected at the bottom of the river so they were picked up by an ancient Ford lorry and taken to the top of the river again. It all worked very well, and saved a lot of trouble. Some of the rapids were really terrifying when you went down them the first time; but the boatmen were so clever that after a bit you took little notice.

On one occasion in the top pool I hooked a good fish just at the edge of the rapids. I gave him line in the hopes that he would come up, but not a bit of it: he turned and ran down the rapids as fast as he could go. My boatman turned to go after him but funked it and said it was not safe, and I don't think it was. I scrambled out of the boat, and then began the roughest bit of walking I have ever done with a fish on the end of my rod. I had by this time about 120 yards of line out, so if I was to kill my fish I had to keep moving pretty quickly over a quarter of a mile of boulders. So I did keep moving and killed my fish. Now for the return journey. Believe me or not, I took three times as long to crawl back as I did when I had a fish at the end.

One day I saw a very big fish come to my fly; just before he took it he hesitated, then took it with a bang. I left the fly in his mouth, a No. 1/0 'Jock'. Well, one gets careless at times—not very often. I had just changed my fly without putting on my glasses. This cost me a big fish. There was no break in the cast—it was sheer carelessness. By the look of him in the water he was one of the 'Portmanteaus'!

To my great surprise and pleasure I found that Thor Thoresen had a house the other side of the river. I had stayed with the family in their lovely home at 'Visthus' in 1923—this was just over the hills in the other valley. We all went over there to lunch one day, by car. What a sumptuous lunch they gave us. The centre of the table was piled with lobsters, and the assortment and abundance of drinks was tremendous. Finally, after white wine, burgundy, champagne, Thor produced a bottle of very old Green Chartreuse. After lunch he proposed that we should return round the coast in his fast motor-launch so that we could see the scenery. The boat had a cabin: the journey took about two hours, the day was very hot and I slept in the bottom of the cabin! So did the others!

As the weather was so hot, we gave up fishing in the day and went out in the early morning and late in the evening. In this way we managed to get quite a number of fish, which we certainly should not have got if we had fished in the day. After a few days of this the gillies struck, and we had to give up the early morning part of it. The head gillie was a grand chap; but he occasionally went off on the drink. When the fishing got very bad, he got very drunk, but after two or three days he was back again. He said he could not help it when the fishing was bad.

The last week of the fishing was hopeless—all the sea trout had disappeared and most of the salmon, so on 21st September we left for home.

There was one grand-looking pool which never held a fish. I asked why this was, and Conrad told me that at one time it was a very good pool; but that a certain gentleman fishing there was always getting his fly caught up in the trees, so he asked the farmer if he could have them cut down. The trees were mostly cut down, and from that time on no more fish were caught in that pool. There is a great danger in cutting away trees: I know of other cases. Why can't people learn to cast when there are difficulties behind them?

We returned to Bergen by the *Prince Olav*—a converted yacht. She was sunk by the Germans in 1940.

Season 1938

I took the Grantully Castle beat on the Tay from the opening day on 15th January to the end of the month. Sometimes it is very good on the opening day. I got an attack of the 'Flu' and could not go out on the 15th. It did not matter much as the river was in flood and it was snowing and raining. There were masses of kelts about: what a blessing it is to have your Golden Sprat mounted in a 'Scarab'. When the fish strikes, the hooks stay in the fish—or they should do so. I find they always do with kelts and the bait runs up the gut trace and is not damaged. If you don't use a scarab, you may easily use up two bottles of sprats in a day. If the mounting is properly carried out, you can catch kelts galore and not lose your bait.

I did not get a great number of clean fish: the river was too high most of the time.

In the middle of April I went down to fish the Wysham beat on the Wye. There I ran into an old Cambridge friend. His father was Austrian, his mother English. He had been very rich in days gone by, but now practically all his property had been confiscated and he was left with very little. What he was doing in Monmouth I do not know. We talked about old times until one o'clock in the morning. I have never seen him since.

Fish are curious: I saw a nice fish rise in Colmans Pool. As it was early in the year I had on a No. 3 fly. I did not move him. Then I tried a No. 5—no good. I went down to No. 6 and he came with a bang, gave me a great dance over the pool and at last I got him in. He was only sixteen pounds and was caught in the outside of the cheek. I repeat, fish are funny creatures!

In April I had one of the most amusing trips I have ever made. The whole thing was a joke from start to finish. A party of us took a house and fishing at Castle Lodge, Clare, Galway, which is about five miles from the town of Galway. The house was not too bad and the Clare river ran at the end of the garden. Everything was truly Irish. We only saw one salmon in the Clare river during the whole time we were there, and got about half a dozen trout. The gillie—so called, by name of Dougan, was something that might have stepped out of one of Canon Hannay's books. If you asked him to do anything he always said 'No—that is woman's work'. I asked a farmer who had a house quite 400 yards from the river if he had seen or heard of any salmon. He said, 'Sure, your Honour, when the grilse are running they make such a noise that it keeps me awake at night by their splashing!'

Finding no fish in the river we decided it would be rather fun to run over to Galway and fish in the famous 'Drain' just above the town. This fishing to me is something like a comic opera. I think one paid a pound a day and kept one fish in three, but you had to catch three fish before you got one. I don't remember quite how it went, but I never got a fish for myself.

Looking over Galway Bridge you see hundreds of salmon. I remarked to the owner that there was a grand lot of fish. He said, 'That's nothing—when there are really plenty of fish in the pool they are lying in layers of three deep!'

The fishing extends for about 150 yards above the bridge. There is a concrete path along the bank about five feet above the water. Behind you, there is a stone wall, and half-way down there is a large sink such as you have in your scullery. As far as I can remember, four rods are allowed in this 150 yards, and you go down in a procession. There are seats by the way, and most of the anglers, both male and female, sit on the seats while their gillies do the fishing, mostly, I must say, with a small shrimp. Now there is a great art in this shrimp fishing. First of all you must learn to thread your shrimp on a single long-shank hook. Having broken up half a dozen in a feeble attempt to get the shrimp straight on the hook, you at last thread one to your satisfaction. A gut cast about 7/5 and a small strip of lead above the shrimp, completes your cast. You require a fine, dressed, level line and a light rod, bamboo for preference, about fourteen feet long. The cast is a difficult one: I cannot describe it properly, and I doubt if anyone could. It is a sweep round with about fourteen feet and a shoot of line you have gathered in. The clever man can cast about twenty yards of line and drop his shrimp within a few inches of where he wants to. I was quite unable to do this, and only got one cast in three that was much good. I came to the conclusion that it was much more difficult than casting a fly.

Well, the procession goes down the bank, generally the gillie hooks the fish and the fisherman then gets up from where he has been sitting reading the *Times* and takes the rod. I had not been able to get a gillie and so fumbled along as best I could.

When you catch a fish a very long-handled gaff is used to get him out from the height where you are standing. Immediately, the fish is taken to the sink and a label stuck on its side, bearing the name of the proud captor. Sometimes a fly is used, but I did not see many. The drain, as it is called, is a deep cutting in the rock about fifteen to twenty yards broad. On the other side of the river there is a shallow extent of water, so that when the river is not too high you can approach the drain from the other side. Nobody seemed to try this, so I made the attempt with a fly rod and had some interesting fishing, as the fish will rise to the fly if they have a chance.

One day I saw a man hook a fish above the bridge. The fish ran through the bridge and down below. 'What are you going to do now?' I thought. My thought was very soon answered, as his gillie ran down below the bridge where there was a wooden platform and with a very long gaff, gaffed the fish, released the bait, and the fisherman wound in his line. During the few days I had on this water, I don't think I ever laughed so much.

I made many excursions on to Lough Corrib, but I never found a place where the fish were taking well; and there was very little May fly about. The best places seemed to be about ten miles away. As a May fly Lough, I don't think it compares with Arrow, Sheelan or Derg.

Taking it as a whole and from the fishing point of view, this was the most disappointing quarter I had been to in Ireland. But it made up for it by being one of the most amusing.

On one occasion I was driving back from Galway to our house when I came to a long procession of cars, carriages, donkey carts and a hundred or more people walking. It was a funeral. The road was rather narrow and there was hardly room to pass. I followed this on low gear for about a mile, hoping that the procession would turn off. No luck, so at last I stopped and asked some of the walkers if they would think it discourteous of me to drive through, as I was late. I did not want to offend anyone. As they assured me that no offence would be taken I drove through as best I could with my hat in my hand. There was no offence taken.

When I got home the May fly on the Kennet was in full swing. Poor Anthony Crossley was fishing at Barton Court. I think this is the last time I saw him. In 1939 he went by plane to Sweden to fish his favourite river, the Em, where the big sea trout are—his plane crashed on the way. He was a most likeable person and I never met anyone who had picked up fishing so quickly as he had. His gift lay in the fact that he was the most painstaking hardworking fisherman I have ever met. His observation was intense, and his book on *Greased Line Fishing* is a proof of this.

My note at the end of the May fly season is 'I fear the Kennet is going downhill very much'. This I attribute to the lack of stocking with new blood.

I was off to Norway again on 16th July to fish that wonderful big-fish river, the Evanger, at the kind invitation of Edward Corbett. It came about in this way. I had never had the pleasure of meeting him, but in 1937 I had an invitation from him to go over to the Evanger. Unfortunately, I was already booked up to go to the Eira, so with great regret I had to refuse.

In June, 1938, I was in Hardy's shop, and in walked Corbett. I went up to him and reminded him, and he said, 'Oh yes, I remember, and you wouldn't come'. 'No,' I said, 'It wasn't a case of wouldn't, but I couldn't come'. 'Well', he said, 'Will you come this year?' Of course I jumped at it, and arrangements were made for me to leave on 16th July.

The start off from Kings Cross was bad: when I got to the train my ticket was gone! I went back to the old ticket collector I had known for years, and together we searched the floor of the ticket office. He found it, quite thirty feet away from where he had clipped it—what a piece of luck!

We crossed by the new ship *Vega*, such a luxurious boat, like a miniature *Queen Mary*. On arrival at Bergen we took the night train to Oslo, and for the privilege of stopping the express at Evanger you pay the modest sum of fifteen kroner. We got to Evanger at midnight and were met by Edward Corbett, had some supper and got to bed. It is a delightful house, overlooking the river. From the balcony you can see what looks like a large clock on the opposite bank, but by looking through a telescope, which is set on the balcony, you can see that it is a water gauge, and read quite clearly the rise and fall in inches. Nobody but Corbett would have thought of a thing like this.

The fish on this river average thirty-one pounds, and I once got into trouble by producing two lovely fish of twenty-five pounds each. 'Look here, young man, this won't do. You are bringing down our average!' I felt small! I finished up with a grand fish of thirty-three and a half pounds, on a 'Mar Lodge'. I did not connect with one of the 'whales'.

On 25th July I had to leave, which I did with sorrow as I had had such a wonderful time, but I had to meet my friends at Bergen and go up the coast to a river near Narvik. Narvik has since become history.

On the 29th we arrived at Narvik and went off to see the Consul Aagaard, and his wife. I wonder what has happened to these kind and friendly people.* We changed into a small boat and after three hours arrived at our destination. The head gillie, Petersen, met us. Such a nice man, and I am sure led the Germans a dance when they went there in 1940. This is a fine river, best known for its sea trout: there are few salmon, but the sea trout run up to sixteen pounds and more. The weather was hot, and the river was coming down like milk as a glacier fed it: in cold weather it was clear. This is the great drawback to glacier-fed streams—when the weather is lovely your water is cloudy: when it is cold and wet the water is clear. I don't mean to say that you can't catch fish when the water is milky, because you do. In some extraordinary way the fish see your wet fly but, of course, the sport is not so good. In clear water these fish take a dry fly, which, of course, they won't in a milky one.

We did not do too badly in the month—240 sea trout, twenty-three of which were six pounds and over; only six salmon. The best sea trout was fourteen and a half pounds.

I find that I wrote the following note when I got home in September: 'This has been a trying month. We were very near to war with Germany, and on 30th September things looked

* Consul Aagaard died soon after the German Occupation.

pretty certain. However, owing to Mr Chamberlain's per-
sistence, war was averted'. How much we have to thank that
good man for. When history comes to be written, we shall
appreciate him all the more.

So ends 1938 season.

XXIV

THE FLY FISHERS' CLUB

I AM devoting a short chapter to this, our most eminent Fly Fishers' Club, because I think that fishermen ought to know something about it.

When I was at my Prep. School at St. Davids, Reigate, I had two great friends, Arthur and Agnew Severn. Their father was Arthur Severn, the artist, and they lived with John Ruskin at Brantwood Coniston. They were related through Mrs Severn to John Ruskin.

When we were boys at school we were always talking about fishing and mostly about pike and perch. They told me about John Ruskin—I was very ignorant, I had never heard of him before.

There came a time, as in the lives of all small boys, when we parted from school. One went to one Public School, one to another, and we saw nothing more of each other. Time went by until the year 1907: I was walking through the courtyard of Victoria Station when someone came up to me and said, 'Aren't you John Rennie?' 'Yes', I said, 'Aren't you Agnew Severn?'

So the friendship which had been forgotten for about eighteen years was renewed.

Agnew Severn then said to me, 'Why aren't you a member of the Fly Fishers' Club?' 'I don't know', I replied, 'No one has ever asked me to be one.' So I was proposed and seconded by these two old friends and became a member in 1908.

The object of the Club is to bring together those who were devoted to fly fishing generally; to afford a ready means of communication between those interested in this delightful art; to provide in the Reading Room papers, periodicals, catalogues and books having reference to fishing, and a means of obtaining knowledge about fishing places, and supplying information on all points relating to the art.

In the Club no introductions are needed, and a stranger may enter into conversation between members with the assurance that his remarks will be welcome.

The actual birth of the Club was in 1884.

In 1885 rooms were taken at 10 Adelphi Terrace: before the end of 1885 there were no less than 264 members. Many distinguished fishermen had by that time joined the Club—their names are too numerous to record here.

In 1887 the Club moved to the Arundel Hotel, and the membership rose to 324.

In 1889 an American Split Cane rod was presented to the Club for the use of 'office bearers': one wonders what rivalry there was for the use of this innovation.

It is worth recording that in the year 1896 one member died, having, it was said, spent during the last ten years of his life no less than £30,000 on guns, rods and fishing tackle. He left 367 rods, his salmon flies ran into thousands, and his trout flies into hundreds of thousands. I understand that as he got older he got busier—having no time to fish, his hobby was to collect tackle, as others collect pictures.

It only shows what a wonderful attraction there is in fishing.

In 1899 the Club moved into premises in the Haymarket, and in 1908 into No. 36 Piccadilly, W.1, and remained there until they were 'blitzed' out in 1941. The premises have since been demolished and, from that date on, the Club has been housed by the Junior Carlton Club, for which kindness members are very grateful.

When I joined in 1908, the Thursday dinners were of the most frugal kind—it was usually a chop and fried potatoes followed by bread and cheese. Six or eight people were about as many as sat down to dinner. In 1910 I asked to be allowed to provide a cook for the occasion, and the dinners improved so much that the attendance doubled itself in a short time. Although the cost of the dinner was only two shillings and sixpence, I was able to hand over to the Secretary at the end of six months a profit of £5.

So the dinners improved as we went on, and nicer little dinner parties it would be difficult to find.

Those dinners became a great feature of the Club, and continued all through the first World War, and most of the time during the second World War.

After dinner, fly tying was popular, and discussions on fishing matters took place. There was no bridge in those days to devastate all conversation and controversy in matters relating to fishing.

Our great performer in trout fly dressing was Hassam, the greatest trout fly tyer that ever was. I learned much from him. Graham Clark was probably the most finished salmon fly dresser in the Club in those days, and it was he who gave me my first lesson and started me off in the right way. I have tied flies ever since, to my great enjoyment and profit. I should not have caught nearly so many fish unless I had learned to tie my own flies, and, may I say, that many of my friends would not have caught so many if I had not tied flies for them!

In 1912 I was asked to go on the Committee, and I was much honoured. I have been on the Committee ever since.

In 1914 the Club honoured me by making me President, which post I filled until 1917, when I relinquished my duties to Mr Walter Coggeshall, our American member. Coggeshall was always the life and soul of a party: he was full of stories and American witticisms. I always remember one evening Coggeshall was very pleased with himself because he had just had a grandson. By chance it happened that General Sir Desmond O'Callaghan also had a grandson on the same date, and they argued as to which was the finest child. 'Coggy', as we called him, said, 'Well, mine weighed X pounds'—as quick as thought Sir Desmond said, 'My dear fellow, we always put them back at that size!' Poor Coggy, for once in a way, the wind was taken out of his sails.

This will give some idea of the fun we used to have amongst ourselves.

In 1920 the Club had prospered so much that its membership had risen to 550 and a rule was then passed limiting the membership to 600. The membership has remained round about this figure ever since.

In 1927 I modelled a jumping salmon as a mascot for my motor-car. So many members kindly expressed their approval that I gave it to the Club for their members' use, and replicas now adorn many motor-cars. The dimensions of the fish I took from a large Shannon salmon.

The Club has a fine journal of its own, edited by that gifted writer, Dr E. A. Barton, and gives us excellent articles on fishing and many interesting letters from members.

The Club had its 'Jubilee' year in 1933.

And here I end my few notes on the Fly Fishers' Club. It has been a great source of joy to me for over forty years and I hope to enjoy many more years in its pleasant company.

Let us hope that the Club will soon have its own premises again and be surrounded by its own belongings, most of which were saved from the 'blitz'.

NEVILLE CHAMBERLAIN

Season 1939

ON 1st March I was fishing at Grantully Castle water. This Upper Tay fishing is always chancy work and, as a rule, March is not a very good month. This winter was one of the coldest I can remember and at home we were practically snowed up at Christmas. Plenty of snow in Scotland generally means good spring fishing, and unless you get snow on such rivers as the Dee and Spey, the chances are that your season will be short, as the fish run up with the warm water. I have known the temperature of the water on the Dee in May as much as ten degrees higher than the air, and the fish started running in thousands. By the middle of May most of the fishing was over.

I did not think much of our chances at Grantully as the weather was so cold and the fish remained lower down. However, we finished up with thirty-one fish of an average of eighteen pounds; not so bad. It is not often that one catches more than one expects.

I had taken a beat on the Clytha water for the season. I was only down there once in the spring and, as events turned out, I never got down there again.

The cuckoo sounded on the 19th April. It is very interesting to note from my diary that he nearly always makes his call on that date for the first time. I wonder how he remembers the date!

18th April

Our President of the Fly Fishers' Club gave a dinner at 36 Piccadilly to all Past Presidents and members of Committee. We were a party of twenty and spent a most hilarious evening in very pleasant company, with much fishing gossip.

On 28th April my friend, Percy Hedley, asked me to run up for the week-end to the Tweed, Carham beat. I arrived in time for a late dinner on Friday and was told that the prospects were not too good. The NE. wind was howling and it was bitterly cold. It only shows how little we know about fishing and what is a good fishing day.

On Saturday morning I started at 10.30 and before the day was out at 5 p.m. I had got ten fish, all on No. 7 to No. 9 flies and greased line. Half these fish were taken on the dropper. Now this point arises—supposing I had not used a dropper, would I have got the same number of fish on the tail fly? Personally, I do not think so. A dropper seems to have a great attraction for Tweed fish.

On Sunday I spotted a good fish just opposite the house, and wondered if he would stay there until Monday. He did, and I got him: sixteen and a half pounds. I got four fish on Monday, and returned home by the night train. What a lovely week-end, and all so easy.

As it turned out, this was the last visit I was to pay to Carham, as my friend died soon afterwards.

19th May

This was a wonderful week, and one I shall always remember.

Sir Joseph Ball had very kindly asked me to spend the week-end at Kimbridge House on the Test and to meet the Prime Minister, Mr Chamberlain.

I arrived at 6 p.m., and the P.M. turned up ten minutes later. He had had a very busy day in the House and should have taken things a bit easy, but no—in a few minutes he was running upstairs to change, as he wanted to get the evening rise, and away he went. We all got back at 10 p.m. with a nice lot of fish, the P.M. having caught the largest, which was just as it should have been.

In his enthusiasm, he reminded me much of a schoolboy on a week-end holiday. We sat up till 1 a.m. talking, mostly about fishing, and not Hitler!

I noticed he drank several glasses of port, and I asked him about this and what effect it had on his gout. He said that all the doctors had warned him; but, for the last year he had drunk port and never had a touch of gout! His age was then seventy-one, and a more agile, energetic man on the river bank I never saw at that age.

The next day he was off salmon fishing at Nursling, and breakfasted at 8.15 a.m. He fished all day, and refused to fish with any other bait but fly, and greased line. He rose two salmon but did not connect, and was back again at Kimbridge House by 6.30. This would have been enough for most men younger than he was, but no—on arrival back he wanted to go after the trout again. So off we all went and had a very good evening, returning at 10 p.m. and to bed at 12. Not a bad effort.

Sunday was a warmer day and the fish rose well. We finished up the week-end with twenty-two fish averaging two pounds. What more delightful week-end could any man want.

I am full of admiration for this wonderful man who, after one had known him for a little time, was a most likeable and charming fishing companion. His knowledge of plants, birds and fishes was very extensive, and in many ways reminded me of Lord Grey of Falloden. It is remarkable, considering how little time he had at his disposal. But great men are like that.

Sir Joseph Ball and his wife are the perfect host and hostess, with that wonderful gift of making one feel completely at home.

26th May

Suddenly, on the spur of the moment, I decided to run over to Lough Arrow. It was one of those impetuous decisions which one can't account for. So away I went to my old friends, the Gethins, at Ballindoon House.

I found my motor-boat, *Little Audrey*, leaking like a sieve, so she had to be sunk in water for twenty-four hours. By that time she had 'taken up' and after pumping out, was quite seaworthy. The weather was fine and the sport good. One always thinks one is going to catch far more than one actually does, but the whole thing is so exciting that at the end of the day one finds that one has only caught three or four fish from two to three pounds, and one imagines what one would have got if one had been connected with all the 'whoppers' one had seen feeding and sometimes risen.

I remember one huge fish of seven to eight pounds which I had been chasing for half an hour. At last I got on terms and he was coming to my spent gnat not more than ten feet from the boat. Just as he was taking the fly, I think he must have seen the reflection of my outboard motor—it was aluminium and the setting sun was shining on it—anyhow he saw something, and with a huge lunge in the water, he disappeared.

I made up my mind after this, that any bright parts of the outboard motor should be painted in some dull colour. I shall do this on my next trip to Lough Arrow.

Tuesday, 30th May

My last day. The fly was practically over. The day was lovely with not a breath of wind, just the sort of day a dry-fly man dreams of. I picked up a fish or two in the morning and then went back to pack, for I must leave in the afternoon. So ended a brief but delightful visit.

I was just in time on my arrival home to get a few days' fishing on the Kennet, my best fish four and a half pounds at Barton Court, with Lord Burnham. I always get a good one on this water. A few more days with not much success on other waters of the Kennet, and that finishes the May fly season. I always have a great pang of regret when the May fly is over—I feel as if another year of my life has passed.

Here is a bit of luck—my good friend, Edward Corbett, has again asked me to fish the Evanger River in Norway, and I left on 17th June, on the lovely ship *Vega* which is better than the *Venus*. He has evidently forgotten that I could only catch 'tiddlers' of twenty-five pounds on my last visit, which brought down his average!

I met several fishing acquaintances on board, the present Lord Leicester, Bromley Davenport and Sir Edward Chichester, on their way to fish the Rauma and Aaro rivers.

I arrived at Scorvelin, Evanger, on the following day at 12.30 a.m., when it was quite light. I was half afraid that Corbett would ask me to go out and catch a fish; instead of that he gave me a good supper, a drink, and so to bed.

For the first few days we got a heat wave, temperature eighty-five degrees in the shade, so there was little fishing in the day-time. On the 25th I got two beauties, thirty-one and thirty pounds, both on the fly. But this was not the best of them, for on the 28th I got into a really big fish. He took me just at the tail of 'Scorva'. Now if a fish takes you at the tail end of 'Scorva' it is just as likely as not that he may decide to go down the rapids below, where there is little chance of following him. My boatman was skilful and I never reeled in a yard of line. He rowed very gently and carefully upstream and the huge fish followed the boat. He must have followed quite 100 yards, then back again he went, but not quite so far as the danger spot. At length we got him out into the broad water above the pool. He then took a terrific run and must have taken out 140 yards of line. With much coaxing and gentle rowing upstream we got him round to a little bay formed by a promontory. I then landed, as he was showing signs of getting done.

Finally I walked backwards and towed him in, and the *klepper* made a beautiful gaff. I was overjoyed, as I felt quite certain he was over forty pounds. We got one more fish, thirty-two pounds, and then started for home. Every fish you catch at Evanger has to go through a process conducted by Edward Corbett—the last item of which is taking the weight. I walked up and down outside the hut while the scales of the fish were being taken off and put into an envelope with the date attached. Then the length of the fish was taken and the girth and, last of all, the weight. I felt like a father waiting to hear of the birth of his child, or what I imagine he would feel like. At last I could stand it no longer and put my head into the hut and said, 'What's the weight?' A laconic answer came back 'forty-three pounds'.

So I had done it at last, but what a long time it had taken me to do it. The coveted forty-pounder. I had had many fish of thirty-eight and thirty-nine pounds, but up till that moment the forty-pounders had got away. I often wonder how many people there are living in this country who have caught forty-pounders and over. I should say surprisingly few. I know so many salmon fishers who have fished all their lives and never been able to get their forty-pounders. For one thing, I don't think that there are so many big fish about now as there used to be. The Tay usually had quite a number in the season, but they don't get many now. The Awe still keeps up its reputation and has a few to its credit, but not so many as formerly. The Tweed always had a number of big fish in the late Autumn—you never hear of them now. The Shannon, of course, has been killed.

There is no doubt, big fish give one a tremendous thrill and you can't get away from it.

The Alton river in Norway has probably the greatest number of big fish; then there is the Aaro in Norway. A fisherman once told me, after a visit to this river, that the average weight while he was there was thirty-seven pounds. I once very nearly took a lease of this water for a month. But there were certain reasons why I did not sign the lease, and I say no more.

I keep a collection of big-fish records and their photographs. It is very interesting; but perhaps I have said enough about big fish.

Next morning I had to get up at 5 a.m. to catch the train to Bergen and so back home. So ended a very happy trip in the company of delightful people.

I had now only a fortnight before I left for Iceland, and much to do before. I had grave doubts about going away at all, as the world was so unsettled and war might be on us at any time, and Iceland is not an easy place to get away from. If I had known then what I knew afterwards, I don't think I should have gone.

The river I had chosen this year was the Nordura. I knew nothing about the river, the accommodation or anything else, but I had seen the records, which were good. These records were for the whole season and the best months were June and July. It was not until 21st July that we started fishing. We made the journey to Iceland this year in luxury, as we found that there was one of those cruising ships making the round trip, Iceland, Spitzbergen, Norway. As the ship was not full they allowed us to go as far as Iceland. The ship was the old *Atlantis* of 16,000 tons. There were only 200 people on board: amongst the passengers was my old friend, Sir Harold Gillies, also Sir Percy

"RIVER NORDURA, ICELAND."

From a painting by the author

Bates whom I had met before; they also were bound for Iceland.

We arrived at Reykjavik and found the Borg Hotel the same as usual. Next day we took boat to Borganess and thence by car to Laxfos on the Nordura. We found a nice tin house, of course no bathroom, but this omission is made up by a wonderful natural bath in the rocks with a hot sulphur stream of water running in. At one end the bath was hot enough to cook an egg: at the other end it was just a nice temperature. We pitched a tent and that was our bathroom. Within six feet of the bath, salmon were jumping.

There had been no rain for weeks and the river was very low and what salmon there were had already started to colour a bit. Our tin house overlooked a great waterfall and underneath you could wade across on the rocky bed when the river was low. Above the falls there was a long lake, and then the river began again. We were surrounded by beautiful mountains. There was much riding to be done as, except for the pools below the house, the other fishing pools were a long way apart, too far and too rough to walk.

We were fishing with very light tackle, 9/5 casts and No. 7-No. 9 flies. In this way we picked up a few fish in the low water.

One day, soon after I arrived, I rose and hooked a good fish of about twenty pounds. I saw he had taken the tail fly: I was fishing very fine 9/5 cast and he took me round a rock and smashed me, taking away most of the cast and the dropper.

Three days later Sir William Jaffary caught a small fish of five pounds with my dropper in his dorsal fin. I know I hooked my fish in the mouth with my tail fly, so I can only imagine that the dropper must have caught in the small fish, but you must work it out for yourself.

By the way, this dropper is worth remembering, as I have caught many fish with it. Size No. 10. Tail: a topping. Body: dressed very short, half silver tinsel flat. Head: half black floss silk. Wings: a pair of very small Golden Pheasant tippets, back to back. Hackle: light blue, two or three turns only.

There were very few places we could fish, as the water was so low: we were told that there were thousands of fish down below waiting to come up. I hoped they would, but we had to wait many days before we got rain.

Fish seemed to like my 'Terror' of which I have spoken in previous chapters. It has accounted for quite a number.

One day we went off to see neighbours on the same river we fished in 1936. They wanted to see dry fly fishing for salmon. Fortunately things went well and we showed them how salmon could be caught on a dry fly in very clear and low water.

What with sketching, bathing, fishing and pony riding, the days always passed too quickly.

We were told that, before we left Iceland, we must go to the town of Akuryeri, where there was an hotel. We hired a fine American car and it took us the whole day to get there. The roads for the most part were not roads at all, and it pelted with rain all the way. But the scenery was magnificent, and well worth the trip. The hotel was the most tumbledown place I have ever stayed in, in fact the balcony gave way when I walked out on it. The bath was used for cleaning the boots, and the beds looked as if they had had many tenants in the same sheets!

Next day we went off farther North to see some very fine lakes and rivers. I believe the fishing here is first class in June and July.

We saw little habitation and wondered where fishermen stayed when they went there. If you are young, you can live in a tent, but then there is always the problem of how to get rid of your fish.

I was very glad to have seen all this part of Iceland, and I have now been about three-quarters of the way round the island. It is quite different from Norway, or any other place I have been to.

We left at 8 a.m. next day and got back to our house at 8 p.m. We paid our bill at the hotel, and I find a note in my diary—'Not cheap, almost Ritz prices!'

Looking round the shops in the town, everything was of the shoddiest description, and prices four times that of any London shop. Who buys the goods it is hard to imagine, as the people are very poor. On the way back we stopped for some lunch at a rest house and got some coffee and sandwiches in the company of three lorry and car drivers. The drivers told us that there had been a lot of rain in our valley, so we started again full of hope. When we got back, we found the river in flood. We had given the Postmaster two days' fishing, and we found he had got seven fish, I think on the worm!

All this time we were troubled with the thought of war and what was happening at home. Then one fine morning, when I was fishing on the opposite side of the river, I saw a little man waving to me with a piece of paper in his hand. I waded across under the waterfall and found it to be a telegram. My friend said, 'Telegram, telegram, I think most important'; so he knew the contents all right. It was important—it said, 'Should advise your return as soon as possible'. We knew what that meant, war was upon us. My kind friend, Sir Joseph Ball, had not forgotten us.

As we had an invitation to stay at Langa Lodge on our return journey, we thought the best thing to do was to pack up and get along there, as we knew that they had a wireless set in their house.

We were very sorry to leave, but by the 21st August we knew that the best of the fishing was over as most of the fish we were now catching were coloured.

On arrival at Langa Lodge we found the war news was very bad and, personally, I found little enjoyment in fishing. We all decided that the sooner we were off the better, but the trouble was, we could not get a passage. One felt like a trapped tiger.

I find this note in my diary—'Now note this once and for all: never go to Norway or Iceland for salmon fishing after the end of July: if you do, you will be disappointed. If you are after sea trout, yes, but salmon, No!'

Sunday, 27th August. 'War news is very bad, there may be war at any moment.' We all pack up and leave Borganess by boat for Reykjavik. Everybody with nerves, in different ways.

Monday, 28th August. We had now got passages on a small boat, very overcrowded. I spent the morning trying to persuade the shipping people to land us in the North of Scotland, instead of Grimsby. This they decided to do at Peterhead, provided we were willing to pay the harbour dues, and we agreed. As a matter of fact they never charged us, as events turned out.

We sailed at 9 p.m. Our skipper, I feel sure, was a German,

anyhow he looked it and behaved as such. Our journey was a nightmare—I somehow felt that the skipper, by altering his course a bit, might land us up at Hamburg, which was his next port of call. In the Pentland Firth we met the *Hood* in all her glory, escorted by six destroyers and a number of planes over-head. She held us up and asked where we were bound for, and told us to go into Peterhead. We arrived at Peterhead at mid-night, and thanks to the forethought of Sir Harold Gillies, who had sent a wireless telegram for a motor-bus, we were able to get to Aberdeen that night.

We arrived in London the day before war was declared. So ended our journey, and I was glad to learn that our ship and skipper never did get to Hamburg, nor the cargo which it carried. Most of the cargo consisted of tons and tons of old fishing nets. Presumably for camouflage purposes for the Huns.

I went to the Fly Fishers' Club to sleep and the whole of Piccadilly was crowded with people walking about all in dark-ness, many of them very drunk. I have scarcely seen a drunken man since that night. Everybody was worked up, waiting for the morrow.

Next day war was declared at 11 a.m. What an impressive announcement it was. How much I felt for Mr Chamberlain.

One is apt to forget those early days in 1939, so I may be forgiven for recording from my diary my impressions. 'Since the war started, London has been extraordinary. The odd part about this war is—nobody seems to know anything. As an example, I met to-day Captain C., an old Member of Parliament and a distinguished one. He said, "I have come up to London to try and get some news. I have seen many of my old friends, men dis-tinguished in the last war at the Admiralty, War Office, and in Parliament, and if you will believe me, Rennie, there is not one man who knows anything more than you do".'

I find the Fly Fishers' Club has got very dull, and nobody puts on a dinner jacket when dining at a restaurant; in fact if one did so one would probably be turned out.

We had a delightful dinner party at the Garrick Club, when Sir Harold Gillies showed us his Icelandic movie films, all in colour. Really quite beautiful. Then Joseph Ball showed us his movie film of the Prime Minister fishing at Kimbridge when I was down there. Amongst those present were: our host, Sir Harold Gillies, Sir Joseph Ball, Sir Andrew Caird, Wimperis, Lord Harmsworth, Sir Frank Newnes, Fortescue, Sebastian Earle, Dr Thomas and several others, including myself. We did not leave the Garrick Club until midnight. I finished up my diary for the year with this quotation, made by King George to his people: 'I said to the man who stood at the gate of the year, give me a light that I may tread safely into the unknown, and he replied, "Go out into the darkness and put your hand into the Hand of God, that shall be to you better than the light, and safer than a known way".'

XXVI

WEIGHED IN THE BALANCE

1940

THIS has been a very trying winter, but then I always think winters are trying. This one seems to have been more so than others, hard frost and no rain since November, thermometer down to zero, and even below that in Sussex.

It is interesting to look back at one's thoughts in 1940; they seem to go up and down like a thermometer.

In March I decided to go to the Dee, and had taken Carlogie for the last fortnight. Before I left we had a dreadful spell of weather. It rained and froze as it fell, and all the trees, shrubs, telegraph wires, were covered with thick ice: birds on the telegraph wires were frozen into a ball of ice. The destruction of trees and plants was awful. I have an avenue of poplars, and they were nearly stripped of all their branches. Trains were twenty-four hours late from the North, no light or telephone: one has almost forgotten it all by now. In spite of all this a snowdrop appeared the next day.

On 17th February it started snowing again, and soon there was nine inches, so I started overlooking my fishing tackle, which I had not looked at since my return from Iceland. I generally do this in the Autumn.

I am not sure that half the trouble of sticky lines does not arise from the grease one puts on them when one is fishing

222

greased line. At the end of the season they should be well rubbed down with a silk handkerchief. I have noticed that lines which have never been greased never get sticky, so there may be something in this.

I am in despair—I have just lost one of my best friends, 'Woolley', a poodle. Every night we had a cocktail together—he had the biscuit, I had the cocktail. All the pleasure of this 7 o'clock drink has gone. Why does one give one's heart to a dog? Because they are always the same and never change.

On 14th March I started out for the Dee. Carlogie is a delightful water, moreover there is a grand fishing hut and a very nice keeper. This adds to one's pleasure enormously.

By the size of the water and the low temperature, I feared it was mostly spinning, and this proved to be the case, as the fish would not pull the fly most of the time I was there. There is a very good rule on this water: unless the gauge shows a certain height, no bait fishing is allowed before 1 o'clock. This rule is observed on both sides. One day I got into a good fish at the tail end of a pool. Below this there was broken water and rapids. The fish immediately went downstream. I thought I could follow him under the bank, which was overhung with trees. Suddenly my feet found nothing underneath them, and floated up. I grasped the branch of a tree and started shouting. The salmon was still running down and by this time had some sixty yards of line out. Mercifully, the keeper heard me down below and came running up. He took my rod and I scrambled out: then we passed the rod round from tree to tree and finally I was able to run after the fish which had now taken out about eighty yards of line. We killed him in the pool below, a lovely fish of fifteen pounds. If the keeper had not turned up, I don't know what would have been the end of the story. I had three fish that day, twenty-five and a half, nineteen and a half and fifteen pounds; not a bad day.

All our baits were mounted on 'Scarabs'. It saves no end of baits and time, as one is constantly getting into kelts. But you must fix your Scarab so that it runs up your trace.

On 28th March a blizzard started and there was nine inches of snow: fishing was very painful. On 1st April I left for home: in spite of the weather it had been a jolly trip and most enjoyable.

In May I went to the Wysham beat on the Wye but, as so often happens, I found this river in flood. Morgan, the keeper, said it would take some days to clear. He was right—I never unpacked my rods. But to make up for this there is some nice sketching at Monmouth and I spent most of my time on painting the old Monmow Bridge, a photograph of which appears in most G.W.R. carriages.

On the 12th of May I set sail for the Delfur beat on the Spey, at the kind invitation of Sir Edward Mountain. I had never fished this part of the Spey before, and for several years I was to enjoy Sir Edward's hospitality. Delfur Lodge overlooks the Spey, and you can see the fish jumping from your bedroom window. Such a glorious bit of water, and many of the pools can be fished from the bank, which I much prefer to any boat. One is more independent from the shore, and one gets more exercise. I was only there for a week, and it passed all too quickly. On the Saturday, before I left in the afternoon, I was fishing 'Broom' pool. Rather stupidly I put up my Leonard eleven-feet rod with a 9/5 cast and small fly. Well, of course I got into a really big fish. I had him on for some twenty minutes and then he took out sixty yards of line and stopped. I felt a 'grating' feeling and knew that he had rocked me. I knew I had little chance with a 9/5 cast and heavy water, so we parted—the best of friends, but very sad.

I think the most successful angler was Miss Hay—she was always getting into fish.

I was very sorry to leave—one always is when one's company, surroundings and fishing are good.

I got home in time for the May fly, and on 9th June I had a great event, fishing with Lord Burnham at Barton Court. There had been little fly or spent gnat all day, and in the evening I spent an hour gossiping with Joseph Ball on the river bank. He is a first-class person to gossip with, and the time went by quickly. I said to him, 'It is time we went fishing'. I strolled down 'Shermans' and saw a fish move on the opposite bank. Just a tail or a dorsal fin moved very slowly. I thought it was a chub, and threw a fly, a spent gnat, somewhat carelessly, but as it turned out, very accurately, just where the fish moved on the opposite bank. It was taken in very quickly, so quickly that I could hardly see the rise in the failing light. I gave him lots of time and moved my rod quietly over my left shoulder. Immediately I knew I was into a 'steam roller'. He went off down stream for about thirty yards and then jumped. I was quite right—he was a 'steam roller'. He got me into some weeds and the heads came floating up like rhubarb. What a cast I had on! and it was only 2X. He ran down nearly as far as the railway bridge, and through this you cannot follow. This is 100 yards below where I had hooked him. There he stopped, and I wound him quietly in. My net, which I had had for twenty years, is one of those in which the head of the net runs down the shaft. There is a screw at the end of the shaft which you screw up and it expands at the end. Whether it was not screwed up enough I do not know, but as soon as I got the fish into the net, the net slid off the shaft. My fish got out of the net and went off again. He was very done by this time, so I thought I would put my fingers into his gills to lift him out. This put new life into him, and away he went again. Then I saw the head of my net in the bottom of the river. I plunged my arm down to my shoulder and grasped it, then I brought the fish in again and slipped the head of the net under him, and so he was landed. That fish had no luck.

I weighed him, and he was six pounds two ounces. There was much rejoicing when I took him back to Barton Court. He was weighed on the house scales, a beautiful nickel-plated new spring balance weighing up to twenty pounds. The scales made him five pounds fourteen ounces. I could only accept this.

But, next morning, being a Monday, I sent him down to the local chemist to be weighed. The verdict was six pounds, so I don't think my scales were far wrong at six pounds two ounces for the night before.

I always mistrust new spring balances that weigh up to twenty pounds, when you are weighing fish from two to six pounds. I remember a spring balance I had for many years, which weighed up to forty pounds. On one of my trips to Norway my partners used to say at the commencement of the trip that my scale was a little liberal in its measurement of weight. Later on I always noticed that they weighed their fish on my scale. No, spring balances are not always reliable, especially when the occasion arises and you have to sell some of your fish to the local fishman. Invariably, when you get the result of the fish sent in, there is a difference of a pound or two on each fish!

I remember once, this year, when I was obliged to send a fish of twenty-one pounds to the market, I weighed it on three different scales, the kitchen scale and two spring balances. But all I got from the fishmonger was nineteen pounds!

There is no redress.

September 14th

London is now being bombarded and is an inferno. So says my diary. The Fly Fishers' Club has had some narrow squeaks. I walked round to see how another club of mine was getting on, the Arts Club in Dover Street. It was in ruins. I found the Fly Fishers' roped off—a time bomb had landed nearby.

So ends my diary for 1940, with the words 'it may go on for years. To-day the Italians have gone for Greece—28th October'.

During the first week in November I had occasion to go down to South Wales on business. I passed by the Clytha Arms hotel, where I had spent many happy days fishing the Usk. I found that a big flood a few days previously had undermined the hotel and practically the whole building had tumbled into the river. This for the sake of a few hundred pounds not having been spent in protecting the banks.

XXVII

THE LADY ANGLER

1941

THE first part of my diary this year is taken up with war news, speculations on what is going to happen, bombing, food, invasion, Home Guard, of which I am a member! But as this is a book on fishing and not a history of the war, I will leave all this alone.

It was my intention to run up to the Dee or Tay in the early part of the year, but as things were so unsettled I decided not to go. I was glad I did not go: on the Tay they had the most severe winter in memory, ten degrees and twenty degrees below zero—what a lucky escape.

My first fishing trip appears to have been on 4th April. I went down to the Wye for the week-end, on the Whitney Court water. I left my house at 4.30 a.m. by car: it was bitterly cold and foggy. When I had gone a mile or so I found that I had left my petrol licence behind, so back I had to go. What a good beginning. At 4 p.m., having fished all day and caught nothing or seen nothing, I decided to walk back to the hotel. My host, who had fished blank all day, decided to go on fishing. Soon after I left, the fish began to move and he came back with two fish, thirty-two and eighteen pounds. This is a good example of showing that you should never give up as long as you can go on fishing, but I had a cold on me and felt rather miserable at the time, otherwise I generally stick it out. We stayed at a funny old inn, dated 1360, the name 'Rhydspence', very comfortable in an old-fashioned way, and the feeding was excellent. In the evening I had my first lesson at 'Darts'. I was not much good—the locals were, and it cost me several pints of beer. My kind host gave me the eighteen-pounder, and a better fish I have seldom eaten.

I left on Thursday, 1st May, for Delfur on the Spey, to fish once more with another kind host, Sir Edward Mountain. Sleepers and dinner on the train were quite easy in those days, just as if nothing was happening in the world. I got to Delfur next day at 12.30 p.m., changed, had lunch and got away fishing. What a joy to be on this lovely river again amongst friends. I was very unlucky for the next three days, I think I was fishing with too small flies. Others were getting fish and I could not meet them. It is funny how things go this way at times.

On Sunday we went for a picnic lunch: I shall always remember this for the following reasons. We took a salmon to the R.A.F. mess near Lossiemouth. We arrived at the aerodrome, went in at the gates, walked about looking for the Mess. Nobody stopped us nor asked us what we were doing. I remember I had a camera on my back. Eventually we found the Mess and a cheery lot of officers, and delivered the salmon, had some drinks and departed. Can you imagine that in Germany? On the way back I stopped and looked at Ramsay Macdonald's house, a very ugly and depressing looking house. It is interesting to see where the well-known have lived and been brought up.

On Monday I tried fishing with larger flies, Nos. 4, 5 and 6, and started doing much better amongst them at twenty-nine and a half and nineteen and a half pounds, then a twenty-six pounds; next day a twenty-eight and eighteen pounds. One morning when they were not pulling I put on my old friend, the 'Terror'. The fish came at it with a great lunge and splash and generally a pull, but out of quite a number of rises I got only one fish. Anyhow, it woke them up a bit.

A fly that I did well on is as follows: Tail, a topping; body, flat silver tinsel; hackle, a black heron; wings, two strips of Golden Pheasant tail. It is a simple fly to tie and did very well. Hook No. 5 and 6.

My time had come to an end. I don't know when I have en-

joyed a visit so much. I caught my train on the 14th May on my
way to fish the Dee at Ballater. I stayed at the Loriston Hotel,
Ballater, a most comfortable place and very well run.

I started my fishing on 15th May on the Invercauld beat. This
is a nice bit of water but has been neglected. The banks have
fallen in and many of the pools are silted up. The yield of fish on
this beat used to be enormous, and I understand that as many
as 1,000 fish had been killed here in one season. Well, these
baskets are not made now, and unless some attention is given to
this water, I doubt if they ever will again.

It was snowing hard when I started the first day, and it was
evident that the fish were not in the water. I did not get a fish
until the 17th. I heard that there were loads of fish down below,
and with a change of weather they might come up. As a matter
of fact, they never did come up until 1st June, the day after my
fishing was over. I spent a long time on the bridge at Ballater
watching them coming up in hundreds, but I heard afterwards
that the rods did very badly on this stretch, as the fish ran
through the water. I put this down, to a great extent, to the
silting up of the pools. Nevertheless, during my fortnight I
generally managed to pick up a fish or two each day; but it was
not what one expected.

The scenery is wonderful in this part of the Dee, and a trip up
to Balmoral and the old Brig of Dee is delightful.

The most successful fly was as follows: body and hackle as
a 'Logie'; wings, light Brown Turkey, split, the same as 'Ackroyd'—whether there was anything in this pattern of fly I don't
know. I must again say that my old friend, the 'Terror', accounted for several fish, but only after having tried the fish with
many other small flies.

Towards the end of my time I got a telegram from a friend,
'Will you come and fish at Cairnton 1st to 7th June'. Here was
a bit of luck. Of course I accepted. On 1st June I took the motor-
bus to Cairnton and met a taxi, by arrangement, which took me to
the house. I arrived before my host, so spent the time looking up
and down the pools. It was Sunday, so no fishing. Presently my
host arrived with two ladies. None of them know much about
fishing, in fact none of them had ever caught a salmon! We spent

Sunday afternoon practising casting on the lawn. We overhauled tackle and rods. I found I was the only one with long waders. We got some rods from my friend, Playfair, of Aberdeen.

Cairnton is a lovely fishing lodge. It stands about 150 yards from the river and is about half-way on the water. Everything is beautifully arranged for the fisherman, even for the man who comes down late for breakfast, although I cannot understand any fisherman coming down late here: but if he does, there is a cupboard in the dining-room electrically heated, where the breakfast is placed! The rod room is a dream, all the details thought out by Wood—great big line winders, trays to soak your casts, etc., etc.

The bathrooms had enormous taps: your bath filled in about two minutes. All these things were designed by Wood.

I felt that the whole atmosphere was pervaded by Wood. When I walked back in the evening, and it was nearly dark, I felt sure that I would meet him at some turning. I should not have felt surprised or nervous. I would have chatted to him in a natural way and asked him all kinds of questions. I was disappointed that I never did meet him; but somehow during the whole of that week I felt his presence very near.

That week at Cairnton was sheer delight. We fished from Monday until midday Saturday. I killed twenty-seven fish. The weather was heavenly, the fish were very shy. They came and nibbled the fly, as they do in prawn fishing: but if you gave them plenty of loose line, they eventually took it. The 'Grey Mare' pool was the best, and here I saw one of the prettiest exhibitions of casting from the opposite bank—this from a lady. I sat down and watched her. She had a perfect figure and rhythm. When she had finished I could not help taking off my hat and saying to the man who was with her, 'That's the prettiest exhibition of casting I have seen for a long time'—his reply was not very encouraging to my most sincere appreciation. Jealous perhaps!

The last night I fished the 'Grey Mare' I had on my cast a 'Black Heron' No. 6. It was getting very dark and I kept getting pull after pull, but nothing held on. At last I reeled up, and it was then that I found that my cast had hitched up over the wing and hackle, and I presume that was why they would not hold on.

This was the end of my Cairnton visit, all too short, but lovely all the time.

It must have been a very late season, as any amount of fish were running up to the time I left on 7th June. I should think you could do quite fifty per cent of your fishing at Cairnton without wetting your boots. There are very few beats on the Dee that can boast of this; most of the beats I know are pretty rough going.

On the way back I stopped the night with friends in Edinburgh. Edinburgh hospitality is something to remember and I did not get to bed until the small hours in the morning.

I have little to tell about the May fly season on the Kennet this year, except that, for some unaccountable reason, it was ten to twelve days late in coming up.

On 11th June I fished at Barton Court: there were no fly or fish to be seen. Usually the fishing is mostly finished by this time. On the 15th I fished at Benham, a moderate day and many fishermen on the banks. I found quite a number fishing down stream with a wet fly.

Barton Court on 16th June: no fishing all day.

19th June, Barton Court. The evening before they had a wonderful time for a couple of hours. The four best fish were six pounds, five pounds, four pounds, three and a half pounds. Lord Burnham got the six-pounder; I was so glad. The five-pounder was caught in the famous pool known as the 'Hog Pen'. Anyone who has fished at Barton Court will remember this place. At the top end of the Hog Pen runs the railway bridge, then there is a stretch of about fifty yards and a foot bridge, and below the foot bridge the stream enters the canal. I should think that this piece of water has accounted for as many big fish as anywhere on the Kennet.

Well, the five-pounder was hooked by a lady in the 'Hog Pen' and after playing up and down took a dash under the foot bridge into the canal. Fortunately her husband was with her, and between them they managed to pass the rod under the bridge and follow the fish into the canal.

By this time the fish had got into a fine bank of weeds and was securely fixed there. After a long time the husband decided that the only thing to do was to strip and go into the canal. It was now nearly midnight so there was no one on the towpath. He went out with his net, felt with his hand down the cast and got his net under the fish and to bank. What a triumph of perseverance and gentle handling, but then the lady is one of the best fishers on the Kennet.

But to go back to my day which followed this event. There was little doing most of the day so we went back to dinner. A bottle of 1840 brandy was produced, which gave me plenty of hope for the evening rise. I got three lovely fish, the best four and a half pounds. So to bed at 1 a.m.

I had several more days after this, but there was little fishing in the daytime. This I attribute, to some extent, to the excessive weed cutting. In hot weather fish will not come out into the open in a river that is shaved of weed. Moreover, with no weed, they can see the nymph hatching out far more distinctly, and so they rush about picking up the nymphs and not bothering to let them rise to the surface. Perhaps I am wrong, it is only my observation that leads me to think this way.

This year I have taken a small piece of water on the Test, Houghton Lodge water. There is about 800 yards of fishing in the middle of the Houghton Club water. It is a pretty little bit of water, but I found it lacking in trout, but a good many grayling. Owing to the war, it was difficult to get down there and I only managed it four times in the season for week-ends.

In August I badly wanted to get away up North again, and I thought of Woodend on the Dee. My kind friend, Major Wybrants, sent me a wire to come up, but I knew full well—or rather I thought I did—that there was little chance of sport on the Dee in the first week in August.

Things often turn out differently from what one expects, and so it happened at Woodend this August. I went up on the night of 1st August, got a 'sleeper' and dined on the train. There was time next morning to do some shopping before leaving for Deeside. The shopping consisted mostly of hunting for 'Three Nuns' tobacco. By going into eight shops, I managed to get half a pound. in London I had drawn blank. On arrival at Woodend I found the water dead low, and a few old black fish splashing about. This is just what I had expected, so I was not disappointed.

On 5th August it started raining hard and next morning the river had risen two feet. It was a question of bait fishing, as the water was so thick. Got two fish, and not bad ones either—they must be running up.

On 7th August the river was in lovely order and if any fresh fish had run up, we should get some.

This turned out to be the case; there were plenty of fish in the water and good ones, just as clean as June fish, and plenty of fight in them. I suppose it is something very exceptional, this late run.

I had on a small No. 8 'Butcher'. This little fly used to work wonders on the sea trout at Elvegard, Norway. It worked wonders here, and I got four nice fish before lunch. They came very gingerly, and unless you had a yard or so of slack, and let them have it, they would not take hold at all. I rose a large number of fish, and the fun was great.

If I had not stopped to go back to the house for lunch, I might have got several more. Anyhow, I finished with seven fish for the day on a 9/5 cast and eleven-feet Leonard. What more could you want?

The next day, the fish were more particular. I never kept count of the number of fish that I rose, but there were a great many. I finished up with two fish, eight pounds each. I wonder why one rose so many fish—one tried them at all angles, but they rose just as well at one angle as another. I think the answer is light and gut flash.

Saturday, 9th August, I rose quite a dozen fish on 'Hardy Shrimp' fly, size No. 6, but, like the day before, they would not take hold. In the afternoon I walked down to Cairnton and watched the Grey Mare and other pools. I saw quite a number of fish jumping and they were all very black. Why were these fish black, just a mile farther down, and our fish at Woodend almost like springers?

I notice that the Government are cutting down a tremendous amount of timber opposite Cairnton on the Blackhall side. I wonder if it will make any difference to the fishing? I have known this happen in other places. Salmon are very curious in their likes and dislikes.

We got two fish in the evening, eighteen pounds and nine pounds. The larger fish is a stale one.

The only time I ever felt pleased about packing up and going away was in 1939 when we left Iceland!

A short week-end on the Test in September, and this is the finish for 1941.

I won't say what I wrote in my diary about the war in December, 1941, but it is amusing to read these words now.

1942

And so we come to another year. Singapore is about to fall, Rommel is galloping back towards Egypt. The three German battleships have just steamed up the Channel—what a dreary winter. The less said about it the better.

15th March. I am going to stay at Woodend. 'Sleepers' are still obtainable, with a cup of tea and bread and butter in the morning.

When I got to Woodend, I found that a flood had started, the first one for weeks. The gauge is four feet six inches, which is high water, so I took out a spinning rod. I got a large kelt: one hook in his mouth, the other in my finger. So I had a very sore finger for three days!

Now there is a big flood, eight feet. I don't know how many kelts have to be landed and returned, certainly over twenty. So one was pretty busy all the time. This is where the 'Scarab' comes in, and I don't suppose that I used more than three Golden Sprats in the day.

On 18th the water started to go down and the fresh fish were appearing. I got a 'botcher'* of twenty-one pounds. It was like an autumn fish, and the flesh quite pink, so I was told: another nice clean fish of eight pounds.

After this we began to get fresh fish every day, and on 25th March it is a spring day. Four fish to-day, nine, ten, six and seventeen pounds. The last one was a 'gallery' fish. All the fishing party happened to be around me. Several times he took out sixty and eighty yards of line, and very nearly went down the rapids. Such a grand fish.

On 30th March we started off well, five fish by lunch, then the

* *Botcher*, a salmon which has never spawned.

wind changed and not another touch. This change of wind is a very curious thing. Two days before, it was blowing from the East and no one got a fish. Late in the afternoon, when all the others had gone home, it suddenly changed to the South. I got two fish very quickly and thought I was going to get several more, but—the wind changed again to the East, and not another touch did I get.

31st March, my last day. The river started rising, and fresh fish were to be seen running everywhere. In spite of the rise I got two fish. So ends a very happy trip.

On the 6th May I was again fortunate enough to be on my way to the Spey at Delfur with Sir Edward Mountain.

This place is always delightful. You never know what you are going to get into. Thirty-pounders are not scarce and occasionally you see something very much larger, which sends a tremor all down your back when your rod is only twelve feet and your cast is 7/5!

My last morning I was fishing alone, and I did a shameful thing. I saw a large fish rise. He took me well and for thirty minutes he gave me a grand fight, all over the pool. I had no doubt he was a clean fish: the sun was in my eyes when I gaffed him. He was one of those wonderful kelts which one meets with sometimes on the Spey, quite different from the ordinary kelt, and if it were not for the colour of his eye, anyone might have been mistaken. He was near thirty pounds.

I cannot remember any time or place when I lost so many fish. Fish that ran me for ten and fifteen minutes and then came unstuck. Bad fishing I suppose, but why on this particular trip?

On 16th May I departed, feeling rather small and depressed.

On 17th May I was at Woodend again.

On 21st May nine fish, on 22nd five fish, after this it tails off. Then the river goes down to nothing. Without doubt, the safest time for the mid reaches of the Dee is the last fortnight in April and the first fortnight in May: after that it is chancy.

For some reason this year fish on the Dee and Spey seemed to favour flies with black bodies and black hackles. I killed several fish on the Dee and the Spey with the following fly on No. 5 long hook; tail, a topping; body, half yellow floss, half black floss;

hackle, black cock, or small black heron for preference; wings, two strips from a Cinnamon Turkey. But, such is one's fancy, one rod on the Dee got most of his fish on the 'Demon', a contraption of three small hooks tied in the same manner as the 'Terror': length of body one and a half inches, the wing a bunch of peacock herl with two narrow strips of Golden Pheasant tail, and a topping. It is wonderful how large fish may be caught on these very small hooks.

I sent a number of salmon away by post, but those sent by rail never arrived.

The May fly season on the Kennet this year has been a complete failure. The summer was a very poor one: we had only one really hot day, the rest of the time it was cold, cloudy and rainy.

As there is no means of getting about now, there has been no fishing for me. I envy those few people who live on their water.

By September, that restless spirit came over me again and I felt that I must have one more throw at a salmon before the long winter shuts me down. The difficulty in the autumn is to know where to go. There are so few places which have an autumn run of fish. Finally I settled on my old friend, the Awe. I had not been there for many years and I wanted to have a look at it again. It was now the 25th September, which was rather late. I spent the first day walking up and down the river, looking at old pools and going over old battles I had had with fish. It is thirty-three years since I was on the lower water, and it was much like turning over an old book one had read years before.

The beat I had taken was on the left bank from Awe Bridge to the Brander Pass.

On the 30th September, my birthday, I got into a nice fish on the fly, seventeen and a half pounds, and not at all a bad colour. The next day was quite exciting. There were a lot of fish moving about, so there had evidently been a fresh run up with the high water. I rose several fish in Garavelt but hooked none until I got into a big fish of thirty pounds or more. He gave me a fine dance all over the river. The river is very rocky here and after twenty minutes he suddenly stopped. I went below, I went above. I did all I could to move him, finally the line came back—the fly was gone and the end of the cast was like a grey mare's tail! After this I got a couple of smallish fish.

It was very amusing fishing, the fish kept on 'nibbling' the fly, just as they will do sometimes with a prawn. If you threw out a yard of slack, they very often took hold. The next day I got three fish, nineteen, eighteen and six pounds. They were all well shaped fish and quite worth catching. Practically all the fish were caught on the 'Morgan' fly. This fly was invented by a boatman on the Wye. Although I tried many other patterns, this seemed to be the only fly they cared about, so I give its dressing: Tag, silver; tail, a few strands from Golden Pheasant breast feather; body, dirty yellow seals' fur; ribs, oval gold tinsel; hackle, coch y bondhu; wings, two strips of Turkey black or dark bronze with white tips. I have killed fish with this fly in all kinds of rivers and I can recommend it without fear.

I finish up my diary for this year with the following remark: 'My chief thought this year is the number of fish I have lost. When I say lost, I mean fish that have been on for some minutes, not merely "plucks".' I don't think it was my fault, as I was conscious of having fished better this year than in other years. There is always this comforting thought, if I had not fished well I should not have hooked so many fish! But the fact remains, and what I am certain of is this, that if I had not been fishing greased line all the season, I should not have hooked nearly so many fish.

Travelling has now become almost impossible, and one wonders if one will be able to travel at all next year.

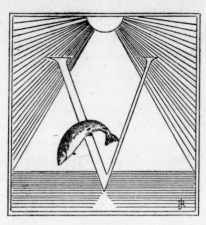

XXVIII

A GOOD YEAR

A NEW diary begun. It is 1943 and I have taken a beat on the Dee at Dinnet, Glentana Water, and left London on 29th March. I stayed at 'Profit's Hotel', Dinnet. Most comfortable, and obliging people. This water was new to me, so I spent the morning going over the river with a gillie. He was a nice man, by name Alec Thompson, very keen, and ties a good fly. I found out from him that as a rule the fish do not get up here in any quantities until May. You live and learn. He was quite right, there were very few fish in the water. Part of this water, known as 'C' beat, I like very much: other parts are dull to my way of thinking. The famous Logie pool, about 400 yards above the bridge, is a dream to the greased line angler. If only it had held more fish when I was there!

Waterside, at the bottom of the beat, is a fine great pool, but the drawback to fishing it from the right-hand bank is, first, you are fishing from a high bank with deep water below you and shallow on the other side, and second, you have the road just behind you, where there is a procession of timber lorries and cars passing by. It would be a bore to hook a lorry in your back cast, but this I managed to avoid. I think that Waterside is a pool trading on its past history. Most of the other pools held no fish.

Certainly the weather was not kind, and for the first few days we had heavy snow, but afterwards it cleared and there was little excuse for the lack of fish.

238

The result was fifteen fish for the fortnight, very poor work. Knowing that anything in the form of drinks was hard to come by in Scotland, I sent up a case of what I thought necessary, by advanced luggage, together with my rod box. The rod box arrived, but not so the drinks.

I tried to convince the porter that the other case had arrived, but he assured me with the sweetest of smiles that it had not. The Police called on me late one night and produced an 'otter' which I had packed up with the drinks. The 'otter' gave the show away and the culprit was convicted and sentenced. I still have the 'otter', but I never got the drinks.

Just as I was leaving, my old friend, Arthur Severn, turned up to fish the same water. It was Arthur who had proposed me for the Fly Fishers' Club many years earlier. He and his party did not do very well after I left. This double summertime upsets the fishing: the gillies down tools at 5 p.m., which is really 3 p.m., and the sun does not get off the water until after this time. One gillie would stick to the 5 p.m., G.M.T., so when I said that it was quite all right, and I was perfectly happy fishing alone, in fact I preferred it, he was 'as sick as mud', as they say. But Thompson was a grand chap.

From Dinnet I went on to Woodend, and in spite of the recent flood I found that there were plenty of fish in the water. I started off with five fish the first day and six the second. Not too bad. Thank goodness I had not got a gillie: I am much happier without, except for the trouble of having to carry one's fish home, but with the help of a bicycle it is not too bad. I was catching them all on a 'Blue Charm' No. 6 and 7, and no losses. Other rods were getting them on the 'Logie' and 'Jeannie': size is all that matters. The next day I got seven fish, all on 'Blue Charm'. When the evening came I put on my night fly. It is a large fly—hook, 1½; body, half yellow and half black floss; ribs, silver twist; hackle, a long black heron, as long as the bend of the hook; wings, two narrow strips of Light Buff Turkey, tied flat. It is a wonderful killer at night.

For the next few days I went on averaging six fish a day. On 21st April I had one of those experiences never to be forgotten. There is a pool called the 'Morrel'. At the tail of the Morrel there is heavy broken water, big rocks and rapids which continue for about 500 yards before you come to the Hut pool. I had caught two fish in the Morrel and when I had got to the tail end, just before the rapids, it was 10 p.m. and it was almost dark. At the very tail I got a long heavy pull. I knew it was a good fish and I was frightened. It was so near the rapids, and my cast was 7/5. If I pulled on him, I knew he would go over. I kept a light strain and started to edge my way back. The wading was none too good in the dark, the water pretty strong. Foot by foot he followed me up some twenty yards, then back he would go to the brink. The process started over again, with the same result. At 10.20 a terrific 'blitz' started, and I imagined that Aberdeen was getting it. There were planes going overhead, and the sky was lit up, but on went the battle of the salmon. There was a great noise of bombs and gunfire. This went on until 10.45 p.m., and by that time I had worked my fish up eighty yards. It was now 11 p.m. and pitch dark. I could not get my fish to come into the shallow water and I could not see the top of my rod. At 11.10 I did see the water break three yards away from me. I got out my gaff and made a good shot and dragged him through the shallow water to the shore. I had this fish on for an hour and ten minutes, and I am sure that if I had been rough with him I should have lost him in the rapids. I left the fish, the rod and tackle in the fishing hut and got home at midnight. What a lovely day. Altogether, the three rods got 157 fish for the fortnight. One does not often hit it off like that.

On the 1st May I went to the Spey to fish the Delfur water. I caught few fish and the river was too high. It was very cold and there was snow on the ground, but it is always a pleasure to be entertained by Sir Edward and Lady Mountain.

The Kennet did not behave itself in June and I have only one recollection of a huge trout I saw in the half water on Geoffrey Turner's water. This stream is fairly shallow, and at the head there are hatches and a deep pool. I saw this fish about thirty yards below the pool on the opposite bank. It was moving along slowly, not feeding. Suddenly it appeared to have a 'brain storm'. It rushed out into the stream, plunged about and worked towards the pool. I was so taken aback, I did not know what to do as, as far as I could see, it was not feeding. Then suddenly I thought that the fish had furunculosis—I had seen a fish behaving like that at Barton Court and after a bit he had floated down on his back. So I thought this fish was doing the same and I waited to see him float down. Nothing more happened. The keeper, Brown, came up soon after and we waited for about an hour. We never saw him again. I said, 'Brown, that fish was about seven pounds'. Brown saw him next day and said he was eight pounds! I can only conclude that he was after minnows, but I was so petrified at the time I could do nothing, and it was all over in a minute or so.

On 3rd July I went down to stay as the guest of Sir Harold Gillies and members of the Houghton Club at Stockbridge. It was very, very hot and very delightful. Quite one of the nicest week-ends I have ever spent. Such grand company and perfect hosts. I shall thank them always for their kindness and hospitality.

We caught quite a nice basket of trout in the evenings, getting back to the Club rooms at about 10.30 p.m. and so to bed, after having stayed up until midnight telling each other stories about the day's sport. This is the perfect club and perfect fishing.

There is one little incident I would like to record. I was fishing with the keeper, Lunn, a delightful companion with eyes like a hawk. Thanks to him, I got several fish, which I don't think I should have got without him. As a fisherman on strange water one is always at a disadvantage, at least I always feel so, and on a water like Stockbridge, where the rise is often quick and short, by the time you have found out what the fish are taking, the light has gone, the rise is over. This is where Lunn was so helpful. He told me one thing which intrigued me. I saw a rise under a footbridge, just one movement—no more. I cast several times with no result. Lunn said, 'Put on a very small sedge and give it a good bang on the water'. I did so and up came the fish: it was hooked but not landed. Quite a new idea to me—I shall remember that.

In August it was impossible to go anywhere, stations were invaded in their thousands. So I went down to Henley for three days to stay at my old Club, Leander. I had not stayed there for thirty years. It was just the same and I met several old friends that I had not met since my Cambridge days, amongst them one or two fishermen. But if there was no change in the Club, there was a great change in the river. It was Bank Holiday, and hundreds were camping out up the river above Henley. They seemed to be enjoying themselves, and the scarcity of their garments was most remarkable. One young lady, having enjoyed her bathe, threw off her bathing dress and proceeded to dry herself without one stitch on! and appeared to be quite unconcerned. Then a terrific thunderstorm and wind came down on us: it blew down the tents, it turned over boats. I fled—I did not want to see any more; but a picture of 1899, which was my last rowing year, kept coming up in my mind, and I know that I now belonged to a past generation.

North Esk. Through the kind invitation of a friend I was asked to fish the North Esk. I had often heard of this river and what a capital autumn river it was. So on 20th September I started off for Montrose. The river runs into the sea two and a half miles north of Montrose and the beat which I fished was from the Bridge up, for I suppose, about two and a half to three miles. I found it most charming water to fish and what was more to the point, the fish were almost as bright as spring fish, in fact I have caught many fish in the spring which were not so good. I do not know what they were like to eat as we had to send all the fish away to the owner, except one each. We smoked ours and they were excellent and of good colour, but what they were like fresh I don't know.

The first week we stuck to the fly and although we saw plenty of fish they would not pull the fly well and I only got two. The second week we took to bait. We had no prawns, but I did have a couple of artificial ones, which I had had for many years and never used. These had a celluloid spinner at the tail. The result was almost immediate, four fish, twenty-eight and a half, twenty, twenty, fifteen and three-quarter pounds, and all good fish. As we were fishing with 'Elarex' reels and nine-pound lines with nine-feet light rods it was very good fun. The appearance and fighting qualities of the fish were all that you could wish for, and so the fun went on.

A few days after this, someone sent me a dozen fresh prawns. I thought this might be even better. It was not, we never got a fish on the fresh prawns and as soon as we put on the artificial, we got fish again. I think it must have been the colour. The fresh ones were light pink, the artificial dark red. I have tried the artificial on two occasions since this on other rivers, with no result.

There was a lunatic asylum close to one of the pools and some of the inmates would come round and watch us. They were quite simple and well behaved, and I am sure they thought we were the lunatics. Perhaps they were not far wrong!

This river is netted for some considerable distance up and there is no rod fishing until the nets are taken off in September. It seems such a pity that a beautiful water should be treated in this manner. Attempts have been made to get the nets off, but with no success.

On 30th September—I always catch fish on my birthday—I was fishing below the 'Goyle' which is a dam, and a large fish took me on a small No. 6 Prawn fly and 7/5 cast. I hooked him in the rough water below the 'Goyle' and he ran up under my feet, gave me a slack line and I said, 'He's off'. I reeled up slowly, feeling sure that the fish had departed, when, to my surprise, he took a run out of sixty yards. For forty minutes I had one of the best fights with that fish you could want. Time after time he went across and up the river into the heavy water. He would not give in: he was twenty-seven pounds, and a lovely fish.

The average weight of our fish that week, leaving out the two small ones caught the first week, was over twenty pounds.

On the 5th October I finished my fishing for 1943.

I came away with the feeling that Montrose was a delightful little town and the civility of the shop people was such a change after London. The hotel was excellent, and more obliging people you could not find. The name of the hotel was 'The Star'. Certainly the fish were the best autumn fish I have ever caught.

I lost very few fish this year. At Woodend I hooked fifty-seven fish in eleven days and got fifty-four. This is exceptional: I think it is owing to my new method of striking, or rather not striking but allowing them a free running reel when they take and then a swing of the rod over to the bank without touching the line or reel. Anyhow, this method suits me.

I met a young man at the Fly Fishers' Club who said to me: 'I must thank you for your tip about striking: I had wonderful success this season'. I did not remember having given him the tip, but it was nice of him to remember.

People have been writing to the fishing papers saying that they have yet to find a means of catching fish when they pull you from below. Now, I must have caught quite forty per cent of my fish taken from below, or nearly so. I put this down to the method which I have described. I hope I do not appear to be dogmatic: I am only trying to help those of no great experience.

POTARCH. R. DEE

XXIX

PASSING REMARKS—1944

I DECIDED this year to go up to the Dee in May and June so that one could see the country at its best, and enjoy fishing under more favourable weather conditions than one gets in March and April. In this I was mistaken, as it hardly stopped raining and blowing during the whole six weeks I was away. The first fortnight in May was not too bad but the temperature for the most part was low, and the water temperature was higher than the atmosphere. This made the fish run, and after the 15th May the fishing at Woodend and thereabouts was practically over.

This is the sort of thing I find in my diary:

29th April. Morning bright, two fish. Afternoon cold wind, no fish.

1st May. Howling gale, water fifteen degrees above air temperature, no fish.

3rd May. Air forty degrees, water fifty degrees, no fish.

4th May. Easterly gale, air forty-two degrees, water forty-eight degrees, blank.

And so it went on. When the weather improved a little, then we got fish.

By the 15th May, most of the fish had moved up: they were running in hundreds.

1st June. I thought we might catch the fish a few miles up at Carlogie. There were plenty of fish there the week before, but a flood on 2nd June took most of them away, and so it went on for a fortnight, a succession of floods and gales. In spite of this we managed to pick up an odd fish here and there.

245

Is there anything in a fly or not? or is it only size? My last day at Carlogie looked like being a blank: I had risen a number of stale fish on a No. 9 fly, but nothing would take hold. We had all been down the Calm Pool many times in the day: the other rods had packed up and were waiting for the car. I remembered a fly given to me by Mr William Barry, a 'Gled Wing' on No. 7 hook. I fished all the way down the Pool to the end of 'Lucky Hole': it was my very last cast, when bang went the reel and I knew I was into a good fish. He was on the edge of the rough water and as I had only a 8/5 cast, it required gentle handling. He was all over the river, up and down, across and back again. A very lively fish. At last I was able to draw him into shallow water by walking back twenty to thirty feet. He was a beautiful fresh run fish of twenty-one pounds. The car came up for me at that moment: the day was not a blank.

Now although I had been down that pool three times before and used a similar sized fly—and others had done the same thing—not a touch had any of us had. Was it the 'Gled Wing', or was it not?

That finished my fishing for the season, as I hardly count a later visit to Faskally at the end of September, as the fish were so red we started putting them back: they were not worth catching.

I was too late for the May fly when I got home on 17th June. They had a poor year on the Kennet. I have only missed one other year on the Kennet, which was in 1898, the year I went to Central Africa.

As the lower part of the Test, from Stockbridge down, was out of bounds, there was no question of a visit down to these parts.

As I have said, at the end of September I had the opportunity of going to Faskally on the Tummel. A more lovely bit of fishing you cannot imagine. The River Garry runs into the Tummel just below the falls. Every pool is a dream, and for the most part you can fish almost every one without wetting your feet.

The late autumn run of fish on the Tay never seem to get as far as the Tummel; in fact they told me at Perth that most of them do not go beyond Dunkeld: whether this is so or not I cannot say.

One of my reasons for going to Faskally was to try and find out something about the new power scheme which the Government have in hand. If this takes place, goodbye to all the fishing above Pitlochry, because the whole valley, up to the Loch Tummel, will be one huge reservoir, created by a big dam at Pitlochry. As we all know, this is one of the beauty spots in Scotland. Thousands come to see the Queen's View, the Falls of Tummel, the Soldier's Leap and Glen Garry. All this will be destroyed with disastrous results to all the inhabitants and hotel keepers in Pitlochry. But the Bill will not go through without a fight, and let us hope the rivers will win.*

* The Bill was passed in Parliament in November, 1945, so the Tummel is doomed for ever.

HUNGERFORD BRIDGE.

XXX

SEASONS 1945 AND 1946

I DO not suppose that any salmon fisher has experienced two such unfortunate years in the whole course of his salmon fishing career, indeed, there were few fish to enter the rivers in 1945 and it would appear from all reports that 1946 has been even worse.

What is the cause of this shortage of fish for the past two years? I have heard no reasonable explanation. One has read and discussed a number of theories to account for this universal shortage; but I do not think that any of them are the correct answer. These speculations have undoubtedly accounted for a great many fish; but not the failure, which has been so widespread in the British Isles and also in all parts of the Atlantic coast.

Let us examine some of them. In April, 1945, I was on the Brora in Sutherland. There was much discussion as to the depth charges from planes, which seemed to be continually ranging the coast. It may have been practice or not, but that is beside the point. These depth charges may have done some harm during the past four or five years, but surely they could not have accounted for the universal damage which has taken place.

I understand that the fish of the sea are more plentiful than ever and they have not suffered.

Now let us examine a cutting from the *Daily Express* dated 3rd June, 1946.

It is headed 'The Salmon Mystery. Grenade poaching made this famine' and I have taken extracts from the article.

'The Scottish salmon famine is worse this year (1946), although in 1945 the salmon yield was the worst since 1800. Yet it will not improve for several years.'

'Thousands of millions of young fish, which by now would have been returning to their native rivers after their first trip to the sea as smelts three, four, or five years ago, were destroyed by hand grenades and other explosives used by troops in Scotland to kill the grown salmon.'

'I have found irrefutable evidence of this in north, west and east of Scotland.'

'Mr Dyson, of Cambas O'May Hotel on Upper Deeside, told me that in the latter days of the war, he visited an army camp on Upper Deeside where 2,000 men had salmon twice a day in October. He asked a sergeant-major how it was done. Smilingly, the sergeant-major made a gesture of unhitching a grenade from his belt and hurling it into the river.'

'In the West Highlands I found incontrovertible evidence of similar destruction.'

'Mr Mitchell, Aberdeen Salmon Exporter, said yesterday: "The season has been twice as bad as 1945. The fish simply are not on the coast".'

'A gillie of forty years' experience on Rivers Dee, Don, Spey and Deverson said "I am not looking for a return to runs of pre-war magnitude until 1950".'

This theory may certainly apply to some of our rivers; but certainly not to all of them, I have not heard that the Tay has suffered in this respect and yet there were no fish there this year.

Another theory which has been put forward is the vast number of predatory fish which have accumulated round our coast from the lack of trawling, I refer to such possible species as conger, dogfish and the like. These fish have been waiting at the mouths of our rivers for the smolts to enter the sea. I think that there is more scope for argument in this theory; but here again, a sea angler informs me that these fish have their homes in rocky places, where trawlers cannot sweep them. But there is no doubt that they increased to a very great extent during the war.

Seals have also increased in number all round our coasts. On the Tay where I was fishing this year, 1946, out of fifteen fish caught, twelve of them had been attacked by seals or some other monster. But seals only account for matured fish, and in my experience, generally the large fish.

I think on the whole, although great numbers of salmon may have perished from these various causes, there must be some other reason for the shortage of fish for the years 1945 and 1946.

But to go back to the year 1945. In April I took the Brora

river in Sutherland. There is an admirable rule on this river made by the respective proprietors. One side takes the top beat one day and the other side the lower beat and they change over each day or at half-time each day. By this means there is no rod on the opposite bank. There are only two rods on either side. No bait fishing is allowed. A more pleasant little river it would be hard to find and most of the fishing is from the bank. The river rises very quickly, but clears very quickly after a flood. The whole of the water can be fished comfortably with a twelve-feet rod. This part of the river runs from Loch Brora to the sea, a distance of about five to six miles. At the mouth of the river there is the little town of Brora, with two very good hotels, a golf course and lovely sands for those who want to bathe. My party went there full of hope, as the records of this river show anything from seventy to one hundred salmon for the month of April on either side.

Although we went on hoping that the salmon would come up and there was every inducement for them to do so, practically no fish entered the river in April. Our total bag was eleven fish. Well, you have to make the best of these things and in spite of the lack of fish, we enjoyed ourselves in the beautiful surroundings and lovely air. On 27th April we had a snow storm, which lasted for two days.

We were not alone in the lack of fish, as the Helmsdale and other rivers north and south of us had fared in the same way. On the 30th April I left Brora in a snowstorm at 6 a.m. I did not get to Banchory until 6 p.m. The Railway Company seems to take a joy in arranging the trains so that you have to wait several hours in Inverness and Aberdeen.

I was on my way to Woodend on the Dee to fish once more, for a fortnight, that lovely stretch of water. I thought that the Dee might prove better than the Brora, but alas! these hopes soon vanished and the accounts which one gathered from various sources were anything but hopeful.

I started fishing on the 1st May and I have seldom been so cold at any time of the year. The air was five degrees colder than the water. It was blowing a gale from the North and I was glad to stop fishing at 5.30 p.m., having drawn a total blank.

On 2nd May things were not much better and although I saw quite a number of fish on the run, I failed to interest them in any way with ordinary pattern of flies in all sizes. Then I put on a 'Terror' tied with two narrow strips of Heron and up came a fish like a tiger—but he shied off. Then I rose two more in the same way. At last I hooked one, a good fish, but he came unstuck—then another came short. Anyhow the 'Terror' does move fish when nothing else will. Then at last one came with a bang and I got him—nine pounds. I got one more rise on this fly—or whatever you like to call it; but as the river was now rising I stopped fishing.

On the 4th May, I was rather pleased with myself, and for the following reason. For many years I owned a huge 'Castle Connell' rod of eighteen feet. This rod had a history as my friend, David Muir, won the Switch Casting Event with this rod at some tournament twenty years ago. His record cast remained good for some ten or fifteen years. Then he sold the rod at one of the Fly Fishers' Club sales and I bought it for £1.

It was too big and heavy to fish with, so one winter I started to cut it down and turn it into a thirteen-feet spliced rod. It took me a very long time to do this; but at last it was finished to my satisfaction. Well, on 4th May I took it out to christen it and I had not been fishing very long before I was into something which was a good deal larger than the ordinary run of spring fish on the Dee. The river was high, I had a 7/5 cast and he was a very stubborn fish and liked the heavy water. He took me forty minutes, as I was alone and he weighed nineteen and a half pounds. In the end I beached this fish. It only shows what one can do with a 7/5 cast if you are careful. I like beaching fish, it is much more fun than gaffing them if you have a favourable place to beach them on. Another little fish of twelve pounds completed the day.

And so it went on from day to day. A fish here and a fish there; but so unlike the Dee on former occasions.

The 8th May—this was V-Day. Except for a bonfire and a few flags about, I saw nothing in the way of celebrations. I heard Winston Churchill on the wireless—short and to the point. No fish that day.

So on the 15th May I write 'Finis', and a more disappointing trip I have seldom had. So little excitement, in fact my only real excitement was when I hooked a wild fish, which turned out to be foul hooked, and when he had run out about sixty yards of line downstream, I thought it was time to get a move on. In my hurry to get ashore—I was wading up to my middle—I unfortunately met a large rock, which I had not met before. So I pitched headlong into the water and found my face on the bottom. I still had my rod and got on to my feet again. My face had suffered from its contact with the rock and I felt pretty awful. I waded ashore and started to reel up. The line was slack and I never thought of a fish. Then, when I had gathered up some sixty yards of line, I found that I still had something at the end. Off he went again. In the end I got him, ten pounds, hooked in the back. I don't know why this fish was hooked in the back, he made a perfect head and tail rise and hooked himself.

What a sight I was, face cut, hands cut, soaked from top to bottom. I stripped in the fishing hut and put on a dry waterproof and in that way went back to Banchory after waiting an hour for a taxi.

There is only one thing to do after these little incidents. Drink half a tumbler of whisky—take an aspirin and go to bed. In an hour I was all right again. So ended the only excitement I had.

On the way home I thought I was lucky to get a 'sleeper' from Aberdeen; but I was not so lucky. The 'sleeper' broke down at Newcastle and I had to turn out and sit in a dirty third-class carriage for the rest of the journey to King's Cross. A lovely finish; but I got my money back from the Company.

The Kennet was unkind as usual at this time of year.

On the 1st June, I went to stay with my kind friend, Geoffrey Turner, at Hungerford Park. From my diary I see that for the last ten years we have had atrocious weather just as the May fly was coming on. In days gone by, during the May fly season I have a memory of very hot days with little wind and gnats biting you; but for the last ten years the climate has changed—no hot days and no gnats to bite. When gnats bite—you get fish.

On 10th June I went over to fish Eddington Mill on the Kennet, with my friend, Sir Joseph Ball. There are big trout on this stretch. Just above the Mill House we saw a fish move and take two or three May flies very quietly right under the opposite bank. My host said to me, 'He's a nice little fish about a couple of pounds, you might give him a fly'—I did so but he ignored my effort.

I moved higher up and got a nice fish of two and a half pounds, but as I saw nothing rising above I went back to my friend just above the Mill. He was still rising and taking spent gnat. About the third cast he had my fly. I then realized that he was more than two pounds—more like three pounds. A little later on I said to myself, he must be four pounds—and when I drew him over the net, I nearly let everything go. He was so short and so fat you could hardly believe your eyes. He was one ounce under five pounds. So let us call him five pounds. He was only twenty-one inches long.

When I got home it was nearly midnight; but I could not resist laying him out on a sheet of three-ply wood, and setting to work to paint a picture of him. It was 1.30 a.m. when I retired to bed, well satisfied with his portrait.

When we ate him next day, and I was almost sorry to eat such a lovely fish, he was as pink and as good to eat as any sea trout. This was the end of my trout fishing. The weather was atrocious all through the summer and there was scarcely a warm, calm evening throughout the season.

I have often heard of Loch Ailort on the west coast of Scotland and its reputation for large sea trout, so when I had the opportunity of going there on 5th September for a fortnight, and having made no other plans, I jumped for it. The rent was high, but if you want good fishing, you must pay for it.

This time my luck was out. I could not get a 'sleeper', so had to be content with a corner seat in a first-class carriage and I was lucky to get that. There were hundreds of people struggling for seats; but I had a clever porter. At my age I am not prepared to stand up in a corridor from King's Cross to Edinburgh. I am prepared to pay anything within reason for not doing so. I did. At 4 a.m. we arrived at Edinburgh and there I had to change. When I went to look for my luggage in the van, I found at least

100 sailors' kit bags piled on top of my luggage. After some time the sailors came along and slowly my luggage was revealed. But where were the porters? There were none. My train for Glasgow and Loch Ailort was waiting. I wondered how long it would wait, but these things all work out in the end and I got the train and got to Loch Ailort at lunch time.

The river Ailort runs out of Loch Eilt into the sea at Loch Ailort. The length of the river is about five miles. It is a small winding river which is easily covered from the bank.

During the fortnight I was there I came to the conclusion that Loch Eilt and the river Ailort were living on a past reputation. All the stories of great catches of sea trout dated back more than ten years. For my own part I spent many days on the Loch and several days on the river. There was nothing to complain of in the conditions, plenty of rain and nice little spates and yet the fish did not appear to be there.

The only fish of any size were mostly caught on the troll. The day before I left I learned from the gillie that the sluices which regulate the amount of water running out of the Loch into the river were constructed ten years ago. My own feeling is that these sluices have in some way affected the run of fish. Why, when the Loch was so good up to ten years ago, should the sport have altered so much? This, of course, is only my personal opinion and I may be quite wrong.

I saw hardly any bird life on the Loch, even the gulls were absent.

One day I picked up a buzzard by the roadside, he had flown into a telegraph wire and was only just killed. He was a huge bird with a span of wing I should say of four or five feet. On another day, walking up the Loch side, a wild cat suddenly jumped out in front of me, only about twenty yards away. I have seen dead wild cats, but never a live one in all the years I have been to Scotland. He stood on a rock and looked at me for some time. He was a grand specimen. I was told afterwards that they were fairly common in that district.

This is the end of fishing for 1945 and I must write it down as a thoroughly unsuccessful year. There is only one consolation, everybody seems to have fared in the same way.

Year 1946

My diary has begun with these words: 'This is a new fishing year, let us hope that it will be a better one than last year; but from all accounts up to the present, it would appear to be much worse'.

I think everybody will agree with me it has been the worst on record for most people.

Personally, I have had little to complain of and I think that I have been one of the few lucky ones.

On the 14th March I left London to stay with my friend, Sir Edward Mountain, who had lately acquired Dunkeld House and fishing on the Tay, also the Stanley Water and a lease of Murthly Castle Water.

I had always wanted to fish these grand waters and at last the opportunity had come.

Those of you who can look back thirty and more years will remember the wonderful fishing which the late Duke of Portland had on these waters. The late Lord Dudley also fished it for many years with his wife.

It was not to be wondered at that I was full of excitement for some weeks before starting, in anticipation of seeing and fishing these historic waters.

Dunkeld House is comparatively modern, having been built by the Duke of Athol in 1890. It stands about fifty yards from the river, with the most superb surroundings and some of the finest trees you can imagine. The pools are magnificent and very large and most of the fishing must be done from a boat.

Within a few hours of my arrival I started off fishing the lower Dunkeld water in a snowstorm. It snowed most of the day and I found spinning a great trial, as my hands were frozen beyond any sense of feeling.

The next day I went down to Upper Stanley and managed to get one fish; but saw only one other.

The fact is, the fish were not there this year. The nets above Stanley were only getting two and three a day, instead of one hundred to one hundred and fifty as I believe they sometimes did.

On the following day it was my turn to fish the lower Murthly Castle water. This was the famous water where Miss Ballantine caught the record salmon for the British Isles in 1922 and which still remains a record.

At lunch time I went down to see Miss Ballantine, who still lives with her old mother, now aged over ninety—at the little cottage at Caputh Bridge.

I was fortunate to find her there and she remembered me after twenty-four years, when I went to call on her soon after she had caught her record fish.

I asked her to tell me the whole story again, as I had heard so many different versions of it from gillies up at Dunkeld. Her story was precisely the same as what she told me twenty-four years ago, so here it is again, so as to put it on record.

It was caught on the 7th October, 1922, late in the afternoon, below a big rock some five hundred yards above Caputh Bridge. She was in the boat alone with her father. She was spinning a 'Golden Sprat'. After the fish had been on for some time, they decided to land about one hundred yards above Caputh Bridge, thinking that they could kill the fish there.

But this fish thought otherwise and with a tremendous rush, away he went downstream and fortunately took the near arch, otherwise the story would never have been told. Down he went for 200 yards below the bridge and there was no stopping him. Her father thought it would be as well if he went back and got the boat. This took him some twenty minutes. It was now almost dark and Miss Ballantine had to manage this huge fish all alone from the bank. It was as well that her father had fetched the boat, as the fish decided to go over to the island, which is about 400 to 500 yards below the bridge. There they landed and eventually killed the fish at 8.20 p.m., when it was pitch dark. The weight of the salmon was sixty-four pounds.

'Did you get that new dress your father promised you if you killed the fish?' I asked her. 'Yes', she said, 'I got the new dress.' Now there are many stories up the river that there was a crowd of people on the bank and one gillie told me that his father was in the boat. I asked Miss Ballantine this question and she said that there was not a word of truth in it. There was no one on the bank and she and her father were alone in the boat.

If ever Miss Ballantine's record is broken, and I have my

doubts it ever will be, I hope the story will be as thrilling as the one she told me on 18th March, 1946.

We had a laugh one day, when one of the party brought back a huge fish which should have weighed thirty to thirty-five pounds, but which actually scaled twenty-two pounds.

The gillies said it was a 'Bull Trout', but after examination I really felt convinced that it was a very well-mended Kelt, and I think I was right.

At dinner that night I asked Lady Mountain if I might have a slice of the fish grilled, as I had never tasted a Kelt and wanted to see what it looked like. So next day I had a slice, beautifully grilled. All I can say is, it was not half bad and I have had many worse in London restaurants.

I will not dwell further on the loveliness of this river and the pleasure I had in spite of the lack of fish. A more generous host and hostess it would be hard to find. Also the greatest courtesy and kindness from all the gillies and others I came in touch with. What a contrast from London.

From the Tay I went on to fish the Spey. There I had a great surprise. From all accounts the Spey was faring little better than the Dee and Tay. My beat happened to be low down, so what few fish came up had to pass through the water and some of them stayed there a short time.

I told my fellow fishers that if we got twenty or thirty fish for the month I should be quite content. Instead of that we got sixty fish. It is seldom one gets more than one hopes for. A large proportion of these fish were big fish, by which I mean fish from eighteen to thirty-seven pounds. From this one might assume that it is the smaller fish that have suffered during the past two or three years and not the larger ones.

I had many a good thrill on this beat, two of which I would like to mention. One a disaster, the other a triumph. The disaster came first, and it was like this. I had seen a big fish break the water when I was wading. It was rough water and I felt that my fly did not hang properly over the fish. So I said to my gillie, 'I will get into the boat and you can hold it farther out than I can wade.' This we did and as soon as my fly was over the fish he took it with a great bang. Then I got out of the boat and he started 'fireworks' all over the river. Then he went over the other side of the river about sixty yards and jumped. He was thirty-five to forty pounds. So this went on for thirty minutes and after this I got control of him. When he was coming over to my side the hook came back. I thought perhaps he had broken me. I was fishing with an 8/5 cast and No. 6 Blue Charm. But the fly was there all right. The gillie took the fly and looked at it. 'The fly has no barb,' he said, and sure enough the hook was perfect, but a barbless hook. It had never had a barb.

I seldom fish with a fly that I have not tied myself, but by some means or other this fly had got into my box and I had picked it up without noticing that there was no barb. One occasionally does these things even after fifty years of salmon fishing.

The other thriller was this. There had been heavy rain for two days and the river had risen four feet six inches. The next afternoon the water had cleared sufficiently to cast a bait. I had my little nine-feet Greenheart, which is almost as supple as a fly rod. The reel was a Hardy 'Elarex' Multiplier and the line a five-year-old, ten pounds breaking strain.

I said that I would stroll to the bottom pool about one and a quarter miles down and see if the boat had been sunk or been carried away. I found the boat almost full of water and it took me three-quarters of an hour to bale her out. There was very little water to spin from the bank and after I had been spinning for five or ten minutes I found my line in the most awful kink I ever met. The trouble was a new trace and the swivels were not working. It took me half an hour to get this set right. Having put on a new trace all was well. I moved down to a patch which looked likely and at the third cast I was into something really big. This was one of the fish of my life. He was savage—he was demented, he did everything that a fish could do. Now a run of sixty to seventy yards down and across, then he doubled back upstream and jumped. When I saw him I thought that he must be some other fish, but it was mine all right and I put him at forty pounds. After forty minutes of this kind of exercise he was cooling off and coming over to my side; but when he came to facing the shallow water, he did not like it a bit and would not come in. The only thing to do was to wade in and gaff him in the deep water. This I did, but he nearly pulled me in, as I was standing on an uncertain bottom. I waded with him to the shore and what a lovely fish he was. It was now 6.30 p.m. and I had to get back to the hut one and a quarter miles upstream. I had nothing but a bit of stout string. The fish was very heavy. I put on my oil skin and flung him over my back. It was a weary walk in long waders, fish, rod, etc. I am not as young as I was. When I got to the hut I was pleased but tired. He weighed thirty-seven pounds. At the end of the walk I thought he was forty-seven pounds.

This ended our fishing. How hard it is, after one has had a delightful fishing trip in a part of Scotland where everybody is nice to you, to pack up one's rods and tackle and all one's goods and to say goodbye. One can only hope for a return next year; but that is a long time to wait. But these dreams keep one going through the winter and, if one had nothing to look forward to, it would be a dull life.

Although I only had one afternoon's May fly fishing on the Kennet this year, I hear from all accounts it was a very bad season. Gales of wind and rain drove the fly off the river and the nights were so cold that the fly died in the trees and there was little spent gnat. When are we going to have a good summer?

PASS OF BRANDA. R. AWE.

XXXI

ABOUT THINGS IN GENERAL

THIS is the end of my story, but I still hope that I shall be able to visit again some of the beautiful rivers I have mentioned. There are certain other rivers which I have in mind, where I would like to fish, in Scotland, Norway and Iceland. There is still time—they may come my way. There are two kinds of salmon fishing, the delicate kind, with small rods and light casts and flies, and the other kind where you require heavy casts, rods and tackle, such as the Alton, Aaro, Evanger in Norway, where you never know when you are going to get into a fifty- or sixty-pounder. The Shannon was another river where light tackle was useless; but taking it on the whole, Scottish rivers do not require heavy tackle. I often wonder what has happened to our big fish in Scotland. Occasionally big fish of forty to fifty pounds are caught, but not often. Is it that the nets get nearly all of them? and why have rivers changed so much? The Tweed, Dee and Spey were autumn rivers at one time: now they are spring rivers; what has accounted for this change? Then there is another problem. In former days bait was practically unknown, fish would pull the fly in the early months of January, February, March. It is not often that they pull it now.

Personally I would like to see all bait fishing stopped after the end of March on such rivers as the Dee, Tweed and Spey.

Every year I hear stories of lovely reaches of fly water being ruined for the opposite bank by people fishing prawn in the months of April, May and June when the river was in perfect fly condition.

If landlords would only take the matter into their own hands, they would have a clause in their leases to this effect. This would put a stop to the 'fish hog' who only tries to get the fish out in any way, and is no fisherman at heart. Landlords need not be afraid of their rents, there are plenty of good fishermen still alive who would rather catch fish on the fly than have their sport ruined by 'bait-sluggers'. If I have caught fish on a bait after March, it is only in self defence. If we were all in the same boat and fished fly only, it would stop that spirit of competition which is so noticeable now. I have had my say, and there it is.

What constitutes a good fisherman? I mean the sort of fisherman who catches more fish than most people. This question always puzzles me. There is the old saying, 'The man who keeps his fly longest in the water is the best salmon fisher' and there is a lot of truth in this. There is generally some time in the day when the salmon will pull. I have seen it so often when all the rods have given it up except one man: that man, as often as not, will come home with a fish or two.

Some people have a natural instinct for where the fish lay. Some never acquire it. Knowing your water and keeping on fishing is half the secret. The right size of fly is just as important. Your beautiful caster is not always the most successful one. He may lack 'fish sense'. He may cast too straight a line, which in modern salmon fishing with a greased line is a mistake. He may not pay sufficient attention to the temperature of the water and size of fly, or he may not think of the way the sun is shining on the pool. No, casting is not everything to be learned in salmon fishing.

I have noticed on some salmon waters and some trout waters that I am always lucky, whereas on other waters I fail to catch fish. I have never been able to understand this. At Barton Court on the Kennet, I always caught fish, whereas on another stretch of water not far away, I was seldom very successful. It always takes me about two seasons to know a salmon river properly.

I consider that a really good fisherman should know all the

branches of the art. He should know all about dry fly and wet fly fishing for trout. He should be a good salmon fisher both with fly and bait, with heavy tackle and light. There is plenty for him to learn and if he likes to tie flies and make up his own tackle, so much the better. I never have much respect for the fisherman who, at the end of the season, bundles his rods and tackle away and never overhauls them or gloats over them during the winter.

Waders are expensive things in these days and hard to come by. Instead of leaving them during the winter in some cold place, exposed to the light, it is as well to see that they are properly dried, folded up and put in some dark dry place. They will last much longer. A good coat of castor oil will keep your brogues soft and pliable. A thorough rub down with a silk handkerchief will keep your lines in good order. I have come to think that half the trouble of sticky lines is caused by leaving them greasy.

Keep your cast away from light and air. They will last for a long time. Never in a tin box. Chamois leather is the best. I once had a cast case with celluloid envelopes. The celluloid envelopes had some peculiar effect on the gut. The gut became as brittle as glass.

After many years, I find that the best type of waterproof is the oilskin. It keeps out any rain, and lasts for years. Mine is lined with a green waterproof lining, and after five years is in perfect order.

After having ruined many a hat and coat lapel by sticking flies in them when I change my pattern, I am now, after fifty years, trying to break myself of this habit. I keep a little box about two and a half inches square with a piece of felt in it. The wet flies are put in this, and opened out to dry after the day's work is done. I feel sure that I shall never break myself of the old habit; but I shall keep on trying. For years I used to put a strip of soft felt round my hat, fastened with elastic. This is all very well in dry weather, but in wet weather it gets soaked. Still, there are some good points in this, as long as you are not sensitive about the remarks that are made when you go through a town or village.

In finishing my book I have the same feeling as when a fishing holiday has come to an end. Time advances, but it is only of late years that I have noticed how quickly time goes.

Let me conclude, however, with the following quotation: 'I shall pass through this world but once. Any good thing therefore I can do, or any kindness that I can show, let me do it now, I shall not pass this way again'. So, if by writing this book I have accomplished something in giving one helpful thought to a few anglers of less experience, I shall be satisfied.

DENFORD MILL R.KENNET

XXXII

A LETTER FROM MR MENZIES

MY own personal reminiscences now concluded in the foregoing chapters, I feel I ought not to close without quoting a letter I received from my friend, W. J. M. Menzies. Its contents are of such obvious interest to all fishermen that I give the letter in full in the following pages.

CALEDONIAN UNITED SERVICE CLUB,
EDINBURGH.

10th June, 1946.

'My Dear Rennie,

'You are indeed fortunate, or shall I say very skilful, to have done so relatively well with your spring fishing this year. The general average has been deplorably low and probably lower than ever before. It is certainly far lower than in any year since the great increase in spring salmon, and unfortunately the corresponding decrease in autumn fish, started in the early years of this century.

'Lest your head be tempted to swell, and I cannot believe that would occur, may I add that you have been fishing on one beat at least which was curiously lucky. In both Spey and Dee (Aberdeen) more than one run of fish stopped quite unexpectedly in one of the lowest beats and gave sport that was almost, or quite, up to the average. On the contrary the middle beats were almost deserted; in one good fortnight a round dozen of anglers on the Dee had five fish between them from some of the best beats!

'All this is in 1946. Last season was almost as bad and, since we know the whole of it, we can write it down as by far the worst year in living memory.

'We poor anglers have not been the only sufferers. Those who make their living from the salmon, the net fishermen, have not lost merely their sport; they have lost their livelihood. You may be sure that loss has not been due to

264

lack of trying or lack of skill in spite of difficulties due to shortages of labour and gear. The weather, too, has not been unfavourable for the netsmen; for much of the spring of this year it has been very favourable.

'The root of the troubles of all of us, rod fishermen and net fishermen alike, has been a very real shortage of salmon and grilse throughout 1945 and again in the past months of this year. Our fathers never knew a shortage such as you and I, and others like us, have experienced.

'Having experienced the results I expect you would like to know, and I certainly would like to know, the causes which have led to this unfortunate scarcity. It is not going to be at all easy to discover the reason or reasons. We certainly cannot blame the Government this time for an alleged result of price control—the fish are not under the counter; they are not even alive in the water or dead in cold store.

'We are likely to be able to assess the cause definitely only if that cause occurred during the early freshwater life of the fish. We have often watched the salmon spawning in the chill November and December days; we have seen the fry and parr feeding and, on those warm April and May mornings we have seen the smolts feeding, too, and behaving as if they were thoroughly enjoying life, especially when the river has been rather small. You and I could have a guess at conditions which are likely to be harmful at those times—excessive floods which lead the fish to spawn in places subsequently to be left dry; excessive frost and ice which may possibly, although by no means certainly, turn up some redds and destroy some eggs. Great spring floods may sweep away fry and parr overland and then leave them in the growing grass as the waters recede.

'You will remember, too, times when the old heron has been fishing for his supper, when mergansers and goosanders seemed not entirely guiltless as the smolts were on the move and when a pair of black-backed gulls stood sentinel on the shallow runs during the weeks of the smolt migration. Are the dippers, too, which we have seen about the redds, entirely concerned with small animal life and oblivious to the edible properties of salmon and trout ova?

'The salmon and grilse of 1945 and 1946 (most of which were two-year-old smolts) were hatched in the springs of 1941, 1942 and 1943. Now, John Rennie, can you remember anything which might have been unusually and extremely harmful in either the winters before those springs or in the spring months themselves when the fry began to feed, or when they were parr or smolts? I think you will not be able to remember any outstanding general feature common to the whole country and to Eire too. We do not have to remember isolated great floods in a particular river, or in particular rivers, or a spell of hard frost which hit perhaps Scotland but not elsewhere. We have to look for something which affected all, or almost all, rivers from the Thurso to the Cork Blackwater, from the Aberdeen Dee to the Usk. It really does not look as if we could lay our hands on anything sufficiently serious, extending probably over more than one spawning season mind you, in that part of the life of the fish.

'We know what has happened to the grouse. They are just as scarce as, or more scarce than, the salmon. Vermin, four-footed and winged, may have contributed to their fall from high estate. Do you think winged vermin, some of which I have already mentioned, could have increased sufficiently to decimate fry, parr and smolts? Personally I more than doubt it. Goosanders and mergansers have probably increased but in many, or indeed most, rivers they are scarce or absent even now. Herons are not really numerous anywhere so far as I know—do you know any river where they could be described as plentiful? The gull population must be much the same as ever though some may have more freedom to reach moors and rivers than in the days of peace.

'Obviously if we cannot find the cause in fresh water we must look to the sea. And here we are up against it. The sea forms a big area, we do not know where the salmon feed, we know little of their actual food, we know only some of their enemies and difficulties. What is worse, we have not the means of finding out more about these things without a great deal of very difficult research and with the added danger of possibly subjecting the stock to additional fishing on their ocean feeding grounds whether these feeding grounds be near or far and the highways to and from them long or short.

'We do know that we were not the only unfortunates in 1945. Salmon fishermen in Iceland, Canada, Newfoundland and the Labrador were equally badly off. In some rivers in Norway they may perhaps have been better off than the rest of us.

'Can you believe that adverse climatic conditions can have fallen on all countries, east, north and west of the Atlantic not in an isolated year but certainly in two, and possibly in three, consecutive years? It does not seem to be possible and again we are driven to the ocean for an explanation.

'Also can you believe that direct wartime actions—mines, depth charges and suchlike death-dealing what-nots—can have affected the salmon of all these countries? If so they must all be feeding in, or travel through, some quite unsuspected places and when so feeding or travelling they must be very concentrated. Mines and bombs and torpedoes make a hell of an eruption but that eruption is only a minute speck in the vast areas of salt water. A salmon caught in the eruption ought surely to be a very unlucky fish for he does not touch the horn, or ring the bell, of a mine or invite the attention of cruising aircraft.

'If the deficiency were confined to Great Britain don't you think we might look at the war and its effects from another angle. Amid the general increase in numbers and size of white fish, coalfish, dogfish and conger eels, to instance no others, must also have increased. You know they have all been recorded as eaters of smolts. Sharks and porpoises also eat adult salmon; they, too, may have increased. The losses in this country might have arisen in part at least from this source. But has there been a corresponding increase in these predatory creatures from the same cause round Iceland?—yes, possibly—off the Labrador, Newfoundland and Canadian coasts—almost certainly not.

'It may be that we should look to two causes. The one a secondary cause for our salmon, and possibly the Icelandic salmon, and the other for the western

Atlantic salmon arising from natural processes unaided by the wars of man.

'If we do have these very serious factors arising in two different ways on each side of the Atlantic the coincidence would be more than curious. Indeed it would be so curious as to seem in the light of our present knowledge wildly improbable. If Iceland and the western countries repeat, or intensify, their 1945 experience in 1946, as we are already doing, then surely we shall be justified in saying that the coincidence could not exist and that the result must be due to a common cause.

'On present evidence I do suggest to you that the cause of the unhappy state of our salmon fisheries in 1945 and 1946 is due to some unexplained happening arising from natural, and not war-like, causes in the sea and that the happening affected practically the whole stock of salmon on all sides of the Atlantic. Do you agree?'

Yours sincerely,

W. J. M. MENZIES.

INDEX

Printed by W. S. Cowell Ltd, at the Butter Market, Ipswich
1949